THE
REGULATORY
CRAFT

THE REGULATORY CRAFT

Controlling Risks,
Solving Problems, and
Managing Compliance

MALCOLM K. SPARROW

COUNCIL FOR EXCELLENCE IN GOVERNMENT

BROOKINGS INSTITUTION PRESS
Washington, D.C.

ABOUT BROOKINGS

The Brookings Institution is a private nonprofit organization devoted to research, education, and publication on important issues of domestic and foreign policy. Its principal purpose is to bring knowledge to bear on current and emerging policy problems. The Institution maintains a position of neutrality on issues of public policy. Interpretations or conclusions in Brookings publications should be understood to be solely those of the authors.

Copyright © 2000
THE BROOKINGS INSTITUTION
1775 Massachusetts Avenue, N.W., Washington, D.C. 20036
www.brookings.edu

Library of Congress Cataloging-in-Publication data

Sparrow, Malcolm K.
    The regulatory craft: controlling risks, solving problems, and managing compliance / Malcolm K. Sparrow.
        p. cm.
    "Council for Excellence in Government."
    Includes bibliographical references and index.
    ISBN 0-8157-8065-6 (pbk. : alk. paper)
    1. Trade regulation—United States. 2. Industrial policy—United States.
3. Compliance—United States. 4. Administrative procedure—United States.
5. Government paperwork—United States. I. Title.
    HD3616.U47 S6 2000   00-008438
    658.4—dc21   CIP

Digital printing

The paper used in this publication meets minimum requirements of the American National Standard for Information Sciences—Permanence of Paper for Printed Library Materials: ANSI Z39.48-1984.

Typeset in Sabon

Composition by Betsy Kulamer
Washington, D.C.

Contents

Foreword

FRANK KEATING
Governor of Oklahoma

How pervasive is regulation in our modern society? The car you park in your garage bears a state license tag, perhaps a locally issued safety and emissions sticker, and all manner of fuel economy and antipollution devices under the hood mandated by various federal regulators. Your television and radio receive signals regulated by the Federal Communications Commission. If Aunt Mabel comes to visit, she flies in on an airline regulated by the Federal Aviation Administration. In your fishing tackle box is a state fishing license. You use electricity at state-regulated rates. The gas you use to heat the tea kettle is regulated. So are the medicines in your bathroom cabinet. The pacemaker the surgeon installs in your chest was approved and tested by the Food and Drug Administration, along with the meat and milk and bread in your kitchen. You have to show proof that Johnny and Susie have been vaccinated for smallpox before they can enroll in a public school, which uses textbooks selected by a state regulatory board. On the schoolbus that brings them home are placards and warnings mandated by regulators. The bus driver needs a special driver's license and has to attend a special training class. So does the crossing guard. Johnny's toys have passed rigorous safety testing. So has the mattress he sleeps on.

As you tuck Johnny in for the night, the regulated airplane following a prescribed path in regulated airspace carrying Aunt Mabel home flies over your thoroughly regulated house with its thoroughly regulated contents. Among its contents is a thick file labeled "Taxes," which help pay for all that regulation. Americans increasingly question whether government's vast regulatory apparatus delivers value for money; whether it focuses on the right things; whether it actually succeeds in protecting consumers and reducing their risks. Sometimes they offer simpleminded prescriptions—such as "less regulation" or "regulation with a smile"— that do not match the complexity of modern society.

Malcolm K. Sparrow, a professor at Harvard University's John F. Kennedy School of Government, has wrestled with the issue of regulatory and enforcement practice and has emerged with a very attractive proposal for reform: that regulators should "pick important problems and fix them." As for unimportant problems, they should leave them alone.

Professor Sparrow and I share a common background, he as a detective chief inspector in Great Britain, I as an agent for the Federal Bureau of Investigation. Neither of us is against regulation: we both know the importance of effective crime control and also the importance of professionally managed and properly directed enforcement actions. But we also know, from our practical experience, how hard it is for regulatory and enforcement agencies to abandon areas that are no longer important and to—circumspectly—move into unfamiliar areas that have become important. Since leaving the FBI, I have had the privilege of serving as a prosecutor; as a state legislator; as an official of the (federal) Justice Department, the Treasury Department, the Department of Housing and Urban Development; and as a state governor. I have seen the business of regulation from many angles. Regulations are essential for public peace and order, for health and safety, and for our mutual convenience. It is wise to prohibit human behaviors that endanger or seriously inconvenience others. Society has a right and an obligation to act collectively, through government, to prevent others from selling rotten meat, or flying airliners into one another, or engaging in fraudulent business practices. Of course we need regulations. There are too many of us, living too close together, to manage without them.

But although we need regulations, we do not need regulators who are, in Sparrow's words "nitpicky, unreasonable, unnecessarily adversarial, rigidly bureaucratic, [and] incapable of applying discretion sensibly." Sparrow also suggests that the competitiveness of American businesses depends to a significant degree upon our ability to reform our regulatory philosophy and practices.

In recent years, Democrats and Republicans alike have tackled regulation. Both groups say we need less of it, and both have created more of it. Many efforts at regulatory reform have turned out, in retrospect, to be little more than regulatory rearrangement. Not enough has been achieved in terms of focusing regulatory attention on crucial matters, taking the focus off unimportant matters, and making regulators responsible for delivering results that matter. Most recently we have watched the Clinton-Gore administration try to "reinvent government." The reinvention approach emphasizes improving customer service (which is valuable) but ignores the core issues of regulatory effectiveness and the management of enforcement operations.

Professor Sparrow provides a beguilingly simple idea: regulatory and enforcement operations constructed around an explicit risk control strategy. He demonstrates how extraordinarily demanding implementation of this idea is, but he also demonstrates how a few pioneering agencies have made significant strides in this direction. I hope many others will follow.

Foreword

PATRICIA MCGINNIS
Council for Excellence in Government

THE COUNCIL FOR EXCELLENCE IN GOVERNMENT is a nonprofit, nonpartisan organization committed to improving the performance of government and promoting greater citizen trust and participation in government and governance. The Council's membership consists of business and nonprofit leaders who have served in government.

The American people, according to the findings of the Council's polling on public attitudes toward government, think government's regulatory functions play a major role in determining their quality of life, especially in the areas of environmental protection, health, and safety. Most say they have benefited from government programs in food and drug safety, consumer protection, and workplace health and safety and think government should play a major part in these areas. At the same time, they regard current regulatory practices as costly—pushing up the price of products and services—and insufficiently oriented toward valuable results.

The Council is therefore pleased to sponsor Malcolm K. Sparrow's useful and engaging examination of regulatory and enforcement practice, which reveals many of the vogue prescriptions for regulatory reform as insufficiently cognizant of the underlying nature of the regulatory task. The regulatory function routinely involves use of the coercive power of the state against individuals or corporations. The satisfaction of those individuals or companies, although important, is perhaps less important in that moment than the broader public purposes that regulation serves. At the same time, those who are regulated (and who may find themselves the target of enforcement actions) deserve fair and dignified treatment. Managing the coercive power of the state, and the inescapable discretion that accompanies it, thus presents regulatory and enforcement managers with challenges largely without parallel in the private sector or in the service aspects of government's role.

Professor Sparrow's study examines a broad range of innovative programs and uses them to tease out the essence of a new—and I think extremely promising—model for regulatory practice. This risk control or problem-solving strategy focuses on task-oriented management, rigorous measurement methods, and new systems of accountability. As a framework for regulatory reform, centered on the core idea of risk control, this book should resonate well beyond its immediate audience of regulatory managers. I commend it to members of the Congress and congressional staff members who design and oversee the regulatory functions of government; and to political scientists, teachers, and others concerned with improving the performance of government.

During the preparation of this book, the council was pleased to host, in Washington, D.C., a series of highly productive roundtable discussions involving regulatory practitioners across government. Among the participants were representatives of federal regulatory programs that have recently won the Innovations in American Government award (sponsored by the Ford Foundation and administered by Harvard's Kennedy School of Government in partnership with the Council for Excellence in Government). These innovators developed their successes in the fields of occupational safety and health, new drug approvals, consumer product safety, sweatshop prevention, pension security, tax collection, and immigration. The Council is delighted with the recognition they receive here. The Council believes strongly in the value, as a learning tool, of innovative problem solving.

We are even more pleased that this collection of regulatory successes, coupled with the experiences of many other pioneering agencies, points so clearly toward a whole new model of regulatory conduct, one that reemphasizes the fundamental purposes for which agencies of social regulation were created: to reduce risks, to eliminate hazards, and to solve some of society's thornier and more intractable problems. Professor Sparrow's analysis shows what it takes, in practice, for regulatory bureaucracies to deliver that kind of performance. Given the current pressure for results-oriented government, this work could not have come at a better time.

Preface

IN 1994, in *Imposing Duties: Government's Changing Approach to Compliance*, I compared the professions of policing, environmental protection, and tax administration, and discovered that the three professions had much in common in both the pressures for reform that they faced and the adaptations they were making in response.[1] This commonality was striking given the almost complete absence of communication between practitioners of these professions.

Imposing Duties was modest in two senses. First, it made no claim of relevance to any broader set of regulatory or enforcement professions. Second, it did not present, nor did it purport to present, empirical evidence that the emerging strategies were demonstrably more effective than traditional enforcement-centered approaches—nor that the strategies described were necessarily the best of the available options. The purpose of that book, quite simply, was to demonstrate to practitioners in each of those three professions that they were by no means alone in the issues they faced, the ideas they embraced, and the aspirations they held. By examining those issues, ideas, and aspirations across professions I hoped to give practitioners a broader frame of reference within which to contemplate their own dilemmas, a richer variety of initiatives and examples to consider, and a new set of colleagues with whom they could usefully converse.

Of the reviews of the book that appeared, one of the more interesting begins like this: "Malcolm K. Sparrow's *Imposing Duties* is one of the most stimulating, profound, and original books to be published in public administration in many a year. At the same time, it is seriously flawed in methodology, and its basic assumptions cannot be verified."[2] With respect to the cross-professional comparison (spanning policing, environmental protection, and tax administration), the reviewer observes: "No one has ever looked at these activities from this vantage point, but when readers see new organizational developments through the eyes of this ex-policeman, they are almost persuaded that some powerfully important changes in the entire enforcement and regulatory landscape are looming."[3]

Five years on, I, for one, remain "almost persuaded" (and quite hopeful) "that some powerfully important changes in the entire enforcement and regulatory landscape are looming." My worry, though, is that they may loom, and continue to loom, and then eventually recede; that a significant opportunity may be missed. If it is missed, the reason, most likely, will be a collective failure to understand exactly what the opportunity was.

The current accumulation of pressures on regulators, coupled with the rich experience of recent regulatory experiments and innovations, presents a very special opportunity: to define, or substantially refine, the professional craft of regulatory practice and to design administrative and organizational arrangements to support a new regulatory craftsmanship. My hope for this (new) book is that it will help regulators, legislators—and anyone else concerned with or affected by the quality of regulatory practice—understand the nature of that opportunity and help them realize the benefits it brings.

But why a new book, and what of *Imposing Duties*? If anything *Imposing Duties* was published too early, before the usefulness of cross-professional discussions was generally accepted by regulatory practitioners and before the congressional assaults on key federal regulatory agencies (early in 1995) brought the issues of regulatory reform into such stark relief. Now, the challenges of regulatory reform confront government squarely and urgently and are seen by many as the major unresolved issue, both political and intellectual, within the realm of government reinvention.

This book is not a reissue, nor an update, of *Imposing Duties*. Expecting that many readers drawn to this work will have already read that one, I have taken care not to replicate material adequately stated there. Some of that material, such as the discussion of information management and analytic support, seems just now to be coming of age. I urge readers not familiar with *Imposing Duties* to explore it, not least because it contains greater detail of the travails of policing, environmental protection, and tax administration than you will find here.

There are many compelling reasons to add to that previous work. First, it has become clear that the issues and discussion have relevance considerably beyond the three regulatory professions examined in that book. Neither occupational safety and health nor customs services were mentioned. Nevertheless, the Occupational Safety and Health Administration purchased a copy for nearly every employee, regarding its discussion as central to that agency's reinvention dilemmas. The problem-solving approach (translated from the police profession) was formally incorporated both into OSHA's plan for the redesign of the agency and into the U.S. Customs Service's strategic problem-solving program (which reconstituted the Customs Service approach to its interdiction responsibilities). Further, the New Zealand Ministry of Fisheries has relied heavily on the ideas contained in *Imposing Duties* in developing a fisheries compliance strategy, despite the fact that the book does not mention fisheries. So I am ready now to be a little less modest about the degree to which these matters apply to other areas of regulation.

Second, the pressures on regulatory practice are international in a way that *Imposing Duties* does not suggest. Over the intervening years I have worked with Canadian federal authorities and have had the opportunity to hold discussions with executives of regulatory agencies in Australia, New Zealand, and Latin America. The Organization of Economic Cooperation and Development, based in Paris, which offers help to its twenty-nine member countries in evaluating and developing public policy, reports that regulatory reform is now the number one subject upon which member countries seek guidance.

Third, I have learned much about the perils of trying to reform regulatory practice. I have had the privilege of working closely with a number of regulatory agencies over a protracted period, as they have grappled with various stages of reform: most intensively with OSHA, the Customs Service, and Florida's Department of Environmental Protection (the largest environmental agency at the state level, having three times the staff of OSHA); and less intensively with the Internal Revenue Service, the Massachusetts Department of Revenue, Revenue Canada, the

Environmental Protection Agency (specifically around issues of perform-ance measurement), and the Health Care Financing Administration (around the control of health care fraud).

I have discovered what I should have known: that ideas—like "pick-ing important problems and fixing them"—which seem beguilingly sim-ple and sensible can present enormously complex implementation chal-lenges. Virtually every piece of supporting administrative machinery (such as budget processes, strategic planning, performance reporting, and information management) serves to hold regulators to past practice, and each has to be substantially perturbed to make room for new regu-latory behaviors. It is now time to share some of that practical experi-ence. Executives of regulatory and enforcement agencies, even if they know exactly how they would like their agency to behave, might appre-ciate a practical discussion of where and how to begin, of the traps that lay ahead, and of how others have either avoided or fallen into them.

The methodology for this book may appear to many academics as flawed as, or perhaps more flawed than, that of *Imposing Duties*. Hav-ing been actively engaged in the field, working inside or alongside these agencies, I cannot offer detached and dispassionate evaluation. I am nei-ther detached from, nor dispassionate about, any of this. The reviewer of *Imposing Duties* appealed for such: "But someone has to demon-strate that measures other than tough enforcement have positive social payoffs . . . solid, causal research into the effect of particular alternative strategies is the best way to go."[4]

Whether and when alternatives to enforcement have positive social payoffs are questions that occupy many regulators, legislators, and oth-ers who have witnessed the proliferation of regulatory alternatives. Some ask, more pointedly, which approach—hard or soft—works best. If regulators were required to abandon their enforcement tools, that might be an important question to ask. However, ever hopeful that I can lay out a vision of a more sophisticated regulatory craft, the question seems no more useful than asking whether the use of antibiotics is supe-rior to surgery; or for a carpenter, whether a hammer is a more effective tool than a lathe. The answer is obvious: it depends what you are work-ing on. The essence of craftsmanship lies in picking the right tool for the job, knowing when to use them in combination, and having a system for recognizing when the tools are inadequate so that new ones can be invented. The opportunity now confronting regulatory executives, given their diverse experiences with new methods and programs, is to learn how best to manage the increasingly complex regulatory craftshop.

I cannot offer here the "solid, causal research" to answer the question of whether softer approaches work better, at the agency or aggregate level, than traditional enforcement-centered approaches. I can, however, explain where that question comes from, at what stage in an agency's reform process it is likely to arise, and the practical damage that getting hung up on it can do. I can explain why it is more advantageous to ask and answer some different and more fundamental questions about the character of the regulatory business. Through working with regulatory executives, I have come to appreciate the realities of operational life, wherein important decisions about resource allocation and tool selection have to be made in a hurry, with imperfect information, without the luxury of control samples, and in the messy environment of the democratic process. My goal is to help practitioners cope with that *operational* challenge.

The topic of regulatory reform touches an alarming number of established academic disciplines. To deal with the subject in a comprehensive way would demand mastery of criminal justice, compliance psychology, public regulation, public administration, public management, organizational theory, political science, institutional analysis, program evaluation, economics, crime prevention, sociology, criminology, regulatory law, and the emerging risk sciences. To speak with any authority, perhaps academic commentators should also be required to know the particular sciences relevant to each regulatory field: biology, chemistry, and physics (for environmental protection); industrial engineering and industrial hygiene (for occupational safety and health); toxicology, radiology, and medicine (for public health). Each one of these many disciplines has its experts and champions, most of whom will be disappointed by this book, for I have dipped into most of these literatures but have mastered none.

Rather than making a significant contribution to any one of these specialist literatures, I have a different hope. In 1967 Harvey Brooks, addressing professional engineers, wrote: "The dilemma of the professional today lies in the fact that both ends of the gap he is expected to bridge with his profession are changing so rapidly; the body of knowledge that he must use and the expectations of the society that he must serve."[5] I have tried to select, from the enormous range of knowledge available, those concepts and insights most relevant to regulatory professionals and to mix in the practical experiences that seem most immediately instructive. I offer this book for those professionals who are trying to figure out what to do, and for those legislators and overseers who are trying to figure out what to ask for and what they can reasonably expect. I hope it helps them make sense of it all.

Acknowledgments

I VIEW THIS BOOK principally as a celebration and presentation of the work of others—practitioners who, amid the din of daily life, found the time to form a new vision and the energy to implement it. My contribution is to present and frame their collective experience, providing structure and language in those places where it still seems to be missing.

My greatest debt is to a number of public sector executives with whom I have had the honor of working closely over many years. Several of these I have come to regard as intellectual partners and co-explorers as well as dear friends. In our work together, the risks and costs of implementing new ideas have been all theirs; the privilege has been all mine. I salute them for their vision, for their intellectual energy, and for their selfless dedication to public service.

In particular I thank Virginia Wetherell, who as secretary of the Florida Department of Environmental Protection (and in her own gracious way) initiated an amazingly broad program of regulatory reforms. By the end of her time as secretary, the FDEP was recognized as a pioneer among state environmental agencies, receiving bipartisan support in Florida for its reform direction and attracting a considerable amount of international attention. I also thank Michael Phillips, who worked for Secretary Wetherell as director of the Office of Strategic Projects and Planning, spearheading the strategic reforms for the department long before they were broadly accepted or recognized—and bearing much of the daily trauma associated therewith. Thanks also go to Kirby Green, Vivian Garfein, Dave Herbster, Steve Adams, and Darryl Boudreau at the FDEP for all their support and encouragement over many years.

I owe an enormous debt to Mike Lane, for ten years deputy commissioner of the U.S. Customs Service. A more thoughtful, dedicated, and humble public servant I will probably never meet. Thanks also go to Mike Stahl, Stan Meiburg, and Ed Hanley of the Environmental Protection Agency (Ed has since moved on to the Office of the Comptroller of the Currency). At the Occupational Safety and Health Administration, I include Joe Dear (assistant secretary), Nelson Reyneri, Joel Sacks, Bob Kulick, and Bob Pitulej (at various times the masters of reinvention); these were the architects of OSHA's reforms—and managed to maintain their bearings and sanity amid the bruising congressional assaults of 1995 and 1996. At the Internal Revenue Service, I thank Commissioners Peggy Richardson and Charles Rossotti for their support and encouragement; and Mike Dolan (deputy commissioner) and Ted Brown (head of criminal investigation), with whom I have had the pleasure of working, on and off, for eight years or so and through many kinds of turmoil.

I also thank George Grob of the Inspector General's Office at the Department of Health and Human Services. He taught me how these lessons apply to the role of inspector general in any agency and has demonstrated in practice how an IG's office can effectively analyze and manage risks. He provided rich case material on risks controlled in his specific domain—health care fraud. The fact that I have elected not to use health care fraud examples in this text (it is the subject of my last book and of my next one) in no way diminishes the value of his instruction or his influence on this text.

A variety of sources have provided financial and sponsorship support for this project. First and foremost, the Council on Excellence in Government sponsored the overall project, convening and hosting in Washington, D.C., a series of discussion forums for practitioners to examine, test, and refine the ideas. These forums, held during the spring of 1999, brought together a wonderful group of federal executives from a range of agencies to pick apart early drafts of this book.

The forum participants, to whom I am enormously grateful for the time and care they devoted to this enterprise, are Ed Hanley (Office of Comptroller of the Currency), Pamela Gilbert and Barbara Rosenfeld (Consumer Product Safety Commission), Howard Fenton (Department of Education), Mike Stahl and Chris Tirpak (Environmental Protection Agency), Rick Blumberg, Linda Brophy, Marie Urban, and Janet Woodcock (Food and Drug Administration), Curtis Copeland (General Accounting Office), Neil Jacobs (Immigration and Naturalization Service), Adrienne Griffin (Internal Revenue Service, representing Commissioner Charles Rossotti), Kevin Jones (Department of Justice), John Fraser (Department of Labor), John Spotilla (Office of Management and Budget), Bob Kulick, Bob Pitulej, and Rich Tapio (Occupational Safety and Health Administration), Andrea Schneider (Pension Benefit Guaranty Corporation), Neil Eisner (Department of Transportation), Bill Remington (Delaware Division of Revenue, representing the Federation of Tax Administrators), Mark Smith, John Spinnello, and Bob Shinn (New Jersey Department of Environmental Protection, representing ECOS), Ellen Hennessy (formerly of the Pension Benefit Guaranty Corporation), and George Grob (Department of Health and Human Servives, Inspector General's Office).

I found these sessions illuminating, invigorating, and enormous fun. They substantially shaped the final product, made it somewhat longer than it otherwise would have been, and taught me much about how to present the material in a more accessible way. I am indebted to Pat McGinnis (president of the Council for Excellence in Government) for her vision and enthusiasm for this project and for hosting the forums; and to Sally Sachar, John Trattner, Dave Sheldon, and Laura Ziff for their support of the project and their flawless administration of the process.

The Harvard Policy Group on Network-Enabled Services and Government (a research project conducted by the Kennedy School's Program on Strategic Computing and Telecommunications in the Public Sector, and underwritten by IBM, AMS, and Cisco Systems) sponsored the writing of a working paper on the nature of analytic support for risk control operations, the substance of which is incorporated into this volume. I am grateful to Jerry Mechling and Tom Fletcher (program director and deputy) for their sustained interest in and support of many different aspects of my research over many years.

The Innovations in American Government award program, with support from the Ford Foundation, sponsored the preparation of two papers: the first, prepared in 1996 as part of a tenth-year assessment of the program, examined the subset of innovations finalists that were regulatory in nature. Some material from that early paper appears in this volume, updated and much expanded. The second paper focused on the search for measures of regulatory effectiveness; some material from that paper appears here.

Among my academic colleagues, my most abiding intellectual debts in this field are to Mark Moore (Kennedy School) and Herman Goldstein (University of Wisconsin). Mark Moore's conception of strategic public management underpins the whole book; indeed one could regard this study as a specific application of his ideas regarding what it means to "create public value." Herman Goldstein, as principal architect of the police profession's problem-oriented policing, deserves to see his ideas and methods applied much more broadly across the regulatory spectrum. One might regard this book as my attempt to do just that.

I am also grateful to the following: David Kennedy, for his companionship over many years in exploring the theory and practicalities of problem solving and for his generosity in providing information and insight regarding the Boston gun project, which he directed; Marilyn Peterson, for her pioneering and persevering work in enhancing the status and sophistication of intelligence analysis in law enforcement, an essential piece of the foundation for risk control operations; my colleagues Derek Bok, Cary Coglianese, and Bill Hogan for their encouragement, for their thoughtful feedback on drafts, and for extending my horizons on issues of regulatory reform; and Brookings editors Nancy Davidson, Chris Kelaher, Janet Walker, and Dianne Hammond for their deft guidance of the project.

Last but not least, I thank my wife, Penny, and our children—Henry, Elodie, Nadine, Patrick, Sandra, Natasha, and Sophie—for their forbearance during the many days over the past decade when I have traveled to far-off places to spend time closeted in hotel basements with federal and state regulators, trying to help them understand and navigate the mysterious currents swirling about them; and during the intense but relatively short period it took to write it all down. Particularly, I single out Sophie, aged four, who—while her more service-oriented friends like to play shopkeepers—prefers to play customs inspector and search through other people's luggage.

Introduction

Eᴀʀʟʏ ɪɴ ᴍʏ ᴀᴄᴀᴅᴇᴍɪᴄ career I discovered that before I get too far into a lecture it is worth checking whether I am in the right classroom, with the right audience, and that everyone agrees what subject is to be covered. The term regulatory reform means so many different things to different people that I should explain carefully, and early, which particular aspects this book addresses, for many regulatory reformers will not find their major interests represented here.

The subject of this book is the reform of regulatory and law enforcement *practice*, so it has more to do with changing the behavior of regulators than with changing regulations. It is more about management than about law. As such, the book is intended for government officials who have regulatory or law enforcement responsibilities, includes police, customs, any other agencies that use enforcement powers, and any internal departments that play a watchdog function (such as the offices of inspector general), even though many of these do not normally think of themselves as regulators. The book is also intended for legislators, overseers, and others who care about the nature and quality of regulatory practice and who want to know what kinds of behavior and performance they should demand from regulatory and enforcement agencies.

The Distinctive Nature of Regulatory and Enforcement Responsibilities

The important features that distinguish regulatory and enforcement agencies from the rest of government are precisely the important features that they share. The core of their mission involves the imposition of duties. They deliver obligations, rather than services.

Society entrusts regulatory and enforcement agencies with awesome powers. They can impose economic penalties, place liens upon or seize property, limit business practices, suspend professional licenses, destroy livelihoods. They can restrict liberty, use force, and even kill—either in the heat of some dangerous moment on the street or through the cold calculation of the execution room. They use these powers not against foreigners in war but against citizens in peacetime. How regulatory and enforcement agencies use these powers fundamentally affects the nature and quality of life in a democracy. Not surprisingly, regulators are scrutinized more closely and criticized more regularly for their uses or abuses of power than for their stewardship of public resources. Their routine use of state authority and coercion distinguishes them from the rest of government and carries its own distinct strategic and managerial challenges.

The nature and quality of regulatory practice hinges on which laws regulators choose to enforce, and when; on how they focus their efforts and structure their uses of discretion; on their choice of methods for procuring compliance. Yet the vogue prescriptions for the reinvention or reform of government, which have been swirling around regulatory executives for close to ten years, say little about these issues and sometimes seem to ignore them altogether. The popular prescriptions for reform focus on service, customers, quality, and process improvement, not on compliance management, risk control, or structuring the application of enforcement discretion. They rely heavily on management tools and methods imported from the private sector, which has few comparable challenges.

Of course, the prescriptions for customer service and process improvement can be useful in the regulatory context and have been applied to considerable effect by many agencies. But they will never be enough; these ideas are unlikely to provide complete or satisfactory prescriptions for regulatory reinvention or reform, because regulatory functions represent an anomaly in the context of customer-driven government. When people are arrested or fined or have their license revoked or their property seized, most often they are not pleased. Government does not seek to serve them in that instant. In many cases government creates an experience for them that is by design unpleasant. Of course, those being arrested, fined, or forced into compliance are entitled to be treated fairly and with human dignity. But when law is put in action against them, they receive treatment they did not request, did not pay for directly, will not enjoy, and will not want to repeat. In this context, the notions of quality governance in widest circulation simply fall short. The notion of customer falls short. Regulators need a broader vocabulary, so they can think in terms not only of customers but of stakeholders, citizens, obligatees, objects or targets of enforcement, beneficiaries, taxpayers, and society.[1] The underlying nature of the regulatory business requires that individual or private satisfaction be weighed against, and often sacrificed to, broader public purposes. Whatever difficulties we face in translating service models to government will be most acute in regulatory and enforcement domains.

Regulators have learned the value of adopting customer service ideas for certain aspects of their business, but most are aware that they need a broader portfolio of ideas as they search for strategies that are at once economical with respect to the use of authority and genuinely effective in procuring compliance and mitigating risks.

A Focus on Regulatory Practice

Why focus on regulatory practice rather than on the quality of the regulations themselves? I am grateful to my colleague Cary Coglianese for his neat partition of regulatory reform issues into four major subject areas: the scope of regulation, its nature, its locus, and the behavior of regulators. The first area (scope) covers issues of deregulation, reregulation, and regulation of emergent risks or markets. The second (nature) covers consideration of alternative forms of regulation, such as the use of tradable permits in pollution control and the establishment of negotiated resolution procedures. The third (locus) covers questions of centralization or decentralization, levels of regional or local autonomy, and in the United States centers mostly on the relationship between federal and state law. The fourth (behavior) covers the strategies, tactics, policies, operational methods, and culture of regulatory agencies.

Whatever changes the first three areas of reform may produce, and whatever amendments to law result, it falls to regulatory agencies to implement them. The style and nature of their implementation can surely make or break any new set of rules. Philip Howard, in his popular assault on the suffocating nature of regulatory law, observes: "Law can't think, and so law must be entrusted to humans, and they must take responsibility for their interpretation of it."[2] Part of the solution to the overwhelming mass of centralized, prescriptive regulations, Howard says, is to give regulators greater latitude and discretion, so they can make sensible judgments in response to individual situations—because the application of blanket prescriptions leads, in particular cases, to foolishness. Twelve years earlier, Eugene Bardach and Robert Kagan were similarly struggling with the problem of "regulatory unreasonableness," and they too pointed to the role official discretion would inevitably play in any resolution:

> Much that is excessive about protective regulation springs, at one level, from the overinclusiveness of centrally formulated rules applied broadly to enterprises that differ in technology, attitudes, capabilities, potential for harm, and costs of abatement. In some degree this problem arises . . . from the sheer technical difficulty of writing suitably differentiated rules, and in some degree it arises from the inflexibility that our legal and moral norms impose on governmental conduct. Whatever the constellation of causes, though, one obvious remedy for the problem is to institutionalize a certain amount of official discretion to mitigate the effects of overinclusive rules either at the field enforcement level or in the course of higher-level appeals and reviews. This could mean creating explicit legal authority for inspectors to overlook certain violations, authorizing enforcement officials (in conjunction with regulated parties) to work out alternative means of reaching regulatory goals, introducing more explicit bargaining over compliance schedules, transforming inspectors from "cops" into "consultants" in some areas, or any number of other things.[3]

Regulatory agencies exercise discretion as a matter of course—and at many different levels. At the higher managerial levels, executives have considerable latitude in allocating resources, constructing programs, assigning personnel, focusing inspection and enforcement programs, choosing where and how to expend the agency's efforts, and setting the nature and style of their interactions with the regulated community.[4] Such latitude sometimes derives from authorizing statutes, having been consciously granted by lawmakers. More often it results from ambiguous or conflicting mandates, overlapping jurisdictions, the need to respond quickly to changing conditions not foreseen in law, or the simple fact that agency resources are insufficient to do everything, so somebody has to make choices.

At the field level, inspectors, auditors, and enforcement officers hold considerable power to do good or evil, to dispense justice or injustice. Police patrol officers and regulatory inspectors work mostly alone or in pairs and far out of sight of supervisors. The enforcement myth, which has so often saved regulators from having to account for their uses of discretion, is that they enforce the law uniformly, across the board, without fear or favor. It is not, and was never, true. They choose not to enforce laws for many reasons, some good, some bad: they did not have time, they were on their way to something more important, there were too many violators and no sensible way of choosing between them, it was a silly law, making the arrest would have provoked a riot, the offender had political connections or was a friend or worked for the IRS or had a sticker on his car acknowledging contributions to a police charity.

Granting broader discretion to regulators may serve to moderate the excesses of centralized, command-and-control-style legislation. It also brings its own dangers. Bardach and Kagan point out how regulatory regimes can appear oppressive, not because the laws are flawed but as a result of the behavior of individual enforcement officials: "The present [1982] discontent with protective regulation, as expressed in most complaints about it, has almost nothing to do with aggregate costs and almost everything to do with particular costs and aggravations imposed by particular enforcement officials on particular institutions and businesses."[5] Even when frontline staff do enforce the law precisely as written, the action may still be experienced as an injustice.[6] Perhaps the law was defective, or obsolete, or ignorant of the particular circumstances. Or perhaps, even if the law was applicable and appropriate, this application of it was inequitable, discriminatory, or vindictive. Or perhaps the official had a bad attitude, coming across as overbearing, condescending, or unhelpful.

Regulatory agencies, by their conduct, can take perfectly reasonable law and produce oppressive regimes. Similarly, by choosing wisely what to enforce, when, and how, regulatory agencies can take an unmanageable accumulation of laws, many of which might be obsolete, and deliver perfectly reasonable regulatory protection. In their 1986 study of the regulation of strip mining in the coal industry, Neal Shover, Donald Clelland, and John Lynxwiler observe: "Now law is writ, and laws are rules. They are paper threats. They represent the state's intent to regulate certain forms of behavior. But laws on the books mean little in and of themselves. They are meaningful only insofar as they are backed by the mobilization of state powers, law in action."[7] These authors also note the relative lack of attention given to regulatory behavior in academic discussions of regulatory reform: "An emphasis on the politics of the implementation process—what goes on behind the administrative façade—is a notable gap in theoretical approaches to regulation."[8]

In focusing on the behavior of regulators, I prefer the phrase *reforming regulatory practice* than the alternative *administrative reform*. Regulators do so much more than administer laws. They also deliver services, build partnerships, solve problems, and provide guidance. They choose not to administer a law. And in addressing important public problems they frequently seek to influence behaviors that are not regulated. Moreover, the term *administrative reform* hints at the unreasonable notion that law is made first and administered second and that the two processes are clearly distinguishable and separable.[9] In practice, lawmakers have to understand the capabilities and propensities of regulatory agencies and design regulatory frameworks that make good use of them.[10] Regulators, depending on their conception of their role, may adopt an energetic and proactive stance in proposing and pursuing the kind of laws they think should govern their work.

Would-be reformers of the Environmental Protection Agency's authorizing statutes press hard (and have been doing so for some time) for a new, integrative, risk-based statute that would more scientifically balance the attention given to environmental and health hazards. The National Academy of Public Administration's 1985 study of the EPA, in advocating such a change, stresses the importance not only of creating the statute but of having the EPA work with Congress to set strategic priorities (presumably on a continuing basis): "Better and broader risk analyses could improve this process; the biggest gains, however, would come from creating an agency that could better convert knowledge into effective action."[11] If the benefits to be derived from better environmental law depend so heavily upon the EPA learning how to use risk analyses in their operations, and if learning that skill would not automatically follow from passing such a law, then one has to wonder how much society might benefit from the EPA learning that skill, even without any change in the law. (Some EPA officials would protest that they already have the skill but are constrained by the array of existing laws.)

In any case, regulatory practice has received less attention to date than other aspects of regulatory reform—and not just in the United States. In 1995, the Public Management Service of the Organization for Economic Cooperation and Development, summarizing its evaluations of regulatory approaches across the twenty-nine member countries, commented:

> Even after the most rigorous decision-making process inside the administration, regulation has yet to pass the most demanding test of all—the public must agree to comply with it. Yet implementation—consisting of strategies such as education, assistance, persuasion, promotion, economic incentives, monitoring, enforcement, and sanctions—is very often a weak phase in the regulatory process in OECD countries, which tend to rely too much on ineffective punitive threats and too little on other kinds of incentive.[12]

So I focus on the reform of practice, because many others focus so heavily on reform of law. Also, so much of the interesting action occurs in the realm of regulatory practice: that is where there is an important story to be told, where so many innovations have recently appeared, and where much might be gained or lost whether or not new legal frameworks eventually appear.

A Focus on Social Regulation

This book is more about social regulation than economic regulation. That does not necessarily mean it has no relevance for economic regulation. Various practitioners within the field of economic regulation have told me it has relevance for them. But I am not an economist, so I am obliged to leave that determination to the experts.

For the sake of those not familiar with the distinction between social and economic regulation (which is somewhat fuzzy): social regulation centers on issues of health, safety, welfare, working conditions, and the environment; whereas economic regulation concentrates on the healthy functioning of markets. Agencies of social regulation tend to cover specific risks or threats but do so across many or all industrial sectors. By contrast, agencies of economic regulation typically regulate a specific industry (such as utilities, financial services, transportation, or communications) and seek to guarantee adequate competition, efficient markets, fair trade practices, and consumer protections.[13] The majority of the cases and examples in this book come from the domain of social regulation. So economic regulators may feel a little left out of the discussion. Please accept my apologies, and read on.

Even among social regulators, there may be some who will find their agency mentioned nowhere here. I hope that will not make the book irrelevant for them. I have deliberately avoided focusing on domain-specific technicalities, and I am in any case not qualified to teach the finer points of tax administration, the scientific bases for environmental protection, or the distinctive technical specialties of any other regulatory profession. Rather, I present examples and lay out arguments with the broadest possible application. In this I follow others more wise and experienced, such as Robert Kagan. In a 1978 study, he examines the roles of the Cost of Living Council and the Office of Emergency Preparedness in the administration of a nationwide wage-price freeze,

> not to assess the desirability of wage and price controls or the relative merits of regulation as compared to the free market, but to provide insight into the nature of the administrative legal decision process and the making and application of rules in regulatory agencies. . . .
>
> A case study of any single agency casts light on the activities of others, insofar as it is consciously comparative in its mode of inquiry and presentation and focuses on *dimensions* of the legal process and the environment of decision that are common to all legal institutions.[14]

I trust, therefore, that regulatory and enforcement officials whose agencies are not mentioned explicitly in these pages will nevertheless find the conceptual frameworks and analytic apparatus they need to navigate their own reform landscape.

Structure of this Book

Sections of this text will be more important for some readers than others. Legislators—particularly those newly appointed—will find that part 1 provides essential background on regulatory reform and explains the accumulation of pressures acting on regulatory practice, including the influence of party politics (chapter 3). Prescriptions for reform, as well as the influence of the reinvention movement, are discussed. In particular, it examines the strengths and limitations of customer service, process management, and other managerial practices imported from the private sector, explaining why these prescriptions are never adequate guidance for reform of regulatory practice and describing the confusion that results when they are thoughtlessly applied within the regulatory arena (chapters 4 and 5).

Part 2 describes something much more promising but less well understood—the emergence of a new regulatory craftsmanship, which brings with it the ability to specify risk concentrations, problem areas, or patterns of noncompliance, and to design interventions that effectively control or reduce them. In other words, to *pick important problems and fix them.*

I suspect some may be puzzled that such an orientation can be counted as new or even worth writing a book about. Are not risk control and problem solving precisely what the public would expect from agencies of social regulation? Surely these agencies were established in order to control risks to human health, to human welfare, and to the environment. If so, then why—when they do it successfully—does anyone regard such behavior as noteworthy, pioneering, or innovative? If public safety officers could not identify issues of public safety and tackle them effectively, then why are they on the job? What value is a tax agency that does not know how to manage taxpayer compliance? Or an occupational safety and health administration that could not identify important workplace hazards and eliminate them? Or an environmental agency that could not identify and effectively address environmental problems?

The surprising truth is that when regulators do manage to focus their attention on thorny, persistent, and specific problems, and when they devise interventions that work, we often applaud such work as if it were *not* expected. One might properly inquire what other work occupies regulators most of the time. Taking this line of argument too far might do regulatory agencies some injustice. Their missions are amorphous and multifaceted, their statutory obligations miscellaneous and poorly integrated. Each of their activities contributes toward some aspect of mission accomplishment, even if the tangled web of causes and effects makes linking specific actions to specific outcomes difficult or impossible. Indeed, we would all hope that most of what regulators do is useful to a point.

Nevertheless, a new direction for regulatory practice clearly emerges, exemplified by a broad range of regulatory innovations (described in chapter 6). Pioneering agencies are reemphasizing the core purposes of social regulation; developing new, systematic approaches that break those broad purposes down into specific projects; and developing managerial systems that oblige staff to invent solutions, project by project. That such actions pop up on the public administration scanner as innovations suggests that they were not easy, that somehow executives had to wrestle the requisite resources and attention away from other, all-consuming tasks, and that the nature of the organizational apparatus necessary to support such actions was not obvious. If it were all easy and obvious, then regulators everywhere would be doing it all the time, and there would be nothing innovative about it.

The central contention of this book is that while apparently simple ideas about risk control and problem solving remain for the most part very poorly understood, they represent the opportunity for profound changes in regulatory practice and should be adopted as foundations for reform. Part 2 teases out the essential elements of this emerging problem-solving capability, describes the various routes by which different agencies have come to it, and considers what it would really take—in terms of organizational infrastructure and managerial practice—to place effective risk control at the heart of routine operations.

Part 3 examines the underlying nature of the risk control, or problem solving, art. Chapters 15 and 16 reveal it as a substantial professional skill, equivalent in complexity to the practice of medicine, to which the spectrum of regulatory professionals should pay increased attention. Chapter 17 shows how adoption of a risk control framework would transform the ways in which discretion is understood and managed. And chapter 18 shows how any effective risk control operation requires, at its very core, a substantially enhanced analytic or intelligence operation.

Part 4 brings the various pieces of the puzzle together and focuses closely on the last major piece—the performance measurement story. Chapter 19 describes the performance account that would naturally accompany effective risk control, problem-solving, and compliance management operations. And chapter 20 shows how a few agencies—those more advanced in the development of these strategies—have recognized the need, and created the organizational fabric, to connect a proliferation of innovative field-level projects so they demonstrably contribute to the agency's high-level performance goals.

Several reviewers have suggested to me that the core of this book—the development of the problem-solving or risk control capacity (contained in parts 2 and 3)—has relevance far beyond the field of social regulation. My colleague Derek Bok, reviewing an earlier draft, commented: "In fact, the process of problem-solving and problem identification that you describe is almost as broad as government itself. Is there any type of government program or any government agency that could not usefully employ the methods you advocate?"[15]

The art of risk control is clearly central to a number of fields not generally regarded as regulatory in nature—the most obvious examples being the related fields of public health, disease control, and injury prevention. But I must remain cautious, at least for now, in claiming any broader audience. Without studying such non-regulatory fields in some depth, I cannot tell whether the art of risk control is already better developed there than it is within the regulatory and enforcement professions. If it is better developed elsewhere (and I hope it is), then the usefulness of this book might lie in helping to transfer some of that expertise into the domain of government regulation. If it is not, then this text may be useful among a broader range of professions.

The Babylonian Test

The core readers of this book, the ones I have most in mind, are regulatory and enforcement officials along with others—particularly legislators and legislative staffers—who need to understand the constraints under which those officials operate and what can reasonably be expected of them.

If there are regulatory practitioners unclear whether they are in the right place, and on the right subject—or whether their time would better be spent elsewhere—I recommend the strategy employed by King Nebuchadnezzar. According to the Book of Daniel, King Nebuchadnezzar "dreamed dreams, wherewith his spirit was troubled, and his sleep brake from him."[16] He was surrounded, not by management theorists or scholars of regulation, but by magicians, astrologers, sorcerers, and Chaldeans. King Nebuchadnezzar sought of them an interpretation of his dreams yet found confusion in the plurality of offerings. The strategy he devised to sort them out was not to reveal his dream to any of them. Any who would proffer an interpretation had first to recount the dream, which, if they had it correct, the King would recognize. "Therefore tell me the dream, and I shall know that ye can shew me the interpretation thereof."[17] The penalty for getting it wrong, commensurate with the times, was that the magicians and astrologers would be "cut in pieces, and their houses made a dunghill."[18]

For the regulatory practitioners still with me, let me tell you (with some trepidation) your dream:

— There are too many laws to enforce and not enough resources. Enforcement, the distinctive competence of your agency, seems to have become politically unfashionable and is now accepted only grudgingly by those who hold political sway over you as a necessary evil, a thing of last resort, and better not to talk of it. Given your agency's traditions of audit, inspection, and enforcement, embracing the new tools of voluntary compliance (education, outreach, partnership, customer service, negotiation, consensus building) has presented considerable cultural challenges, but you and your colleagues have persevered.

— In embracing the new tools, you thought senior management had adopted and communicated a well-balanced approach to compliance, but sometime within the last seven years, and quite unexpectedly, enforcement numbers or judicial referrals dropped precipitously. You do not remember anyone actually saying "we don't do enforcement any more." In fact, you are pretty sure no one would ever have said that. But apparently that is what everybody thought they heard.

— When your agency hit this bean dip phenomenon (that is, your enforcement bean counts dipped dramatically), howls of protest were heard from your traditional allies and advocates of your cause (unless you are a tax agency, in which case you have no traditional allies). Imploring you to return to your old ways, they argued that nothing works like enforcement and demanded an explanation for your agency's apparent inactivity. "Innovation," you replied, "newer, better methods, that reach further and get better results at less cost." "Prove it," they said. And you could not.

— Meanwhile, legislative changes washed over your agency, requiring a clear demonstration of the results achieved by your regulatory actions. To justify agency funding, you now had to demonstrate the connection between specific activities and specific outcomes—a complicated intellectual task, which agency executives divided and delegated to the functional managers.

— The enforcement chief in particular complained this was not fair: in this mode of analysis, enforcement would always be undervalued. For no one (not even the academic experts of whom he had inquired) knew how to measure the broader deterrent effect of specific enforcement actions. Enumerating the direct, local consequences of individual enforcement actions could never capture the broader impact on compliance rates. Besides, the enforcement function was more about delivering justice than producing any other kind of results.

— Other enforcement managers, clearly exasperated that they should have to defend their existence, explained that the reason the agency should maintain its commitment to enforcement was that without a credible deterrent none of the other new-fangled methods would work.

— The focus on the customer, imported from the private sector and pressed on you by the reinvention gurus, turned the developing crack in your organization into a fissure. Camps developed. The enforcement camp, accustomed to dealing with egregious violators, found the new language of customer service (especially the private sector notion that they should "delight people so that they come back for more") plainly ridiculous. Investigators' morale plummeted, and several left. Wiser birds amongst them hunkered down, expecting this too, like other management fads, would pass. The voluntary compliance camp, populated by younger, newer, and sweeter people, regarded the enforcement crew as dinosaurs, remnants of a bygone era.

— As conscientious executives, you all set about trying to pull the agency together, tackling this increasingly confusing mess with the management tools in vogue: quality management and process improvement. You found these tools useful for boosting the productivity and efficiency of functional units and for improving the accuracy and timeliness of your core, high-volume, operational processes (particularly those awkward ones that straddle multiple functional areas). Using *quality circles,* you even saw hitherto separate parts of your organization working together. *Participative management* wafted through, until middle management realized how it undermined their authority.

— An assortment of consultants came and went, adding to the confusion. Most of them, schooled in the private sector, were experts on change but had no idea what changes were needed, because none of them had any experience with enforcement or compliance work.

— But still the drum beat for results, results, results. With a quiver full of process improvements, you could demonstrate efficiency, timeliness, productivity, and customer satisfaction; but the legislature was asking for effectiveness, which meant showing that the world was a better place and that you had made it so.

— Ever eager to help, your loyal staff brought to your attention a few inspiring stories, dredged up from the bowels of the organization. Individuals or small groups acting on their own initiative had identified some important issue, problem, risk, or pattern of noncompliance; had invented a solution and implemented it; and it had worked. The world was a better place! At least, a little piece of it.

— You rewarded these individuals, celebrated them, and let them stand with politicians and dignitaries. Their exploits were written up— and then written off (by your critics) as anecdotes. You wondered why other employees could not behave so courageously and intelligently. But deep in your heart you knew (as all regulatory managers know) that none of the agency's managerial, administrative, or support systems required, supported, or rewarded such actions. These isolated success stories were really stories of organizational subversion. The heroes and heroines, celebrated by the politicians, were "good people locked in bad systems." It was your job to mend the system.

— When you tried to promote such activity by diffusing innovations, your efforts were met with the depressing refrain, "It won't work here," which sounded cynical to you at first. When you looked into the matter, however, you found that they were right: It wouldn't work here.

— You realized how precious it would be if staff throughout your agency routinely identified and tackled important problems, artfully picking the right combination of tools for the job, using enforcement judiciously and sparingly, designing solutions that worked; and how precious if you were able to demonstrate that your agency's normal operations (as opposed to these isolated exceptions) demonstrably made the world a better place—eliminated hazards, mitigated hazards, decreased exposures, reduced death rates, reduced injury rates, reduced accident rates, reduced illness rates, reduced crime rates, or increased compliance.

— You wondered which pieces of the existing organizational or managerial apparatus you could use to make such creative behavior the routine rather than the exception. As you pondered this, your thoughts turned to the strategic planning process and those excruciatingly dull meetings at which your management team periodically reasserted the organization's mission and values in terms sufficiently general and vague to justify all existing activity. At that point, or thereabouts, you woke up in a cold sweat.

Those who recognize this dream may be interested in the interpretation, which follows.

PART I

Challenges
to Regulatory Practice

CHAPTER ONE

Pressures

Rᴇɢᴜʟᴀᴛᴏʀs, ᴜɴᴅᴇʀ ᴜɴᴘʀᴇᴄᴇᴅᴇɴᴛᴇᴅ pressure, face a range of demands, often contradictory in nature: be less intrusive—but more effective; be kinder and gentler—but don't let the bastards get away with anything; focus your efforts—but be consistent; process things quicker—and be more careful next time; deal with important issues— but do not stray outside your statutory authority; be more responsive to the regulated community—but do not get captured by industry.

Conflicting demands should surprise no one in government. Such is the nature of governance. That is what makes the role of a public official rich and interesting, rather than morally barren or straightforward. Even more, such is the nature of regulation. If complete consensus were possible on any regulatory issue—that is, if a solution existed that served the interests of every private party—then the issue would probably not warrant regulatory attention. Because regulation and enforcement, by their nature, elevate broad public purposes above the interests of private parties, one should expect regulatory practice to carry with it irreducible conflicts. Regulators inhabit, and are obliged to navigate, a landscape of conflicting and shifting interests.

The task here is to assess the demands now pressing on regulatory systems; in particular, given the focus on *practice*, the problem is to draw out any implications for the conduct of regulators and the organizational strategies of their agencies. Complaints about excessive regulation, or about the inappropriateness of a command-and-control regulatory style, are often not carefully directed. Are the regulations themselves overbearing? Or is it the inspector? Which is at fault, the style of the regulatory regime or the choice of regulatory tactics? Practitioners take the brunt either way. Even when the fault lies with the law, the fury is directed at regulators. To the public, and especially to industry, regulators seem all too often nitpicky, unreasonable, unnecessarily adversarial, rigidly bureaucratic, incapable of applying discretion sensibly, and (worst of all, since regulation costs so much) ineffective in achieving their missions.

The Major Themes of the Critics

Picking apart the 1990s chorus of criticism, one finds a number of powerful themes.

The Volume and Complexity of Regulations

The regulated community faces an overwhelming accumulation of rules, regulations, and reporting obligations and, associated with them, tedious and time-consuming bureaucratic processes. The costs of having to deal with government regulations, according to industry groups, threaten to damage American businesses' ability to compete in the global market. To many commentators, this means that the regulatory pendulum has swung too far and should be pushed back. Eugene Bardach and Robert Kagan point out that, in the 1960s, the phrase *regulatory reform* would have held quite the opposite sense.[1] At that time, regulatory authorities were perceived to have been captured by the industries they regulated, so the clamor of reform was for strengthening regulatory controls of harmful behaviors, particularly industrial behaviors. Then the pendulum swung, and the 1960s and 1970s produced enormous growth of federal protective regulation. The Environmental Protection Agency was created in 1970, the same year that Congress passed the Occupational Safety and Health Act.[2] The Nixon administration presided over the creation of a wave of new regulatory agencies: the Occupational Safety and Health Administration, the Nuclear Regulatory Commission, the Environmental Protection Agency, the Mine Safety and Health Administration, the National Highway Transport Safety Administration, and the Consumer Product Safety Commission.[3]

Now the pendulum has swung too far, so the story goes, to the point of overregulation; to the point of diminishing or negative returns.[4] The costs of complying with federal regulations have been estimated at $688 billion for 1997,[5] split roughly evenly between social regulation, economic regulation, and paperwork regulations (primarily tax compliance). During the 1990s, social regulatory costs increased substantially (by roughly 82 percent), whereas economic regulatory costs decreased slightly due to deregulation in the trucking and airlines industries.[6]

Being "overwhelmed by regulation" is by no means peculiar to the United States. The Organization for Economic Cooperation and Development (OECD), following extensive reviews of the needs for and nature of regulatory reforms throughout member countries, reported that

> the volume and complexity of laws, rules, paperwork, and administrative formalities now reach an all-time high in OECD countries, overwhelming the ability of regulators in implementing the total load, the private sector in complying, and elected officials in monitoring action. Too often, legislators issue laws as symbolic public action, rather than as practical solutions to real problems. Regulatory inflation erodes the effectiveness of all regulations, disproportionately hurts [small and medium businesses], and expands scope for misuse of administrative discretion and corruption.[7]

Not surprisingly, many countries have launched vigorously into regulatory reform. Australian federal and state governments, for example, have been working since 1996 on a comprehensive review of regulations (due to be completed in the year 2000), to identify and eliminate anticompetitive effects.[8] Australia's pendulum, historically, has swung in sync with that of the United States, their rate of government regulations (the number made per year) tripling between 1960 and 1981.[9]

Naturally the captains of American industry want to keep up, arguing that U.S. businesses will suffer unless the improvement of regulatory structures at least keeps pace with progress abroad.[10] International comparisons and the growth of international trade also bring pressure to bear on domestic regulatory style. In comparative studies, the U.S. approach is revealed as less cooperative and more enforcement oriented than others, with no discernible difference in overall compliance rates.[11] Such comparisons provide leverage for those who press U.S. regulators to adopt less adversarial approaches. The growth of international trade also brings pressures on regulators to align their systems with those of important trading partners. Mutual recognition agreements, whereby signatory countries recognize the regulatory approvals granted by their counterparts, facilitate trade. (For example, the Food and Drug Administration would permit the importation of pharmaceutical products manufactured in and approved by countries with which the United States has an MRA.)[12]

Regulators, too, feel overwhelmed. There are too many laws to be enforced, too many violators, and not nearly enough resources. As they struggle to keep up, regulators feel that legal and judicial systems, already stretched to capacity, drag their efforts down. The court systems are overloaded. Procuring criminal, civil, or even administrative sanctions is cumbersome and time-consuming. Regulators feel not only overwhelmed but less and less appreciated. Complexity, conflicts, and ambiguities—making it impossible to comply with everything—have the effect of bringing the law into disrepute and dulling consciences.[13] Decreasing respect for regulations means decreasing respect for regulators. For regulators, continuing in a traditional, enforcement-centered mode—given the constraints of shrinking budgets, declining public tolerance for the use of regulatory authority, and clogged judicial systems—is now simply infeasible.

The Cost-Benefit Equation

The second major theme is that the costs of regulation, which are mostly borne by industry and which weigh most heavily on small businesses, outweigh the benefits. As Philip Howard expresses it, "we seem to have achieved the worst of both worlds: a system of regulation that goes too far while it also does too little."[14]

The natural answer for cost-ineffective regulation is not less regulation but a higher threshold over which any would-be regulation must climb. Several legislative initiatives—the two most notable being the Job Creation and Wage Enhancement Act of 1995 (House Resolution 9) and the Regulatory Improvement Act of 1997 (Senate Bill 981), neither of which passed into law—sought to establish mandatory cost-benefit analysis in the promulgation of new rules. Senate Bill 981, the more moderate of the two, was introduced by Senator Carl Levin (Democrat of Michigan) and Senate Governmental Affairs Committee chair Fred Thompson (Republican of Tennessee). If passed, it would have required agencies issuing a rule with economic implications exceeding $100 million to conduct cost-benefit analyses (to justify the costs) and to explore whether alternative regulatory approaches (such as market incentives and performance standards) might be more cost-effective. To this and other similar proposals, the Clinton administration responded that the merits of cost-benefit analysis at the rule-making stage were already secured under existing executive orders and that more rigorous requirements would unnecessarily hamper the rule-making process.[15]

To many public interest groups, an attempt to subject social regulation to cost-benefit analysis smacks of selling out morality to economics. The value of human life, of an ecosystem, of an endangered species, or of equal opportunity cannot be captured or expressed in dollar terms, so these "goods" should not be placed in an equation in which the units are monetary. Despite the fact that proposals such as Senate Bill 981 permit the inclusion in the analysis of benefits "quantifiable and non-quantifiable," opponents fear that economic considerations would inevitably dominate, therefore deemphasizing those aspects of public value (such as collective societal aspiration and distributional equity) not adequately captured by summing individual, utilitarian gains. They also point out that up-front cost-benefit analysis often overestimates the true costs to industry, noting that once regulations are in place, industry often produces technological or operational adaptations that reduce their costs.[16]

Given the strength of the U.S. public interest community, and the fact that as societies become wealthier they tend to face political pressure for greater environmental, health, and safety protections, the moral and ideological arguments are unlikely to subside anytime soon.[17] Given their persistence—and the reluctance of industry groups to appear antihealth, antisafety, or antienvironment—the debate progresses to theme three.

The Irrational Distribution of Regulatory Attention

The theme of irrational distribution at least has the advantage of being essentially technocratic or analytic, rather than ideological. Of course, industry is not actually opposed to these kinds of protections— merely frustrated at their lack of rationality. Having to spend $200 billion for environmental, safety, and health protection might not be so bad if it were an effective sacrifice. "More intelligent policies could achieve the same social goals at much less cost or more ambitious goals at the same cost."[18]

A host of academic researchers, together with a number of administration officials and analysts, point out the incongruities in the distribution of regulatory attention. Lee Thomas, while administrator of the EPA, commissioned a comparative risk assessment of all agency programs to see whether resource distributions reflected the comparative seriousness of risk.[19] Comparing regulations always produces costs per unit of harm averted, which vary by many orders of magnitude. In 1993 Stephen Breyer produced a comparative chart of regulations spanning multiple regulatory agencies, comparing the average cost per premature death averted.[20] Breyer estimates that the 1980 ban on unvented space heaters by the Consumer Product Safety Commission cost $100,000 per premature death averted. At the opposite end of the spectrum, according to Breyer, lies the EPA's 1990 hazardous waste listing for wood-preserving chemicals, estimated at $5.7 trillion per premature death averted.[21] Other analysts, given the inexactitude of the sciences involved, produce different lists, but they always show extraordinary variation.

As the risk sciences and risk literature have developed, more sophisticated units of comparison have emerged, such as the widely adopted quality-adjusted life years (also known as years of healthy life).[22] With such analytic devices, regulatory effectiveness can be evaluated in terms of the price paid by society, in aggregate or at the margin, for each quality-adjusted life year saved. These analyses provide a foundation for a range of legislative reform ideas, from redistribution of existing regulatory resources—to make those investments more efficient—to creation of an umbrella regulatory budget, which could then be scientifically and optimally parsed among competing risks. The intent of such legislative protection is clear: government should concentrate on those areas in which most can be achieved for the least cost and withdraw from the opposite end of the risk spectrum.

Inflexible Regulations

Regulatory inflexibility is the field-level variant of irrational distribution. The example cited repeatedly by industry groups is the case of Amoco's Yorktown refinery in Virginia, which was required by the EPA to spend $31 million to recover a small amount of benzene. Apparently, Amoco might have recovered five times as much benzene for much less ($6 million) if the EPA had been able to adopt a degree of regulatory flexibility.[23]

Project XL, one of the EPA's highest profile reinvention initiatives, was instituted in March 1995 to exploit just such opportunities. Under site-specific XL agreements, the EPA would permit project sponsors to implement, on a pilot basis, innovative strategies that produce superior environmental performance in exchange for regulatory flexibility.[24] The idea seems sound enough, but in retrospect the program seems to have fallen flat. Despite energetic support from Vice President Al Gore, who regularly showcased XL agreements as models of commonsense regulation, only ten agreements had been signed by February 1999.

EPA officials were disappointed with industry's XL proposals, many of which they regarded as strong on "regulatory flexibility" and weak on "superior environmental performance." Industry's growing perception, in turning away from the program, was that the EPA was happy with the superior environmental performance side of the bargain but that it—or its lawyers or its overseers—simply could not handle regulatory flexibility. (In any XL agreement, the agency would in effect be granting a facility, or other sponsor, written exemption from existing regulatory requirements.) Much of industry now regards the work of negotiating an XL application—a time-consuming process, with all interested parties being allowed access to the negotiations—as too risky and too much effort to be worthwhile.[25] Critics of the XL program within EPA, and even some supporters, circulated the motto internally: If it ain't illegal, it ain't XL.

Reformers seem cognizant of the shortcomings of command-and-control regulation (allowing insufficient discretion) and one-size-fits-all regulation (insufficiently differentiated). Perhaps a new regulatory flexibility will form part of the answer to these shortcomings. But as the EPA and others have found, the practical exercise of regulatory flexibility, even when rational and championed by politics, is not easy.

Out-of-Date Regulations

Another major theme is regulatory obsolescence. Industry experiences this as continued enforcement of rules rendered inappropriate by virtue of technological advances and insists that such rules be scrapped; better still, that all rules be born with sunset provisions. From the regulators' perspective, obsolescence works both ways: just as unnecessary rules are slow to go, new rules to address new risks are slow in coming. New risks not covered by existing statutory authorities or addressed by existing operational programs include radon gas in homes, the accumulation in water bodies of agricultural runoff from nonpoint sources, and carpal tunnel syndrome and other ergonomic injuries in the workplace. As responsive public managers, regulators are reluctant to ignore new chemicals, new hazards or threats, or new harmful behaviors just because they do not yet have any relevant law to enforce. Should they not be allowed to step into the void and address emergent risks, using whatever tools they have or can invent, stretching existing authorities in ways not envisaged by the drafters, at least until the legislative or rule-making process catches up?

Calls for Alternative Regulatory Techniques

Another voice in the reform debate calls for less use of state author-ity: to do less enforcement, to generate less hostility and mistrust, to develop less-adversarial techniques. At the highest level, this issue touches on the very scope and nature of regulation. These reformers insist that market mechanisms be employed first and that enforcement be employed as a last resort. Further, they say that society would prefer any method over enforcement if that method achieves the same purpose as enforcement. At lower levels, this theme appears as a tactical impera-tive for regulatory agencies. Negotiate, don't dictate.[26] Adopt a coopera-tive stance. Develop partnerships. Use enforcement only when all else has failed. Even when a facility or corporation is found out of compli-ance, reformers press regulators to prefer a variety of nonenforcement methods (technical assistance, education, guidance, or collaborative development of a company compliance plan) for bringing the facility into compliance. In some agencies the number of "returns to compliance without enforcement" has become a favorite metric for reformist (or politically correct) bean counters, as they search for antidotes to the tra-ditional preoccupation with enforcement statistics.

At the field level, the idea that anything is preferable to enforcement, if taken too far, could have disastrous effects on compliance levels. If indus-try discovered the worst consequences of being caught out of compliance were that they would be nudged back into it, without penalty or sanction, then deterrence would be lost and compliance rates would plummet. The perceived wisdom of substituting for enforcement wherever possible must have some natural limits. Yet the pressure to displace authoritarian meth-ods is felt strongly at every level of the regulatory system.

The Importance of Demonstrable Results

Regulatory agencies (along with the rest of government) face increased pressure to demonstrate their effectiveness. At the federal level, the Government Performance and Results Act of 1993 (GPRA) requires all federal agencies to develop five-year strategic plans and annual performance plans.[27] Although the GPRA encourages some use of *output* measures ("the tabulation, calculation, or recording of activity or effort"), its main thrust is to push regulators to define important *outcome* measures ("an assessment of the results of a program activity compared to its intended purpose").[28] Many state-level regulators experience similar pressure from the introduction of performance-based budgeting, which similarly links agency budgets to production of outputs and achievement of measurable outcomes.

The Implications for Regulatory Practice

Taken together, these accumulating pressures exert considerable torque on regulatory systems—and will continue to do so. It is hard to imagine the demands for regulatory reasonableness and cost-effectiveness abating any time soon. Listening to the reform debate, however, one could easily get the impression that the pressure on the structure can be alleviated only by reforming law and that the hundreds of thousands of men and women working in regulatory and enforcement agencies are irrelevant to the resolution. Legal frameworks may take years to change—or may not change. Maybe the EPA will have a new integrative, risk-based statute in the next decade; maybe it will not. Perhaps proposed rules will have to meet more stringent cost-benefit criteria; perhaps they will not.

Meanwhile, how should regulators behave? What can they offer, even if legal frameworks remain unchanged? By the way, does it not seem reasonable that cost-benefit analyses, in order to be definitive, consider the broad range of methods by which regulators might procure compliance? Some of those methods might be hopelessly inefficient and ineffective, provoking endless strife and failing to produce the intended benefit; other methods might be brilliantly incisive, relatively trouble free, and resource efficient. In the calculus of costs and benefits, is compliance simply assumed? Is any thought given to the range of compliance management techniques available? Surely, nontrivial portions of the costs associated with a regulation will be determined by the behavior of regulators.

Proponents of reform seem much clearer about what they want from legislators than what they want from regulators. Even those who appear like-minded in their description of the problems produce very different recommendations with respect to regulatory practice. For example, consider Philip Howard's position on the use of discretion. Beating the drum of excessive, overprescriptive regulatory law suffocating America, he bores in on the central problem, which, he says, is the absence of one indispensable ingredient: the use of human judgment. He blames the absence of human judgment on the adopted credo "that government should be self-executing and dispassionate."[29] He is clearly uncomfortable advocating greater discretion for government officials, but that is his unambiguous recommendation. "It is perhaps a hateful thought to give government officials a measure of discretion, but that's the only way for them to do anything, and the only way for us to know who to blame."[30]

A 1998 report from the Research and Policy Committee of the Committee for Economic Development (an industry group) apparently beats the same drum, recommending the use of markets first, command-and-control style regulations last, and rigorous cost-benefit analysis for proposed rules.[31] But with respect to the behavior of regulators, and in contrast to Howard, it finds that "Congress far too often grants overly broad authority to regulators because it cannot or will not resolve major conflicts over objectives in its legislation, leaving the resolution of such conflicts to the regulators. As a result, administrators have leeway to act in a capricious fashion."[32] Consequently it recommends that "regulatory authority should not be used capriciously, and the delegation of such authority by Congress to regulatory bodies should be limited to ensure this."

One critic says that the system breaks down because bureaucrats are not allowed to exercise their judgment. Another says that bureaucrats cannot be trusted with discretion and that they need to be straitjacketed to prevent them from acting arbitrarily and capriciously. The odd thing is that regulators and enforcement officials exercise their judgment and discretion all day, every day. They always have, and they always will. Regulators and enforcement officers have a great deal of de facto discretion, even if not de jure. Even when bound by restrictive codes such as "if you see it you must cite it," inspectors may still choose whether or not to *see* it. They may even choose to look *later*, offering the opportunity for remediation beforehand.

Given the routine exercise of de facto discretion, which is a form of regulatory flexibility, why should the EPA's lawyers find it so awkward to conclude XL agreements? I suspect it is because they have to *write it down*. While regulators perpetuate the myth that they enforce the law uniformly and everywhere, the only explanation they have to give, in answer to the question "Why did you prosecute me?" is "Because you broke the law." If discretion is exercised mostly informally and by field-level staff (and without ever being laid down in written policies), then neither the agency nor its managers have to explain its use.

But if regulatory executives acknowledge the routine, unavoidable, exercise of discretion—with important strategic choices being made about which laws matter, what forms of compliance count, and what methods to use—those executives would need to offer an account of the criteria they use in making choices, and they might have to describe the managerial systems that distribute or constrain discretion throughout the organization. Critics like Howard, who can scarcely contain their contempt for bureaucrats, would have to explain more carefully the *ways* in which they would like to see regulators exercise their discretion—different from the ways they do so now. Such a discussion would go to the heart of regulatory practice.

Developing a Mandate for Regulatory Practice

Because reformist pressures focus mostly on the nature of law, practitioners might be tempted to let the debate pass by as "out of our control" or "not our business." However, rather than passively allowing these pressures to pass by and leaving them to legislatures to debate, regulators should squeeze from them anything that might be instructive for regulatory practice. There is much.

— Yes, there are far too many laws and regulations and too much noncompliance. Therefore regulators must choose which laws and rules to enforce and should be prepared to explain publicly the grounds upon which they make such choices.

— Yes, judicial and administrative systems are horribly clogged. Therefore regulators should use these more expensive and cumbersome methods sparingly and devise artful and resource-efficient methods to influence relevant behaviors more broadly.

— Yes, laws in place do not rationally allocate regulatory resources and attention among different risks. Therefore regulators should, as far as possible, correct such defects as they make their strategic choices and resource allocation decisions.

— Yes, laws are often out of date. Therefore regulators should ignore those that are obsolete or unimportant and should take the initiative in tackling emerging issues and risks, even before they are recognized in law, building public support as they go.

What do we want of regulators, even while the reform debate continues? If we had to infer a mandate for regulatory practice, it might look something like this (some may find this constitutionally offensive, as it lands much closer to an *expert* model of regulatory behavior than a *legal* model):

> Acknowledge the constant need to make choices. Make them rationally, analytically, democratically. Take responsibility for the choices you make. Correct, by using your judgment, deficiencies of law. Organize yourselves to deliver important results. Choose specific goals of public value and focus on them. Devise methods that are economical with respect to the use of state authority, the resources of the regulated community, and the resources of the agency. And as you carefully pick and choose what to do and how to do it, reconcile your pursuit of effectiveness with the values of justice and equity.

As far as I can tell from the reform debate, this is what regulatory and enforcement agencies should do. But how will they do it? What tools and managerial methods will they use? What kind of report will they give?

CHAPTER TWO

Ideas

A SENIOR OFFICIAL at the Environmental Protection Agency asked if I could help him and his colleagues figure out the relationship among the many different ideas his agency had recently embraced. I asked him to list just the major ones (aware that the number of new initiatives at the EPA during the Clinton administration already exceeded sixty-five). He produced nine: customer service, quality management, ecosystem management, place-based management, total quality leadership, the commonsense initiative, process improvement, voluntary compliance, and empowerment.

Executives are not, obviously, short of ideas; rather they face the never-ending obligation of assessing them and then either absorbing them or disposing of them. Rather than searching for additional theories, executives want time to take stock and to check their bearings. Gurus come and go, often wheeled through on the coattails of politicians, too busy laying out their own theory to stop and ask who came before or what is coming next. Many of the doctrines they leave behind conflict with one another, and subsequently compete—through their champions—for resources, attention, and dominance. A study of management theories notes how those lately applied within government have not always been consistent: "Three most popular fads—downsizing, reengineering, and TQM [total quality management]—are, on many points of substance, mutually incompatible. Downsizing argues that workers are expendable; TQM sees them as invaluable resources. Reengineering depends on ripping up the organization and starting again; TQM is a doctrine of continuous, incremental improvement."[1]

As regulatory executives try to fit the pieces of the puzzle together, they need frameworks that will enable them to see when pieces do not fit, when pieces overlap, and which pieces are still missing. As comprehensive as the list of nine ideas above (at the EPA) may at first seem, this entire collection of ideas offers the EPA little guidance on how to tackle emerging and significant environmental problems, unless those problems just happen to have a shape that conforms to a watershed area (the focus of ecosystem management) or a community (the focus of place-based management, the anthropocentric equivalent) or are specific to one of the six industries covered by the commonsense initiative.

Private Sector Managerial Methods

Management fads in the public sector have been observed to lag behind those in the private sector by about five years.[2] Certainly, the importation of private sector managerial concepts and techniques, while not specific to or tailored to the domain of regulatory reform, has powerfully influenced regulatory practice over the last decade. The Internal Revenue Service embraced total quality management in 1987 and has had at times more than one thousand quality circles up and running. The EPA similarly embraced quality management in the late 1980s. Across the federal government, agencies learned process management and continuous process improvement in the late 1980s, then business process redesign and the more radical process reengineering during the early 1990s. These techniques of process management have enabled government agencies to improve their core, high-volume, operational processes: eliminating glitches, reducing wastefulness or duplication, improving accuracy and timeliness, reaping the efficiencies of automation, and ensuring cross-functional coordination. Seeking to emulate the best private sector companies by building quality in, government agencies turned to their customers, as the theories prescribe, to tell the agencies what quality means.

Regulatory and enforcement agencies, too, have their high-volume operational processes. They process tax returns, complaints, calls, queries, permit applications, requests for drug approvals, reports of crime, 911 calls. Many regulatory agencies have applied process management methods, to a greater or lesser extent, to improve their handling of process loads. But the confusing question in government, and especially in the regulatory domain, is always, Who is the customer? Which customer is government trying to please? In which areas of regulatory practice should the notion of *customer* give way to alternative conceptions, such as *violators, targets, citizens, beneficiaries, stakeholders, society?*

Despite the related ambiguities, improving customer service now lies at the heart of almost every proposal to reform regulatory practice. Note the way the Organization for Economic Cooperation and Development report on regulatory reform, listing a broad range of obviously sensible prescriptions, uses a culture of client service as the overriding promise:

> Reform is based on screening out regulations and formalities that are outdated or ineffective; streamlining and simplification of those that are needed; use of a wider range of market incentives and more flexible and international regulatory approaches; and introduction of greater discipline, coordination, and transparency within regulatory processes. The Canadian government has called this "regulating smarter," while the European Commission has announced "less action, but better action." In the longer term, the goal is to move governments from a culture of "control" to a culture of "client service."[3]

For regulators, figuring out where these private sector, customer-focused, management techniques ought to be used, and where they ought not, is important work. Chapters 4 and 5 address customer service and process improvement in detail. Regulators can neither ignore nor escape the substantial pressure to emulate private industry's use of these techniques in order to provide better service.

Reinventing Government

An overlapping, but not identical, set of ideas flow through the reinventing government movement. David Osborne and Ted Gaebler's 1992 book, *Reinventing Government,* became the manifesto for the work of the National Performance Review (since renamed the National Partnership for Reinventing Government).[4] Although Osborne and Gaebler's work has much less to say about regulation than Philip Howard's, it is at least more optimistic about government. While the stories in Howard's book are of bureaucratic stupidity and nonsense, the stories in Osborne and Gaebler's work are positive, full of initiative, courage, even heroism:

bureaucrats finding a way to do the right thing. The message of "good people locked in bad systems" comes across throughout. In fact, Osborne and Gaebler specify it as a part of their core doctrine. After declaring their belief in government (first) and the need for effective government (second), they say (third), "we believe that the people who work in government are not the problem; the systems in which they work are the problem. We write not to berate public employees, but to give them hope. At times, it may sound as if we are engaged in bureaucrat-bashing, but our intention is to bash bureaucracies, not bureaucrats. We have known thousands of civil servants through the years, but most—although certainly not all—have been responsible, talented, dedicated people, trapped in archaic systems that frustrate their creativity and sap their energy."[5] Osborne and Gaebler lay out ten themes of reinvention, but they make virtually no distinction between the regulatory and service functions of government. Some themes have more obvious implications for regulatory practice than others; the seven that translate most easily are the following:

— Catalytic government (steering rather than rowing)
— Mission-driven government (as opposed to rule based)
— Results-oriented government (preferring outcomes over outputs)
— Customer-driven government (meeting the needs of the customer)
— Anticipatory government (prevention rather than cure)
— Decentralized government (from hierarchy to participation and teamwork)
— Market-oriented government (allowing markets to do the work, or working through market mechanisms)[6]

Translated for regulatory and enforcement responsibilities, these themes resonate with more specific pressures acting on regulation. Customer-driven government echoes the private sector quality movement. Results-oriented government certainly fits with the broader pressures of GPRA and other performance-based budgeting statutes. Mission-driven government begins to prescribe the organizational culture and orientation that might help to produce those results, rather than conformance with rules and procedures.

Decentralized government could be translated as support for the notion that regulatory systems are more responsive (that is, less one-size-fits-all) when the locus of design and operation is moved to lower levels. Also, decentralized government coupled with catalytic government could be used to press regulators to negotiate more local agreements, both to be responsive to local needs and to mobilize a broader

range of nongovernmental resources. Bear in mind that the implied preference for more localized and operational forms of democracy (superseding centralized national versions) relates closely to the reform
debates regarding the appropriate locus for regulation. Decentralization
is associated with local responsiveness, with federal bureaucracies perceived as less capable of local accommodation than state or local apparatus.[7] For this reason the pressure for responsiveness (being associated
with the operation of decentralized discretion) could be seen as potentially at odds with demands for highly technocratic and analytical
rationalization and redistribution of regulatory attention, which would
presumably operate from the top.

Anticipatory government automatically prefers prevention to cure,
another idea that needs examining very carefully in the regulatory
domain. Preventive methods are often equated with nonenforcement
techniques (education, outreach, technical assistance), whereas enforcement actions are seen as the core of a reactive strategy, processing the
"failures" of prevention. Equating enforcement with reaction and alternatives with prevention can deepen the ideological divide between functional units within regulatory agencies, as certain methods get associated in people's minds with certain organizational philosophies.

In fact, most enforcement work is designed as preventive. The vast
majority of enforcement actions result from inspections and complaints,
not accidents. Motorists are ticketed more often for driving in a manner
that *might* cause an accident (but did not) than for causing accidents.
More broadly, violators are more often prosecuted for permitting a condition to exist that might cause some harm than for actually causing
harm. Thus most compliance management techniques, including
enforcement, are primarily preventive. So it does not make sense to
eschew enforcement simply on the grounds that it is not preventive.

Finally market-driven government as applied to regulation fits comfortably with the pressure for adoption of market mechanisms as an
alternative to the use of regulation. In fact, only in a discussion of market-driven government does *Reinventing Government* explicitly discuss
the challenges of regulation.

The Combined Effect of These Influences

The combination of private sector managerial methods with the doctrines of reinvention has produced a dominant prescription for reform

of regulatory behavior, with which practitioners are familiar but by which many remain puzzled or troubled. This prescription pushes the development of cooperative relationships between regulators and the regulated and emphasizes improvement of voluntary compliance through facilitation and improved customer services.

The focus on voluntary compliance (which favors a new set of tools and spawns numerous new programs) deemphasizes reliance on enforcement methods generally or considers them only as a last resort, to be used against recalcitrant or persistent offenders when all else has failed. Regulators are encouraged to pursue systemic solutions that do not involve enforcement, as these are perceived to produce a better bang for the regulatory buck and cause less trouble. Using alternatives to enforcement helps to minimize the use of state authority (although paradoxically it tends to increase governmental intrusion into the affairs of citizens and industry). As a result of these dominant pressures and prescriptions, most regulatory agencies now recognize, and to differing degrees embrace, a much broader range of compliance-producing tools, including education and outreach programs, partnership and mentoring programs, technical assistance, and economic incentives. Pick a regulator at random and ask which way regulatory practice is moving; the chances are that he or she will say, "From enforcement to voluntary compliance."

The Regulatory Pendulum

Historians and scholars of regulatory policy might point to this as yet another swing of a now familiar regulatory pendulum. The dichotomy between regulatory styles has been around for decades, albeit under a variety of labels. What popular lexicon now presents as enforcement versus voluntary compliance appeared in the 1970s and 1980s as deterrence versus compliance or (for other commentators) enforced compliance versus negotiated compliance. Whatever the labels, one style revolves around formal, precise rules and is viewed as adversarial and punitive and is based on an underlying distrust of the regulated community. The other style is seen as softer, more results oriented, and less wed to rules, stressing responsiveness and forbearance and preferring tools involving trade-offs, gaming tactics, persuasion, and negotiation.[8]

Which way reformist pressures push, history suggests, depends in rather predictable ways on the social and regulatory context. When a new industry or risk area is regulated for the first time (in response to some pressing and otherwise uncontrolled threat), implementation of fixed rules, accompanied by credible threats of aggressive enforcement action, generally provides the quickest way of bringing about widespread change in behavior. Then, over time, a natural maturation process sets in. The regulatory regime produces more and more rules, as regulators and legislators feel obliged to extend controls into similar or related areas. As regulated industries adapt and compliance levels rise, public concern over the original problems subside. Regulators try to keep their regulations up to date (by adding to them) and to produce more carefully differentiated rule-based schemes (in an effort to be reasonable). Proliferation is compounded by complexity. Rules beget exceptions and exceptions beget rules. Even reasonable regulatory protections, through some inescapable logic, grow ever more numerous and complex.[9] Eventually, and some say inevitably, the rule-based system becomes top heavy and turns into an economic liability; sympathy for the plight of regulated industries begins to grow, regulators lose respect as their authoritarian stance alienates the public, and reformist pressures begin to push the other way.

At that point, the danger of agency capture arises. Regulatory agencies, pushed into an accommodative and conciliatory stance, draw closer to the very people whose behavior they are supposed to control. "When the support of elected officials and broad-based public groups are lost, the agency, in quiet desperation, turns to its own clientele for support."[10] From that point on (so advocates of the harder, deterrence style would caution), the agency is compromised, neglects its original mission, and is unlikely to pursue enforcement actions when warranted.

The danger of capture arises from a variety of factors. Shortages of resources may leave regulators outgunned by those they seek to regulate. Regulatory agencies may have trouble retaining sufficient, well-qualified staff. The revolving door may place friends and former colleagues on the other side of the fence. Industry may control essential information and expertise. Commentators also list as a contributory factor for capture the "establishment of cooperative relationships for the solution of problems."[11]

To complete the cycle, captured agencies come to be regarded as feckless; and newer, stricter, rule-based regimes may be introduced using separate, untarnished, administrative apparatus. Given the nature of this regulatory cycle, and given the growth of protective regulation during the 1960s and 1970s (both in the United States and abroad), some would say that the current pressure to roll back rule-based systems in favor of more accommodating methods is natural and normal—even predictable.

This fundamental dichotomy can been observed across agencies as well as over time. Consider, for example, the police profession. James Q. Wilson examines policing in eight communities and finds a variety of policing styles.[12] What he terms the *legalistic style* of police behavior corresponds to the behavior of a rule-based, punitive, regulatory regime. In contrast, Wilson's *watchman style*, in which law is used as one device in a textured and context-specific task of keeping order, reflects a softer, more pragmatic, approach. If this stylistic dilemma, in the context of the current reform debate, presents an underlying policy choice, then most reinventers of government would fall firmly in the compliance camp, whereas the majority of regulatory scholars and much of the public interest community remain loyal to the deterrence camp.

Different Styles for Different Things

Rather than adopt the defeatist position that the swinging of the regulatory pendulum is inevitable, or that the two dichotomous styles are irreconcilable, scholars of regulatory policy have long sought to fashion something more constructive. As early as 1978, Kagan observed:

> In the United States, standards of legality are complex and demanding. Administrators are expected to adhere faithfully to the positive law enacted by the elected representatives of the people. But there is also a strong tradition of pragmatism and natural law which suggests that there are explicit limits on positive law. Officials are expected to adapt positive law to the requirements of the particular case in light of competing public policies, constitutional principles, and commonly recognized notions of fairness, even if those values are not reflected in the words of an applicable positive law. Officials are expected to attend to the substantive consequences of rule application and to provide rational explanations and justifications for their decisions.[13]

More recently, Australia's Ian Ayres and John Braithwaite stated that the time had come to escape what they described as "a long history of barren disputation . . . between those who think that corporations will comply with the law only when confronted with tough sanctions and those who believe that gentle persuasion works in securing business compliance with the law."[14]

The first step forward is to realize that each style has its own distinct advantages, so the choice between them is pragmatic, rather than ideological. The enforcement approach can be very useful when getting a program started as it maximizes immediate compliance. A stringent, rule-based system also provides an agency a strong defense against litigation, a strong base from which to pull back, external support (initially), a strong sense of mission, internal cohesion, and an effective mechanism for producing consistency across a far-flung agency without constructing a vast administrative apparatus. It helps to prevent corruption in situations in which regulators live and work closely with the people they regulate. It also lessens or eliminates the competitive advantage gained through noncompliance, by imposing financial penalties and requiring corrective actions. Negotiated compliance also has its merits. It minimizes opposition to the agency over the long term, reduces the burdens of compliance by allowing tailored responses, reduces levels of both localized and organized hostility, reaches further with fewer resources, and may increase the likelihood of agency survival.[15]

Given the attractiveness of these models for various circumstances, is it not possible to gain the benefits of both? Could executives and overseers not gain the benefits of negotiated compliance and at the same time avoid the dangers of agency capture? Perhaps so. In fact, methods for avoiding capture are already known: breaking up relationships between regulators and regulated (by periodic staff rotation and revolving door employment restrictions), expanding citizen groups' rights to participate, stipulating that agency decisions must be made in public session, providing appeal mechanisms for any aggrieved party, allowing private parties to seek judicial orders to force regulatory agencies to take action, opening agency records to reporters and others, providing federal review of state agencies' actions, forbidding advance notice of inspections, and centralizing the scheduling of inspection programs to remove decentralized discretion.[16]

Responsive Regulation

The second step forward is to realize that regulators should be able to vary their stance as they deal with different issues. In some areas, or for some industries, they might reap the benefits of a rigorous enforcement approach, while in other areas they might tread more softly. In other words, there is no reason why regulatory agencies should only have one act. Having several, plus the ability to choose the right act for the right issue, would be better. Such responsiveness could be more finely tailored if the agency learns a range of intermediate stances (between the two extremes) and is then able to select from this broader repertoire, depending on the circumstances. This is the heart of responsive regulation, as put forth by Ayres and Braithwaite: "An attitude of responsiveness does generate different policy ideas that do transcend the divide between regulatory and deregulatory solutions. But for the responsive regulator, there are no optimal or best regulatory solutions, just solutions that respond better than others to the plural configurations of support and opposition that exist at any particular moment in history."[17]

An interesting question then arises regarding the level within the regulatory system at which such choices should be made. Are we talking only of choosing an aggregate style for the times? Or at one time, for different agencies? Or can a single agency simultaneously apply different styles to different industries or regions? Or—working all the way down—can individual enforcement officers choose from a range of responses, conducting themselves in a semimilitaristic fashion with respect to one problem and then brokering a negotiated settlement among multiple parties on the next? Ayres and Braithwaite clearly envisage the possibility of stylistic choices within an agency, as staff encounter differing motivations among industry associations and individuals: "We suggest that regulation be responsive to industry structure in that different structures will be conducive to different degrees and forms of regulation. Government should also be attuned to the differing motivations of regulated actors. Efficacious regulation should speak to the diverse objectives of regulated firms, industry associations, and individuals within them."[18]

Because agency culture tends to accompany agency style, one might expect life to be simpler if agency style was consistent throughout the agency. But if executives want versatility within their agencies, they confront awkward organizational issues involving the merging or mixing of cultures. Should they maintain functional and cultural separation, with a pen of bulldogs kept lean and mean and a separate enclave of educators and conciliators? Or should there be no distinction between "black hats" and "white hats," with field-level staff required to wear "gray hats" and play whatever role and character fits the occasion? (If so, it seems the agency would require field staff with the versatility of a chameleon.)

Developing regulatory versatility, and learning to manage it, appears a more constructive notion than continuing to merely push or pull the regulatory pendulum. However, it begs extraordinarily complicated organizational questions. To reap the benefits of regulatory responsiveness, agencies would need a system for examining different situations, considering the range of possible responses, selecting one (at whatever level) and implementing it, with involved staff fully aware of the decisions made and the consequences for their actions. Who will be authorized to select regulatory styles? At what level? Would these choices require legislative approval, or could they be made at the operational level?

Such discussion brings us back to the central question of how regulatory and enforcement agencies should structure their uses of discretion. The more tools and tactics—even regulatory styles—an agency learns to use, the more critical and complicated this question becomes. If this question is not resolved, what happens then? New methods tend to grow into new, stand-alone, tool-centered programs—each with its own supporters and culture; each existing and working largely in isolation, searching for suitable targets of opportunity; each competing with the others for resources, credit, and attention. An agency that spawns a host of good ideas but fails to manage the regulatory craft shop will appear to outsiders as innovative but hopelessly confused and disorganized; stylistically diverse but not sure of its identity; inventive but not integrated.

Graduated Sanctions

One rather particular version of regulatory responsiveness involves the use of a hierarchy of graduated responses to noncompliance. Braithwaite's enforcement pyramid (developed in the mid-1980s during his examination of coal mine regulation) not only shows a hierarchy of responses but also suggests a balance among them, wherein the softer approaches (at the base of the pyramid; see figure 2-1) are employed more frequently (represented by greater area), and the toughest sanctions (at the apex) are applied but applied least often. Braithwaite's focus in developing this model was explicitly the selection of sanctions: "The goal of this policy analysis is to find the method of punishment

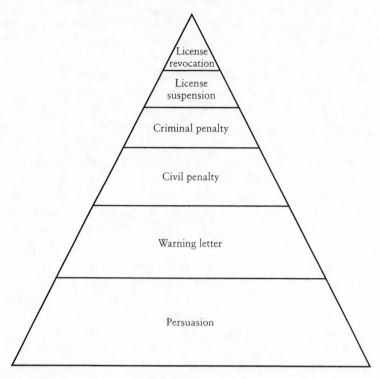

Figure 2-1. Example of an Enforcement Pyramid[a]

Source: Reproduced with permission from the Australian Institute of Criminology, Canberra.

a. Proportion of space in each layer represents proportion of enforcement activity at that level.

(defined broadly as any formal or informal sanction imposed for violations of law) that will achieve the greatest reduction of carnage in coal mines."[19]

Regulators should always retain the capacity to apply tough sanctions, because a strategy based entirely on persuasion and self-regulation will be exploited when actors are motivated by economic rationality.[20] But Braithwaite contends that having the big guns may prevent regulators from needing to use them very often and may make persuasion and lower-level sanctions more effective, a strategy he dubs the "benign big gun": "Regulators will do best by indicating a willingness to escalate intervention up those pyramids or to deregulate down the pyramids in response to the industry's performance in securing regulatory objectives. . . . The greater the heights of tough enforcement to which the agency can escalate (at the peak of its enforcement pyramid), the more effective the agency will be at securing compliance and less likely that it will have to resort to tough enforcement. Regulatory agencies will be able to speak more softly when they are perceived as carrying big sticks."[21]

The enforcement pyramid provides a useful way to think about a range of sanctioning options and about the business of attaining a balance among them. That represents one kind of regulatory versatility and a manner of managing it. However, a determination of sanctions in response to observed incidences of noncompliance constitutes only one aspect of regulatory versatility or responsiveness. Braithwaite developed this model in the context of coal mine safety, a regulatory problem with distinctive characteristics. He found that in virtually every serious coal mine accident, the law had been broken.[22] In the vast majority of cases, the breach of law either caused the accident, was among the causes, or made the consequences of the accident much worse. In only two disasters of thirty-nine examined would better compliance not have prevented or mitigated the accident.

In such a context there is reason to believe that improving compliance is an effective method of decreasing risks. There are, however, situations in which risk is not correlated so closely with lawbreaking. Many environmental issues involve little or no noncompliance; nevertheless, they concern environmental agencies. One of the realizations that drove the Occupational Safety and Health Administration to a redesign program was that a majority of workplace accidents or illnesses did not involve breach of regulations. (Joe Dear, who launched the redesign program in 1993, claimed that as many as 90 percent of workplace injuries and illnesses had nothing to do with noncompliance.) In such situations, effective intervention clearly requires more than carefully structured sanctions. Also, coal mine regulation deals with relatively few, large sites and inspects them all with some frequency. Game-theoretic analyses that led to the enforcement pyramid (as the optimal solution) rest on the assumption that both players are paying attention and monitoring each other's moves. In areas of regulation in which inspection resources are stretched thin, the same calculus may not apply.

The theoretical work on responsive regulation now recognizes that choices have to be made at higher levels of aggregation and need to cover much more than selection of sanctions for observed infractions.

The literature now describes a host of regulatory strategies, and the practical world of regulatory innovation adds constantly to the list. I mention just a few of the newer strategies, which some would label *alternatives to enforcement*, as if displacing enforcement were automatically a good thing. I would rather regulators saw them as new tools added to their tool kit—which really does seem like progress.

— Tripartism: the involvement of nongovernmental entities in the regulatory process.[23] Various methods of involving third parties (other than the regulator and the regulated) bring additional resources to bear on regulatory problems and may also bring pressure to bear on regulated entities.[24] "Overt enforcement of law is but one element in a web of constraint, some of whose strands are barely discernible, and many of which are non-governmental."[25] Tripartism is also perceived to mitigate the dangers of agency capture, especially when external parties can observe regulatory decisionmaking processes, monitor regulatory treatment and disposition of complaints, or force the hand of regulators.

— Information strategies: the communication of risks and risk factors to affected actors and to others in a position to bring pressure upon them to act in socially responsible ways. The use of information strategies allows government to use a lighter touch with responsible actors and allows greater flexibility with regard to specific remedies while focusing on desirable goals: "Decision-makers who are well informed and free to choose different responses have the flexibility to deal with varying situations differently, which is far more efficient than if differently situated people with different preferences are all obliged to do the same thing. . . . Information strategies are non-coercive . . . and life is better for everyone when there is less ordering people around."[26]

— Self-regulation: allowing regulated parties deemed relatively trustworthy to conduct and report their own audits or inspections, subject to some risk of verification.[27] One variation on this theme involves the certification of such audits by an independent third party (in the same way that the Securities and Exchange Commission relies upon certified public accountants to vouch for the truthfulness and completeness of financial statements).[28]

— Positive incentives: influencing behaviors within and beyond the scope of regulations by the use of praise, prizes, awards, and marketing advantages arising from government approval. These may take the form of green stickers, grants, subsidies, bounties, fees and commissions, tax credits, loan guarantees, favorable consideration for award of government contracts, and so forth.[29]

These are only a small selection of the innovative regulatory strategies available. Other methods, including the use of negotiated rule-making procedures, focus on establishing consensus early to prevent conflict later.[30] Partnerships of many kinds, between and among regulators, industries, industry associations, communities, advocacy groups, and other government agencies, serve a host of regulatory purposes. Regulators face no shortage of strategies, methods, programs, and ideas. Rather they face the lack of a structure for managing them all.

CHAPTER THREE

Party Politics

There has to be space for agreement between the left and right that matters such as our economic future and our environmental future are too important to see-saw them away.

IAN AYRES AND JOHN BRAITHWAITE, *Responsive Regulation*

PARTISAN POLITICS HAS naturally played a substantial role in shaping the regulatory reform agenda. To assess the current prescriptions for regulatory practice, one has to understand where they came from. In specifying a new direction, one also has to consider what the world of politics might or might not support. In this arena, at least, political debate seems not so much to generate ideas as to filter them. Politicians and political parties select ideas, champion them, build support for them, and then press them on agency officials. Those officials, accountable to political overseers, feel obliged to give the selected prescriptions greater weight, either incorporating them into agency conduct or explaining carefully (and at some peril) why they should not.

As a result of recent political championing, federal regulators in the United States are quite familiar with the names David Osborne, Ted Gaebler, Michael Hammer, and Philip Howard—despite the fact that Osborne, Gaebler, and Hammer have almost nothing specific to say about the challenges of regulation; and despite the fact that Howard is much clearer about what is wrong with regulatory practice than what would be better. By contrast, scholars of regulatory practice, who have a great deal constructive and specific to say about regulatory policy, remain virtually unknown among practitioners. To understand the strengths and limitations of current reforms, one should understand the role that politics has played in elevating some ideas above others and also the ways in which recent juxtapositions of political forces may have led to proposals or remedies that might be unbalanced, less than optimal, or shortsighted.

One might assume partisan political behavior to be motivated by underlying, static, ideological commitments. In that case Republicans would be defenders of business against regulatory intrusion, champions of capitalism, proponents of small government. Their position on regulation and regulators would be straightforward: less of it and less of them. Certainly, less enforcement. Democrats, whom one might traditionally expect to stand with the little man against the evil corporation, would partner with consumer groups, unions, and environmental activists to counter the social irresponsibility of the business world. Their regulatory policies would rest on a foundation of mistrust, a preference for distance from regulated industry, and an emphasis on enforcement. *Partnership* would mean partnership *against* industry.

Life is not so simple. Now we have Democrats pushing partnership with industry (that is, with employers), deemphasizing enforcement, and claiming that "the era of big government is over"—all of which might more normally be considered a conservative agenda. Perhaps this is a symptom of a broader strategy to take over the political center. In any case, it is worth considering how we came to such a point. During President Bill Clinton's first term, Vice President Al Gore's National Performance Review (NPR) acted as the think tank for the reinvention of government, stressing the need to produce government that "works better, and costs less." It echoed many of the reformist themes of the New Public Management movement influencing Great Britain, New Zealand, Australia, and Canada.[1] In the United States, the NPR team adopted and relied heavily upon Osborne and Gaebler's work (especially for the "works better" piece), supplemented with concepts and managerial tools imported from the private sector and from reforms abroad. To improve government services, the customer service concept provides the guiding light. The early works of the NPR, like Osborne and Gaebler's *Reinventing Government*, drew no special distinction between service provision and regulatory activities. What the NPR had to say about regulation, therefore, principally concerned delivery of services by regulators and scarcely touched on enforcement or compliance management.

By the end of Clinton's first term, the NPR was claiming success—particularly in downsizing government—but had attracted considerable criticism also. Academic observers perceived the reinvention recipe as lacking a satisfactory theoretical foundation and saw the collection of recommendations as springing from a somewhat arbitrary and possibly inappropriate collection of management fads, imported from industry and thoughtlessly translated to government. Much of the academic criticism, curiously enough, focused on aspects of the NPR agenda that might be particularly troublesome in the regulatory arena, even though the NPR, up to then, had paid little or no explicit attention to those issues. For example, Donald Kettl, writing for the Brookings Institution in August 1994, commented:

> The NPR built on ambitious ideas about cutting red tape, putting customers first, empowering employees, and cutting back to basics. Far less clear, however, was what the concepts actually meant. Where do procedural due process and proper administrative safeguards become red tape? Who are the government's customers and how can they be served? Does customer service contradict other public goals?[2]

Kettl and many other observers worried that NPR prescriptions skated past these questions—questions central to the very nature of government—and in so doing placed the whole program in danger of faltering in a "quicksand of fuzzy rhetoric."[3]

The NPR and its reinvention allies did not have to wait long before they were forced to confront the issues of regulation. In the election of November 1994 Republicans gained control of the Senate and the House of Representatives for the first time since 1954. The 104th Congress launched immediately into a Reaganesque campaign to "get regulators off the back of industry," responding to the broadly felt frustration at the clumsy and nitpicky behavior of regulatory agencies and to the burdensome nature of their bureaucratic requirements. The Republican Congress put the Occupational Safety and Health Administration, the Environmental Protection Agency, and the Food and Drug Administration at the top of their hit list, proposing major budget cuts and, in the case of OSHA, recommending the elimination of the agency entirely.

A Focus on OSHA

OSHA came in for an unusually heavy battering. Representative Thomas Ballenger (Republican of North Carolina) took the chair of the House subcommittee on work force protections and filled the committee with the most anti-OSHA members of his party he could find.[4] One of them, Representative John A. Boehner of Ohio, referred to OSHA as the "Gestapo of the federal government."[5] Republicans feasted on Philip Howard's book, which features OSHA heavily.[6] They circulated other OSHA horror stories too: for instance, how "OSHA killed the tooth fairy," claiming that OSHA prevents dentists from giving children their extracted teeth because the blood-borne pathogen standard requires dentists to use extreme caution in dealing with blood. In fact, nothing prevents dentists from giving kids appropriately handled and washed teeth.[7]

The OSHA reform bill that came out of the Ballenger committee early in 1995 would have scaled back OSHA's enforcement capability, exempted large numbers of facilities from random inspection, drastically reduced the application of fines, and forced the agency into a more consultative and cooperative role.[8] Another bill, introduced in the Senate, would have exempted 90 percent of employers from regular inspections and required OSHA to rely on voluntary compliance programs.[9] Meanwhile, the agency's appropriation was held up by the new Congress, forcing OSHA to operate under an interim funding bill that reduced its budget by 15 percent. According to Joe Dear, who had been confirmed as head of OSHA roughly one year before the 1994 congressional elections, OSHA found itself "in a battle for survival." Morale plummeted. During 1995 Dear appeared twelve times before congressional committees, compared with four the year before.[10] OSHA and other regulatory agencies, Dear said, had become politically "red hot."[11]

A Focus on the EPA

Meanwhile, other Republican freshmen set their sights on the EPA, proposing to cut its budget by as much as one-third, restrict its ability to enforce environmental laws, and subject it to paralyzing procedural requirements.[12] They "first attempted to repeal core environmental legislation; then attempted to attach unprecedented riders on appropriations to core environmental programs; then considered—but rejected—tying funding to enforcement direction, and finally launched an assault on EPA's funding.[13] (The Food and Drug Administration came under similar pressure, albeit less severe and less public.)

Naturally, consumer groups, the unions, and environmental advocacy groups all looked to the Clinton administration to respond. And respond it did, picking the EPA as the symbolic point of resistance and warning the public that zealots in Congress planned to roll back twenty-five years of progress in environmental protection. In the spring of 1995 Clinton refused to approve budget proposals from Congress, objecting most strenuously to cuts in the EPA's budget and proposed reductions in its enforcement capacity. During the ensuing impasse (with multiple government shutdowns), and much to the chagrin of Republican freshmen, public opinion polls swung heavily in the Democrats' favor. The public, even if it did not much care for regulatory behavior, retained strong support for regulatory missions; certainly it did not trust industry to do the right thing with respect to worker safety, the environment, or consumer protection, absent some serious capacity for government oversight and enforcement. As one commentator observed, "The freshmen in the 104th Congress misconstrued the popular frustration with regulatory procedure and a complex and often combative bureaucracy for a broad electoral distaste for environmental law in general. Consequently, the main congressional assault on environmental laws fell at the hands of an unexpectedly significant popular outcry."[14]

It took very little time for the Republicans to realize that they had overstepped the mark and to back away from their more extreme proposals. They dropped a flat-out assault on regulation and regulators and started a more defensible campaign focusing on enforcement methods, alternatives to enforcement, allocation of regulatory resources, mandatory cost-benefit analyses for new rules, and a preference for market mechanisms over legalistic regulatory regimes. Had the Republicans looked back over recent history, they might have known that an all-out attack on social regulation would be unsustainable. Reagan's first-term assault on environmental protection produced a backlash that resulted in a dramatic acceleration of enforcement during his second term.[15] During the period 1986–89 the EPA's civil referrals to the Department of Justice more than doubled the rate for the period 1981–85, and jail terms for federal environmental crimes were nine times the rate during Reagan's first term. Such retreats from extreme deregulatory agendas "repeat a familiar postwar pattern of conservative administrations letting business down on this [deregulatory] score."[16] Whether or not Republican freshmen understood the history, by mid-1995 they had abandoned their more radical antiregulatory stance and seemed prepared to engage in debate about "commonsense regulation" and issues of regulatory effectiveness. For public spoils, the Republicans turned the spotlight on a safer target, one that had no vociferous supporters or defenders: the Internal Revenue Service.

The National Performance Review

For their part, the Democrats moved quickly during the spring of 1995 to defuse Republican assaults, using the most obvious tool they had available: the National Performance Review and the reinventing government campaign. They applied the recipe from the NPR, tailoring it slightly for regulators. As well as a government that works better and costs less, reinvention would produce regulatory agencies that behaved more reasonably, worked cooperatively with industry, and shaped behavior more through guidance and support than through enforcement. To announce the new focus, the NPR team distributed a laminated card (dated February 25, 1995) entitled "Reinventing Regulation." Signed by the president and the vice president, the card urged regulators to "cut obsolete regulations; reward results, not red tape; get out of Washington and create grass-roots partnerships; and negotiate, don't dictate." On March 4, 1995, President Clinton sent a memorandum, "Regulatory Reinvention Initiative," to the heads of all federal regulatory agencies, announcing and detailing the same four central themes.[17] The memo also urged a less adversarial approach, the adoption of consensus-building techniques, and better communication with regulated industry. The Democrats adopted Philip Howard's book, urging all federal regulators to read it, sending Howard on a campaign trail within government, and escorting him on the reinvention tour circuit.

Curiously, Clinton's March 4 memorandum does not mention customers or customer service. Clearly, to the drafters, those pieces of the reinvention philosophy were less obviously appropriate in the regulatory context. Focusing on results and using partnerships were easy and obvious applications of principles drawn from Osborne and Gaebler's reinvention philosophy. However, once the issues of regulatory reform fell under the banner of reinvention, the day-to-day responsibility for carrying forward the regulatory reinvention campaign fell squarely in the lap of the NPR, immersed as it was in the customer service mindset. Its favorite reinvention tools—total quality management, process management, and process reengineering—held at their core the private sector customer service motto: Identify your customers and delight them so they come back for more. The NPR team seemed to have no trouble applying the language of customers and customer service to regulation, nor in advocating process management methods as the way to improve regulatory service. Very quickly, customer service moved to center stage in the Democrats' reform efforts. And who was the customer? Regulated industry itself!

Thus regulatory reform issues were assimilated within the broader prescriptions of reinvention, with regulators distinguished from service providers only when unavoidable and at the margins. In 1997, the NPR published a summary of its reinvention philosophy in a booklet entitled *Blair House Papers*. Regulatory issues occupy three of the forty-three pages. The list of four themes for regulatory practice had grown to six:

— Cut obsolete regulations
— Reward results, not red tape
— Get out of Washington and create grass-roots partnerships
— Negotiate, don't dictate
— Reduce regulatory reporting burdens
— Allow fines to be applied to fixes[18]

This composite prescription for regulatory reform appears under the heading, "Focus Regulators on Compliance, Not Enforcement." That, in turn, appears as a subheading under the more general, "Foster Partnerships and Community Solutions." As a reinvention prescription, the shift in emphasis from enforcement to compliance (and in particular to *voluntary* compliance) comes across as sweeping and unconditional, in contrast to a more reasonable focus on compliance *where appropriate,* or *when dealing with well-motivated actors.*

The underlying assumption upon which such a strategy rests holds the vast majority of players to be motivated; thus the bulk of the work of regulatory reform is amply covered in serving regulatory customers well. The *Blair House Papers* lays this assumption out explicitly:

> The president's other five directives deal with what is most important in reinventing regulation—the relationship between regulators and the regulated community.
>
> Not everyone is going to play by the rules. But experience shows that most businesses and communities do want to comply and will, if they can figure out what it is they're supposed to do. Agencies are proving that, working with new partners, agreeing on the goals, allowing room for innovation, and providing all the help

possible to those that want to comply. And because regulatory time is no longer being wasted on the good guys, agencies can better focus their attention on the few cheaters.[19]

Such a prescription is useful in facilitating voluntary compliance, although public interest groups, scholars of regulatory policy, and many regulators themselves remain skeptical of the extent to which such a prescription covers the deeper issues of regulatory reform. One senior federal regulatory executive told me his views on how regulators interpreted this message: "More than any [other] single document, event, or product, the *Blair House Papers* cemented NPR's reputation among regulators. From that point on NPR was viewed as dangerously misguided . . . and a group you needed to monitor carefully and avoid at all costs. The *Blair House Papers* were the 'smoking gun' regulators needed to verify their worst suspicions about the NPR."[20]

The Reaction to the NPR

Regulators remain wary of drawing too close to the regulated community, believing that compliance, for most, is not purely voluntary but coerced at least to some degree. They do not think their audience can be neatly divided between voluntary compliers and a few cheaters or that the tools available to them can be matched in a straightforward way to such a partition. Given the fact that regulators regard the use of state authority as their most precious and contentious resource, they yearn for more sophisticated guidance on when and how to use it than they can find in the vague phrases found in the *Blair House Papers*.

The good news for regulators is that both political parties have shifted away from their stereotypical ideological stances and have come surprisingly close to each other. Democrats are working with industry (to the consternation of some of the party's traditional allies). Republicans, since the bruising of 1995, have backed off their more extreme positions, have compromised on their proposals to eliminate or substantially weaken regulatory agencies or to gut their enforcement capacities, and have turned instead to a search for more sensible, more effective, regulation. The stage is now set for a less partisan, even bipartisan, search for commonsense regulation and more effective regulatory practice.

Of course, some within the government reinvention movement think that the search is already over. They are satisfied that the broader reinvention prescriptions deal adequately with the challenges of regulation and that moving customer service to center stage properly and adequately specifies regulatory style and enforcement practice. Others disagree, viewing reinvention prescriptions, for regulators, as shallow. These critics see the customer service emphasis as fine up to a point but as positively damaging if pushed too far.

Looking back on the political events of the 1990s, one can appreciate how effective the Democrats' embrace of regulated industry (as partners and customers) has been in taking the heat and heart out of the Republican onslaught. Portraying and treating employers and businesses as customers may have accelerated the advent of less adversarial, more accommodative, regulatory styles. Americans might thank the Clinton administration and the NPR for using these devices to ward off, and then help redirect, a particularly dangerous assault on social regulation. But that crisis is past, and the issues of regulatory reform must now be debated more rationally. Executives and policymakers can turn their attention away from crisis management and toward the construction of a more positive, longer-term vision for regulatory effectiveness. For that work, they should pause long enough to make sure they understand both the merits and the limits of a customer service orientation and of the particular managerial methods that usually go with it.

CHAPTER FOUR

Customer Service: Merits and Limits

Of the hundreds of people I arrested during ten years of police service, only one ever thanked me for arresting her. A young woman, who worked with her husband in a dairy company, had defrauded a wide range of customers—most of them elderly people—over a protracted period. Eventually one of her victims (a pensioner who, each week, would leave a blank check for the milk delivery man, trusting him to fill in the amount) called the police station to complain that her bank account was suddenly and unaccountably empty. As the junior detective on duty at the time, it fell to me to investigate and intervene.

Other arrestees occasionally thanked me for treating them fairly and honestly. A few even thanked me for not beating them up or not "stitching them up" (fabricating evidence). Only this woman thanked me for arresting her. However, even she felt this wave of gratitude only later, not at the time of the arrest. After she was convicted and sentenced, she expressed relief at having put this criminal phase of her life behind her—the scam had been gnawing at her conscience, and she used the intervention to change her ways. In retrospect, she told me, she felt I had done her a service. My object, however, was not to serve her. My job was to deal with her on behalf of those to whom her breach of the law had done harm. I was never sure that the woman's husband (codefendant) viewed the intervention in the same positive light. The vast majority of defendants do not view enforcement actions taken against them as a service, even in retrospect. Many are sorry only that they got caught.

The Customs Service

In 1993, the U.S. Customs Service had to figure out whom it served and whom it should expect to be pleased, or not pleased, by its actions. Recently released from congressional restrictions that had prevented them from attempting reorganization for more than a decade, the Customs Service sought to make up for lost time by using the radical methods of process reengineering and a sweeping reorganization of the management structure. The reorganization study report called for the Customs Service to develop new managerial and organizational approaches and to define a mission-oriented vision to enhance compliance with applicable laws. The report announced that customs would "formally move to and implement a system of *management by process.*" Further, that "in recognition of the concerns and recommendations of the NPR, and in response to the problems and issues raised by our workforce and customers, Customs should establish *partnerships with our customers* to enhance organizational effectiveness. Process owners will be responsible for identifying the full range of customers, determining customer needs, developing measurable customer service goals and standards, developing strategies to achieve the goals, and maintaining systems for obtaining continuous customer feedback."[1]

The agency group most disturbed by this prescription was the Office of Enforcement, consisting of special agents (who are a distinct group from inspectors and import specialists). The role of special agents centers on control of smuggling and money laundering; their targets are criminals and criminal organizations. At first glance, it seemed that the Office of Enforcement had escaped reorganization; in a structural sense, it had. In a cultural sense, the special agents perceived organizational adoption of process improvement and customer satisfaction as a devaluation of the enforcement role and dismissal of their professional expertise and experience. In particular, the focus on *voluntary* compliance made agents bristle, and the more attention it got, the more they felt left out in the cold. Because voluntary compliance seemed irrelevant to their work, they inferred that their work had become irrelevant to the organization.

A bitter internal debate broke out on the question of whether drug smugglers should be regarded as customers; and if so, what that would mean for the behavior of special agents trying to destroy their trade and their organizations. Had the smugglers been canvassed about what they wanted of customs officials at the border, the answer (everyone knew) would be, "Don't be there," "Stay out of my way." Ultimately, Deputy Commissioner Mike Lane intervened—much to the relief of the special agents—decreeing that drug smugglers and other criminals should *not* be regarded as customers for the purposes of customs' management of its processes. That left the legitimate travelers as the determiners of quality for the passenger-related processes. Oddly enough, though, when questioned at the airport (as they were) these travelers gave answers surprisingly similar to the hypothetical answers of drug smugglers. Exhausted after long international flights, struggling with luggage and grouchy children, what did these people want from customs? "Get out of the way." "Help me with my luggage." "Do something for my kids." "Be nice."

So customs set about being nice to passengers, especially at international airports. In 1992 their pilot Air Passenger Customer Service Program was launched in Dallas–Fort Worth, Detroit, and Los Angeles. This program, advertised as "Customs with a personal touch," created passenger service representatives (PSRs) whose job it was to offer assistance. In 1993 the program was extended to Boston, Chicago, Honolulu, and Houston. In announcing an extension of the program to Atlanta in 1994, a customs press release quoted a female PSR explaining her role: "All airports are basically the same in that the people in them are always in a hurry. But sometimes they have problems. That's where I come in."[2]

The PSRs were not just friendly faces: they promoted voluntary compliance by circulating brochures among outbound passengers (so they would know what they should or should not buy abroad) describing duty-free allowances, and they helped customers with customs procedures. But the advent of PSRs did nothing for the comfort of the Office of Enforcement's special agents, who saw the diversion of personnel as another sign that the agency had gone customer service mad and was substituting customer satisfaction for accomplishing its mission. According to the special agents, their customers were the schoolchildren they sought to protect from drugs and the crime victims who suffered at the hands of international syndicates; the agency ought to think more about its obligations to citizens than to travelers, they claimed.

Of course, many travelers are also citizens. While traveling, they display preferences focused on their own personal needs and comforts.

Suppose they were canvassed as citizens, not at the airport but at home, after they had put the children to bed, taken a shower, and had time to relax. If asked what they wanted of customs officials, they then might say something more like, "As citizens, we expect customs officials to hold us all up for just long enough to do a quality job of discriminating between the smugglers and law-abiding travelers." That notion, according to special agents, they could swallow. In fact, that notion, they felt, more appropriately defined quality in the context of an inspectional process than immediate, direct customer satisfaction.

In almost every regulatory agency—not just customs—adoption of the language of compliance produces internal stresses and strains. The phrase "From enforcement to compliance" would not be objectionable if everyone agreed that it was a statement about goals. Shifting emphasis from counting outputs to measuring compliance levels is consistent with the search for results, for mission accomplishment, for effectiveness. Enforcement officers might not object if the shift were clearly spelled out that way, in terms such as "From a focus on counting enforcement actions for their own sake, to a focus on increasing compliance." That would leave open the possibility of using enforcement, along with other methods, to increase compliance. But then the word *voluntary* creeps in, and the shift in strategy becomes "From enforcement to voluntary compliance."

All of a sudden (and without anyone necessarily intending the change of sense) this seems now to be a statement more about *tools* rather than about *goals*. And the tools of voluntary compliance are the newer, more politically fashionable, and less adversarial methods: education, outreach, partnership, consensus, and facilitation. For enforcement officers and criminal investigators, these are not subtle questions of semantics. What they hear in the phrase "From enforcement to voluntary compliance" is an announcement of their own obsolescence and the ascendancy of compromise. They view the assumption that everyone wants to comply as naïve regarding human nature, and they worry that the focus on voluntary compliance will mean that the worst offenders—upon whom they spend most of their energies—will be ignored (allowed to get away with it). They see the agency's swing from enforcement to facilitation as corrupting and immoral and feel betrayed by their own bosses.

Hence the precipitous drop in morale among Customs Service special agents—and among equivalent groups in other agencies—when asked to march under the banners of voluntary compliance and customer satis-

faction. This semantic distortion also explains the bean dip phenomenon (when traditional enforcement activity measures, or bean counts,
decline), which surprises and dismays regulatory executives. They think
they have urged their staff to adopt a balanced approach—embracing all
methods as needed—to improve compliance. What people heard, however, was "We don't do enforcement any more." Statements about goals
are interpreted as an *ex ante* preference for particular methods—for just
about any method, in fact, other than enforcement. This, after all, is the
ex ante preference of the regulated community, to whom the agency
more closely attends.

The Internal Revenue Service

It is remarkable how easily a genuine concern for mission accomplishment (expressed as a desire to improve compliance) can undergo this
distortion, to the point at which the message becomes positively antien-
forcement. The IRS has teetered on the brink of this calamity for some
time. In 1991 Commissioner Fred Goldberg began enunciating a new
vision of compliance management, which he distinguished from the way
the IRS operated at the time. Speaking of "a decade of fundamental
reform," he told Congress:

> At present the focus of our compliance effort is principally after-
> the-fact, case-by-case enforcement. Examinations, collection
> actions, and criminal investigations are, and always will be, an
> essential part of what we do; indeed they should be expanded in
> the years ahead. But they cannot be pursued in a vacuum. We are
> changing the way we approach our compliance activities. We are
> devising, implementing and assessing comprehensive strategies to
> improve voluntary compliance—strategies that combine traditional
> enforcement actions with education, outreach, and simplification
> of regulations and legislation. The ultimate objective is not to max-
> imize yield through costly, intrusive, and burdensome enforcement
> efforts. The objective is to enhance voluntary compliance.[3]

The need to retain enforcement is clear, as is the desire to design comprehensive strategies aimed at improving compliance rates. But the word
voluntary has crept in, and the overall objective ("To improve voluntary
compliance") seems to narrow to a subset of taxpayers—the willing
ones. A broader, more clearly goal-oriented statement of the overall

objective would have been "To enhance compliance: sometimes purely voluntary, sometimes enforced, usually coerced at least to some degree." By 1993 Goldberg's new strategy had acquired a name—Compliance 2000—and was being taught throughout the IRS. According to one of the earliest Compliance 2000 teaching manuals, the reasons for change were inescapable: "In today's world, there are too many returns, too many complex laws and too few enforcement resources to permit us to continue 'business as usual.' We must modify our approach to tax administration."[4] The document, in a summary description of the strategy, states that "Compliance 2000 is a mission-based approach to tax administration designed to improve voluntary compliance. It seeks organizational solutions that remove barriers to compliance while minimizing burden on taxpayers." Such compliance would be accomplished through (1) "ongoing analysis of market segments to identify patterns and trends of noncompliance" and (2) "tailored strategies including maintaining accounts; educating, assisting, and informing; and the focused use of enforcement."[5]

Early in the life of the Compliance 2000 strategy, a new executive-level position was created, the Compliance 2000 Executive, to help promulgate the vision, but the first piece of substantial organizational apparatus created toward implementation was essentially analytical. The thirty-three DORA (District Office of Research and Analysis) sites and the one NORA (National Office of Research and Analysis) site were given the task of analyzing market segments to identify patterns of noncompliance. Despite the explicit inclusion of enforcement as an option, the heavy emphasis on preventive systemic solutions (form redesign, clearer notices, advance taxpayer education) soon became exclusive, which meant that the DORA and NORA sites thought their role was to identify noncompliance issues and propose systemic solutions *not involving enforcement*. The enforcement-oriented branches of the IRS (criminal investigation, examination, and collections) were seldom involved in the work of the DORAs, nor affected by their proposals. After all, if prevention worked, why would anyone need to worry about a cure?

By 1996, the IRS had replaced the EPA, OSHA, and the FDA as targets of choice for Republicans in Congress. In fact, here was one agency perceived as so unpopular that both political parties were eager to recommend reforms. Democrats and Republicans—now not quite so far apart in their ideas about regulatory reform—collaborated in a bipartisan National Commission on Restructuring the IRS. After an extensive round of public hearings, the commission produced its report. The introduction states the assumption upon which the commission based its work: "Most American citizens are willing to pay their fair share of taxes; the Commission's recommendations will make it easier for them to do so."[6] The sum of the recommendations "is to make it easier for citizens to interact with the IRS." The three strategic objectives that the IRS should pursue are improving customer service, increasing voluntary compliance, and finding efficiency gains. (None of which put much emphasis on catching and punishing tax evaders or deterring tax evasion).

Should targets of enforcement actions be regarded as customers? Absolutely. "Customer satisfaction must be a goal in every interaction the IRS has with taxpayers, including enforcement actions. Taxpayers expect quality service in all interactions with the IRS, including taxpayer assistance, filing tax returns, paying taxes, and examination and collection actions."[7] Such is the general tenor of the report. Perhaps this is not objectionable (unless you work in an enforcement function for the IRS and you are struggling with your professional sense of self-worth)—but surely it is unbalanced.

The complexities of regulatory responsibility do surface in the report. The commission notes the tendency of DORA sites to focus on nonenforcement solutions to noncompliance and recommends that the sites work with examination and collection offices (embracing the enforcement tools) to increase their efficiency and effectiveness. In another section, Commissioner David Keating (of the National Taxpayers Union) appears to dissent on some central themes:

> The Commission's report repeatedly refers to "customer" service. While everyone supports the goal of improving service to citizens, I'm sure many, if not most, taxpayers certainly don't feel like they are customers. Real customers have a choice about the products and services they buy. Yet taxes are, after all, involuntary payments, and there's no choice about which IRS to use. That's one reason why taxpayers' rights issues are so important.[8]

Referring to the IRS as a schizophrenic institution, Keating says that, "on one hand, the IRS is a law enforcement agency, and as such it is one of the most effective and feared in the world. But on the other hand, it is now supposed to be customer-friendly, service-sensitive and technologically innovative, and as such it is a travesty."[9]

To add to the pressure, in September 1997, just a few weeks before a new IRS commissioner, Charles Rossotti, was sworn in with a mandate to reform and modernize the agency, the Senate Finance Committee held hearings focused on IRS taxpayer abuse. In the Arkansas-Oklahoma IRS District Office, the committee was told, managers in the Collections Branch had used quotas to evaluate employees (a practice expressly forbidden by written policy albeit established in agency culture), thus allegedly encouraging inappropriately harsh treatment of taxpayers, excessive seizures of property, and abuse of taxpayers' rights. Another round of hearings held by the same committee during April and May 1998 again highlighted allegations of taxpayer abuse, but this time it focused on the Criminal Investigation Division. Commissioner Rossotti, meanwhile, moved quickly to formulate his own reorganization plan, spurred by the intensity and bipartisan nature of congressional criticism. He asked his review team to consider all available options. One of those options, seriously considered for a while, was the removal of the criminal investigation function (source of the latest round of embarassment) from the agency altogether.

The National Performance Review (by then renamed the National Partnership for the Reinvention of Government) spotted an opportunity to push its reinvention agenda and submitted its own proposal for IRS reform.[10] Entitled "Reinventing Service at the IRS," this booklet pushes any balance that might be struck between mission accomplishment and customer service to one extreme. In fact, the report uses the language of customer and customer service with such frequency and persistence that reading it feels vaguely like brain-washing. In the report's ninety-two pages, the word *customer* is used 365 times (on average, four times a page). By way of contrast, the words *criminal, evade*, and *evasion* do not appear at all. The root *investigat-* appears just once. The word *enforcement* does appear in the report, twenty-three times altogether. But of these twenty-three appearances, the majority (seventeen) have a context that is negative with respect to enforcement (for example, "from enforcement to . . ." or "rather than enforcement"), or is describing enforcement as a feature of *past* practice, or is relegating enforcement to an option of last resort. One begins to understand why enforcement officers and investigators feel belittled and embattled; and why, given these pressures, many look around for alternative employment.

In defense of the NPR proposal, one might point out that this was a report of the *Customer Service* Task Force, so one might expect the focus on customer service. But bear in mind that there was no Mission Accomplishment Task Force or Compliance Management Task Force to provide the necessary balance. One could perhaps justify this focus on customer service as a device of the times, useful in correcting the imbalances of the past; but, in the broader discussions of regulatory reform, the foolishness of lurching from extreme to extreme, and the value of setting balances and integrating competing ideas more carefully and thoughtfully, have already been established.

The impression of most regulatory practitioners, unfortunately, is that pure customer service prescriptions are not conceived as artful devices for the times nor as judiciously selected positions along the spectrum of regulatory style. Rather, they see these prescriptions as stemming from the application of private sector ideas by people who do not grasp the nature of regulatory responsibilities. They watch with alarm as these prescriptions are thrust upon them, producing schisms in their agencies, alienating significant parts of the work force, and disorienting and demoralizing enforcement personnel. Even after studying them carefully, and even after using them to some advantage in the service aspects of their business, they find these prescriptions too narrow to act as a foundation for regulatory strategy. Customer service prescriptions say too little about mission accomplishment and provide almost no guidance on the issues of how to manage a growing regulatory tool kit.

Executives of regulatory and enforcement agencies struggle to keep some balance as these powerful forces swirl about them. Many do keep their balance. Commissioner Rossotti, relatively new to the regulatory world, commissioned a review of the Criminal Investigation Division by Judge William Webster, the former director of the Federal Bureau of Investigation and an acknowledged expert in enforcement matters. Webster's report emphasizes the importance of criminal enforcement as a compliance management tool and recommends that the Criminal Investigation Division remain within the organizational structure of the IRS. The Webster report also recommends that the commissioner not require criminal investigators to assess customer satisfaction until other federal law enforcement agencies develop acceptable measures in this area.[11] Commissioner Rossotti's plan for an IRS reorganization seeks to balance the obvious imperatives for improved taxpayer services and treatment (around which the political debate has recently revolved) with the need for preserving and enhancing the agency's ability to deal with noncompliance problems, including criminal evasion.

Quite obvious to most regulators is the fact that, much of the time, the person with whom they deal is not the person they seek to please. Regulatory transactions involve multiple parties, some present, many not. All parties need to be treated with fairness and dignity, but not all parties will like what happens to them.

The U.S. Department of Education has a unit called Institutional Participation and Oversight Service (IPOS), which felt the need to clarify some distinctions for the sake of its own staff. IPOS has the task of certifying schools for participation in federal financial assistance programs and then overseeing those that qualify (roughly 5,900 domestic and 600 foreign educational institutions). Describing the results of its internal reforms, IPOS explains whom it serves: "While the IPOS focus is the institution, the ultimate beneficiary is the student, our primary customer. We work *with* institutions, but *for* students (and taxpayers). To institutions, IPOS is many things: monitor/observer, teacher, enforcement agent. . . . The IPOS goal is a simple one: compliance improvement, achieved through a variety of strategies."[12]

To understand the merits and limits of customer service for regulatory and enforcement functions, practitioners should pass the idea through a number of filters. First (and this applies broadly within government) they should not assume that emulating the private sector's treatment of customers will automatically improve government. As Henry Mintzberg points out, commercial companies aim to sell as much as they can as often as possible.[13] One would not want to replicate this aim in the context of regulation, nor in the context of health or welfare. Commercial companies also use a range of tactics (planned obsolescence, bait and switch, promoting dependence) that no one would want government to emulate. At the same time, government should certainly imitate those less sinister aspects of customer service—timeliness, technical competence, courtesy and respect, and being willing to consider others' points of view and preferences.

Second, in most regulatory contexts, the person or party the regulator encounters directly is not paying for the service, often does not want it, and will not be pleased by it. As my colleague Mark Moore puts it,

> These [regulatory] organizations meet individual clients not as service providers but as representatives of the state obliging clients to absorb a loss on behalf of society at large. Of course it may be valuable for regulatory and law enforcement organizations to

think of the citizens whom they regulate as customers and to design their "obligation encounters" with as much care as "service encounters" now are. Nevertheless, it is unreasonable to imagine that regulatory and enforcement agencies find their justification in the satisfactions of those whom they compel to contribute to public purposes.[14]

Regulators must adopt a broader vocabulary, so they can think not only in terms of customers but also of stakeholders, citizens, obligatees, objects or targets of enforcement, beneficiaries, taxpayers, and society. They must contemplate the broader public purposes that their missions encompass and the numerous individual sacrifices necessary to deliver them.

Third, regulators should not permit a customer orientation to lead to exclusion or neglect of enforcement capacities. Scholars of regulatory policy warn that an unconditional preference for negotiated compliance renders an agency susceptible to capture.[15] They also say that "using persuasion on people with no will to comply can be as counterproductive as using punishment on people who are trying their best" and that the problem with a strategy of persuasion, "based as it is on a model of man as basically good . . . fails to recognize that there are some who are not, and thus will take advantage of being presumed to be so."[16] Failure to enforce the law swiftly and effectively against deliberate or persistent offenders undermines the incentives for compliance in the rest of the community and may bring a regulatory regime into disrepute.

Fourth, regulators should understand that corporate behavior moves quickly to take advantage of any perceived softening. Social norms act less upon complex organizations than upon individuals. Those who study organizational deviance warn that, to understand corporate crimes, one needs to think of corporate officials as actors who assume certain roles, the requirements of which are defined by the organization, not by the actor's personality. Thus corporations driven by the profit motive can act in ways that most individuals in the organization would not condone, simply through each person playing the role defined by the organization and no one person being responsible for causing the outcome. This renders corporate behavior somewhat impervious to the normal pressures for socially responsible behavior. Corporate lawbreaking is further facilitated (in comparison with individual crimes) by the distance in time and space between the decisionmaker and the victim of the decision.[17]

With these cautions in place, regulators should feel better able to apply customer service ideals and methods where appropriate, confident that they are not crippling their enforcement capacity or turning their backs on their public responsibilities. Exactly where the balance between customer service and mission accomplishment should lie may depend on the times, the problem, the industry in question, or the political winds. Whatever the weights assigned to each, the implementation should not split the organization, with enforcement shuffled off to some back corner. In most regulatory encounters, no matter how apparently consensual, coercion lies not far beneath the surface, and the possibility of coercion plays on the minds of all involved. The merits of customer service have not only to be balanced with mission accomplishment but integrated within it. All the tools—from the gentlest persuasion to the harshest enforcement campaigns—should be melded within coherent strategies for producing broad compliance.

Balancing and integrating customer service with mission accomplishment is one of the central challenges of the regulatory art—a much less straightforward proposition than some suggest. A serious mistake for regulatory practitioners, though, would be to assume that mission accomplishment and customer satisfaction—especially when regulated industry is viewed as the customer—are one and the same. Paying insufficient attention to customer satisfaction may result in heavy-handed, unresponsive, and low-quality service, a message that has been drummed into the consciousness of virtually all regulatory executives.

Not so well understood, though, are the dangers of pushing the notion of customer satisfaction too far, or applying it to areas of regulatory practice where it does not belong. Overemphasizing customer service can lead those on the receiving end of regulatory encounters to feel entitled to be pleased; and they will then use every avenue open to them to retaliate against inspectors or enforcement agents who displease them by taking a firm stance. When frontline officers discover (often to their cost) that senior managers care more about conflict minimization than mission accomplishment, morale plummets, experienced investigators leave, and an agency's long-term capacity to fulfill its public responsibilities suffers significant damage.

CHAPTER FIVE

Process Improvement:
Merits and Limits

THE DEBATE WITHIN U.S. Customs over who was and who was not a customer arose because of the agency's adoption of process management. Process management requires process owners to identify their customers and ask them to define quality. Customs adopted the language of business process redesign, identifying four core, high-volume, processes. For each, a process "owner" was appointed (a senior executive who already had functional responsibilities), and a redesign team was assembled to pick the processes apart and recommend improvements. The four designated core processes represented goods and people moving either way across the border. Formally, these processes were termed cargo compliance process for imports, cargo compliance process for exports, inbound passenger processing, and outbound passenger processing.

After debating the meaning of *quality* in the context of an inspection process, the redesign teams realized the need to balance facilitation against compliance, using the notion of slowing processing down just long enough to do a quality job of discriminating between compliant and noncompliant traffic. That means that there are two kinds of errors that can be made: holding up legitimate traffic for longer than necessary (measured in delay times or costs) and allowing illegitimate or noncompliant traffic through (measured in terms of the proportion of noncompliance passing undetected). Plotting these two error rates against one another (see figure 5-1) produces a curve representing the policy trade-off between the two error rates (curve A).

This basic analysis applies to virtually all regulatory inspection settings: one would want the Food and Drug Administration to take just long enough over drug approvals to enable them to detect those that should not be approved; and one would want the Immigration and Naturalization Service to process citizenship applications as fast as possible, provided they still weeded out terrorists and criminals.

In the context of Customs Service management of ports, any one port's inspection process could be represented as a single point on such a two-dimensional diagram. To measure the error rates, customs would need to obtain valid estimates of what it was missing, in order to calculate the detection rates for the vertical axis. For this purpose, customs implemented a new suite of statistically valid measurement programs, using a purely random secondary inspection process (placed behind the primary inspection operation), to obtain valid compliance rates. As a result, it was able to see exactly what its routine inspection programs accomplished. In January 1997, John Hill—who had directed the Customs Service development of performance measurement techniques—reported:

> The technique of random sampling is now built into our processing system and hundreds of inspectors are familiar with it. Here's what we can say from these data from FY 1996:
> — Significant violations occur about 5 per 10,000 vehicles
> — We apprehend about 19% of these violations
> — The inspector's selection is about 9 times better than purely random selection.
>
> The most interesting thing we learned this year was how to explain this sort of measurement technique to hundreds of inspectors and dozens of field managers. If I knew then what I know now . . . the math was easy, the marketing is hard.

Actually, the math, in this particular business, is not so easy. Very low violation rates (say, 5 per 10,000, or 0.05 percent) are difficult to estimate efficiently, and it is even harder to detect changes over time. But with a little expert statistical guidance, customs figured out how to combine information from focused and random inspections to produce lower variance estimates of the underlying compliance rate and how to

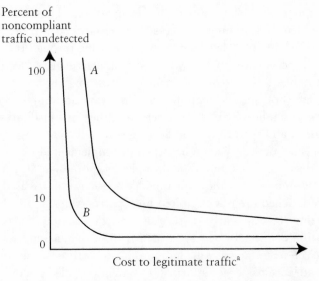

Figure 5-1. Quality in the Context of an Inspection Process: Two Types of Error

a. Measurement units are percent of traffic held up, average length of delay, or average cost of delay.

estimate apprehension rates and measure the targeting efficiency of the primary inspection selection process.[1]

Before this heightened degree of analytic sophistication, customs managers had watched their agency's policy shift first one way then the other, along the facilitation-enforcement trade-off curve depicted in figure 5-1. A succession of commissioners, some of whom favored smooth relationships and passenger satisfaction and others who took a hard line against lawbreakers, endlessly pushed one way or the other—from the top left corner of the diagram, where detection is poor but delays are minimal, to the bottom right, where seizure rates soar and so do passenger complaints. Genuine improvement, redesign teams knew, would mean doing better on both counts at once, finding a way to move from curve A to a curve closer to the origin (curve B), where the trade-offs are not so severe.

Having clarified the goals of customs' process improvements, the agency produced some stunning successes. It also produced some bewildering failures. The most dramatic success involved a complete overhaul of the passenger (inbound) process at international airports. Before redesign, the average delay for passengers passing through the customs clearance process was roughly twenty-six minutes. After collecting their bags, passengers would queue up at the Customs Service desk to be asked a series of questions about their itinerary and purpose of their trip—largely duplicative of the conversation they had just had with the Immigration and Naturalization Service—as well as having their baggage inspected or searched. When customs implemented its redesigned process, the average waiting time dropped by more than 80 percent, to roughly five minutes. At the same time, detection rates increased.

The redesigned process exploited both partnerships and technology. Recognizing the duplicative nature of their questioning, customs and immigration connected their systems. Much of the passenger selection work moved from the customs hall into a back office—and went high-tech. An advance passenger information system provided customs inspectors with passenger lists long before planes landed. The computerized lists were automatically cross-matched with law enforcement databases (including customs' own), and passengers of interest were flagged by name. When these passengers checked in with immigration, customs was alerted automatically and was then able, through a closed-circuit television system installed throughout the baggage claim area, to monitor the movements of these passengers until they approached the customs inspection point. At that point a customs official would appear, armed with a history of these passengers' travels and prior encounters with law enforcement. In redesigning the process, customs did not abandon its tradition of behavioral monitoring (inspectors' acquired skill of picking out people who had something to hide)—they relocated it. Instead of watching passengers only as they moved through the customs hall, now plainclothes officers mingled with passengers as they left the gate and moved through the arrivals concourses, unaware of the surveillance.

Similar gains, albeit less dramatic, accrued within the processing of inbound cargo. A new national Automated Commercial System (ACS) tracked the importation of shipping containers across the country, permitting adjustment of the inspection risk for each container according to a wide range of features—such as the importer, the exporter, the track record of the shipping company, the nature of the load, its value, and so on. The ACS also provided customs the opportunity to administer a random program of container inspections, integrated within the same inspection scheduling system, enabling customs to measure compliance rates across different industry segments and across different ports of entry.

The agency used process reengineering to streamline the hiring process, the handling of correspondence at headquarters, property disposal, the procurement process, and space acquisition, but Deputy Commissioner Michael Lane grew concerned that once again, in the process of reinvention, the Office of Enforcement (the special agents) seemed to be left out. He urged the agents to apply process improvement methods to one of their primary responsibilities—interdiction.

Customs Service Interdiction

Focusing first on narcotics, special agents set about trying to map the existing drug interdiction process. To their consternation, they never got past that stage: the various maps they produced looked like spaghetti, jumbled and confused, and no matter how hard they tried to be all-inclusive, some type of smuggling was not covered by the diagrams or someone's contribution was left out. The agents had expected this redesign to be complicated; they knew that narcotics interdiction involved virtually every piece of the agency, including inspectors. The methods used to smuggle drugs were so diverse—from low-altitude flights across the southern border, to air passengers swallowing heroine packed in condoms, to loads concealed inside the gearboxes of imported tractors—that they could never all be captured on one diagram. Besides, methods changed constantly as smugglers played cat and mouse with law enforcement, so the value of specifying and implementing any improved process, if it ever became static, was clearly questionable.

Wondering whether the agents simply were not trying hard enough, Lane took charge himself, trying to move the process along: more charts were produced, more spaghetti, with no clear flow of work from left to right and always with contributors complaining that they had been left out. Being omitted from a process design was an alarming prospect, especially given the pressures of downsizing; it meant that one's job was in jeopardy. Neither Lane nor his otherwise successful redesign experts could make this one work. They began to realize that, for some reason, the conceptual apparatus and practical methods of process management did not fit this particular aspect of customs' work.

Theorists and experts on process management might argue that customs did not do it right or that the special agents adopted a superficial interpretation of process management. In fact, customs' interpretation and application of business process redesign seems consistent with the writings on which they depended for instruction (particularly Michael Hammer and James Champy's *Reengineering the Corporation*)[2] and with the way most other government agencies were interpreting and applying the same principles. Process management techniques enabled agencies to view their core, high-volume processes as an integrated whole, rather than as independent and uncoordinated functional contributions. As Hammer and Champy put it,

> In most companies today, no one is in charge of the processes. In fact, hardly anyone is even aware of them. Does any company have a vice president in charge of order fulfillment, of getting products to customers? Probably not. Who is in *charge* of developing new products? Everyone—R & D, marketing, finance, manufacturing, and so on—is involved, but no one is in charge.
>
> Companies today consist of functional silos, or stovepipes, vertical structures built on narrow pieces of a process.[3]

They define *reengineering* as "the fundamental rethinking and radical redesign of business processes to achieve dramatic improvements in critical, contemporary measures of performance, such as cost, quality, service, and speed."[4] With the more radical reengineering version (as opposed to *continuous process improvement*), the organization is ripped up and reorganized around its processes: "Process teams don't contain *representatives* from all the functional departments involved. Rather process teams *replace* the old departmental structure."[5] Michael Lane, in his book on customs modernization, describes how customs applied business process redesign:

> Whereas most organizations have tended to organize and manage by occupational series or functional specialty, process management requires that our perspective of work be broadened to visualize a stream of work, or process, that flows from inputs (merchandise, consignees, or passengers) to finished products (cleared goods and passengers in compliance with customs and other agency laws) in a timely fashion at minimal cost to government and industry. With process management, organizations view their work flow horizontally across organizational lines and view those processes from end to end as a whole.[6]

For each of their four major processes, customs followed Hammer and Champy's methods, appointing process owners and then a reengineering team to set about the business of process redesign.[7] In the first stage of redesign, according to Lane, "the processes would each be mapped or flow-diagrammed to determine areas where processes could be improved by introducing controls or eliminating redundant steps."[8] Attempting to map the process was as far as the Office of Enforcement ever got in its efforts to reengineer the interdiction process.

In 1994, having met Mike Lane at a customs "visioning" event hosted by the Brookings Institution, I worked with him to see if we could extract the special agents from this quagmire and prevent them from being totally alienated from reinvention. The immediate question was, Is interdiction really a *process*? If not, then perhaps process management techniques are the wrong tools. Hammer and Champy define processes as "a collection of activities that takes one or more kinds of input and creates an output that is of value to the customer."[9] Their examples consist of a series of defined steps, each conducted by different functional specialists. Dictionary definitions of *process* make clearer the sense of a sequence of steps through which work passes: for example, "a series of actions or operations conducing to an end."[10] Because process management texts invite organizations to look at their own internal processes (rather than any other actions or operations), government agencies naturally apply these techniques for improving the performance of established internal mechanisms, in which work goes in one end and a product flows out the other.

But the work of interdiction is less about perfecting internal processes than about controlling external behaviors. Drug smuggling is a pattern of human behavior, external to the organization, that customs officials needed to pick apart analytically and address intelligently, piece by piece, as they sought to constantly disrupt smuggling patterns. Smooth, predictable, uniform, well-oiled, and customer-friendly importation processes would never constitute a solution. Customer service ideals and process management tools did not even provide a useful way of thinking about interdiction responsibilities. A different mind-set and a different managerial tool kit was needed.

Who could teach that mind-set? What were those tools? I suggested Herman Goldstein's *Problem-Oriented Policing,* a core text from the police profession, describing attempts to move beyond a preoccupation with process. Goldstein, a professor of law at the University of Wisconsin, had been writing on this theme since the 1960s. His argument is that policing becomes more effective if police, rather than processing 911 calls one after another and in isolation, could learn to identify underlying patterns and then fashion tailor-made solutions that prevent recurrences. *Problem-Oriented Policing* is Goldstein's most complete account of the problem-solving, or problem-oriented, philosophy and the ways it differs from the profession's traditional focus on rapid, and procedurally correct, responses to calls for service—a focus that Goldstein critiqued:

> The majority of changes . . . in policing . . . reflect a continuing preoccupation with means over ends; with operating methods, process, and efficiency over effectiveness in dealing with substantive problems; with the running of the organization rather than with the impact of the organization on community problems that the police are expected to handle. Concern over this imbalance led to development of the concept of problem-oriented policing.[11]

Many scholars of police management and practice observe that the advent of three technologies (the patrol car, the telephone, and the radio) led to the creation of centralized dispatch systems, which focus the majority of police attention on process: receiving, prioritizing, and handling 911 calls. The promise of modern, technology-enabled, policing (with the promise, "You call, we'll come") organized around centralized dispatching operations, generated such 911 call volumes that police struggled to escape their slavery to the system they had created.[12] The community policing and problem-solving philosophies were conceived as antidotes to the dominant focus on call processing and to the insulation from community and community life that seems to accompany that focus.

As Goldstein points out, the ability to deal effectively with problems is not just a question of having the right mind-set. Most police agencies lack the requisite infrastructure and systems:

> Relatively little in the current organization and staffing of police agencies reflects a regular, continuing institutionalized concern for substantive matters. Some agencies and administrators get closer than do others. Some get involved when a problem becomes a crisis. But the field as a whole has seldom taken a serious, inquiring, in-depth interest in the wide range of problems that constitute its

business, nor does it have a tradition of proceeding logically from knowledge gained about a particular problem to the fashioning of an appropriate response.[13]

Deputy Commissioner Lane wanted the Customs Service to develop a tradition of proceeding logically from knowledge gained about a particular drug smuggling problem, or other form of noncompliance, to the fashioning of an appropriate response. He not only read Goldstein's book (and required his senior staff to read it too) but also invited Goldstein to Washington.[14] Ultimately, customs embraced the problem-solving approach as well as process management. The two, they learned, served different purposes. In the summer of 1995, with an injection of $2 million of the commissioner's discretionary funds, the agency launched an agencywide Strategic Problem-Solving (SPS) program, managed principally through the Office of Enforcement and focused on the identification and control of specific smuggling problems. The focus was not on law-abiding customers but on lawbreakers—criminals, smuggling organizations, and their various illegal activities.

In designing the SPS program, the agency faced questions for which the process management doctrine provided no answers. How to structure such a program. Whether to reorganize again and, if so, around what? How to specify and allocate the work. How to record and report performance. How to integrate this new kind of work with the work of the core processes. Suffice it to say that by 1995 the agency had realized the limits of process management. The work of the Office of Enforcement was recognized as in many respects different from that of the rest of the agency and as needing to be thought about differently.

Internal Revenue Service and Managing Compliance

The Customs Service was not alone. The Internal Revenue Service, during the same period, was also beginning to question whether the tools of process management equipped the agency to deal with serious noncompliance problems. Some noncompliance issues (such as failure to sign a tax return) could be dealt with within the confines of a core, high-volume process (returns processing). Other noncompliance issues, however, aligned less readily with core processes. In fact some did not align at all.

In the fall of 1991, IRS Commissioner Fred Goldberg convened IRS senior managers, including regional commissioners and heads of the major functional branches, and asked them to list the major noncompliance problems in the federal tax system. It took them less than half an hour to agree on the problems and to rank order the top seven problems.[15] At the top of the list was nonfilers—not taxpayers who forgot to file or who skipped a year, but people who never filed and who remained invisible to the IRS systems. The number of nonfilers, estimated in various tax-gap studies, was believed by IRS managers to number roughly 11 million, consisting mostly of self-employed individuals and cash-based businesses.

Goldberg asked the managers a series of questions about the nonfiler problem. Who in the senior management team was responsible for tackling the problem? What data was available within IRS systems that would help the agency come to grips with the problem? The answers were discouraging. None of the senior management team had specific responsibility for this, the most serious, noncompliance problem because their jobs were defined in either functional or geographic terms. IRS databases contained no information about nonfilers because they had never filed. So how could the IRS tackle this problem? The answer, they assumed, was through quality management and process improvement, as these were the tools pressed upon agencies looking to improve their performance. But which process to improve?

The whole IRS (and especially its computer systems) creaked under its process load. In 1992, the agency handled roughly 200 million tax returns each year, issued 80 million refunds (which had to be out on time, otherwise congressional overseers quickly turned nasty), answered 36 million telephone calls and 40 million letters, and conducted roughly 3 million collection actions. No agency ever had better cause to embrace process improvement. Under this staggering operational load, IRS executives dreaded a breakdown in the system such as they had seen in 1985, when information systems failed to handle the volume, and millions of tax returns could not be processed in a timely fashion. The IRS clearly had to guarantee accuracy, efficiency, and timeliness in these core processes and to use automation extensively toward that end. Among federal agencies, the IRS had been an early adopter of quality management techniques, with as many as a thousand process-centered quality circles operating by 1985.

But what of the number-one noncompliance problem? These 11 million nonfilers not only did not file; neither did they call or write letters.

So step one in grappling with the nonfiler problem was to realize that this problem was not represented in the agency's process loads and that no amount of process improvement would bring it under control. To tackle it effectively, the IRS needed a different mind-set, a different approach to analysis, and a different concept of what the work was. The development of the Compliance 2000 philosophy, and the subsequent creation of the DORA (District Office of Research and Analysis) and NORA (National Office of Research and Analysis) sites to analyze patterns of noncompliance, constituted the beginnings of a formal and systematic approach to noncompliance problems.

The nonfiler problem at the IRS presents an extreme case: a noncompliance problem almost completely disconnected from all the agency's processes. Processes deal with the work that comes in, and the nonfiler problem—like many other problems within the jurisdiction and responsibility of regulatory agencies—does not come in. Process loads present only partial and usually distorted representations of the problems to which regulators should address themselves. Many problems and issues they need to go out and look for. Many (for example, domestic violence, corruption, and white-collar crimes) may not reveal themselves, even in retrospect. The usefulness of the IRS nonfiler example, because of its extreme nature, is to disprove a hypothesis that tempts the reinventers of government and the gurus of quality management, the hypothesis that functional expertise and process management (provided both are done sufficiently well) will automatically take care of all important problems. To disprove a theorem one only needs a single counterexample, and the IRS's nonfiler problem does the job admirably.

The Limits of Process Management

The dismissal of that hypothesis should provoke considerable unease among regulatory practitioners, especially those who rely heavily on the techniques of quality management and process improvement to accomplish their missions. Dismissing the hypothesis raises some fundamental questions about regulatory work. One hopes that serious environmental problems are all represented in the routine process work of environmental agencies: permit applications, inspections, and routine monitoring. One also hopes that important hazards in the workplace have been considered in the design and operation of the Occupational Safety and

Health Administration's responses to complaints and incidents and in the design of its inspection schedules. Likewise, one hopes that the 911 call load alerts police to all their important responsibilities.

The experiences of the Customs Service as it contemplates its interdiction responsibilities, however, and of the IRS as it faces up to major noncompliance issues suggest otherwise. These two agencies and many others (including the police profession) have realized that process work is different from, and sometimes not even a good reflection of, the problems that regulators should handle. In which case, regulators would need to determine what systems and machinery are needed to reveal the full range of problems, and what managerial tools are needed to structure and coordinate the response. Given that existing functional responsibilities and process loads already occupy agency staff more than full time, how can they possibly find time to pay attention to yet another form of work? And how does that new form of work relate to those forms already more familiar?

In the summer of 1995, before the congressional assaults on OSHA finally abated, the *Washington Post* published a rare article in support of the beleaguered agency. The article revealed how lobbyists paid by companies previously cited by OSHA, some of them for serious violations, had worked their way into positions from which they could influence legislation governing OSHA's fate. The article defended OSHA's record:

> There were significant gains in some areas, however, which have strengthened the resolve of OSHA supporters this year as they fight for the agency's life. The impact of OSHA intervention in certain high-risk industries is clear. There have been 58 percent fewer deaths in grain handling and 35 percent fewer deaths in trench cave-ins since OSHA cracked down on those industries. The number of textile workers suffering from brown lung—a crippling respiratory disease—fell from 20 percent of the industry work force in 1978, when OSHA set limits on worker exposure to cotton dust, to 1 percent seven years later.[16]

In the context of OSHA's redesign program, already well under way, Joe Dear and the OSHA redesign team initially focused on process improvement to streamline OSHA's response to employee complaints, to facilitate response to accidents, and to introduce the use of video technology rather than paper reports to create inspection records. These investments were intended to make OSHA inspectors more efficient, help them deliver timely service, and maybe free up resources that could be reinvested elsewhere. What OSHA's early redesign plans were missing, however (and which was added when they too discovered problem solving), was the ability to organize around specific categories of hazard, patterns of noncompliance, and types of accident and injury with a view to achieving measurable mitigation, or even elimination of those risks.

In other words, OSHA wanted to produce more of what their few defenders appreciated: *significant risks identified and then controlled.* Like the Customs Service and the Internal Revenue Service, OSHA had to figure out what kind of organizational structures and operational techniques could make *that* kind of work routine.

PART II

The Emergence of
Regulatory Craftsmanship

CHAPTER SIX

Innovations

INNOVATIONS IN REGULATORY and enforcement practice are breaking out all over, which is no surprise, given the clamor for reform. Some innovations respond to calls for enhanced customer service and process efficiency; some focus more explicitly on mission accomplishment; some merge the two, by focusing on mission areas in which facilitation and cooperative enterprise might help.

The Ford Foundation's annual Innovations in American Government competition, open to federal, state, and local public sector initiatives, has been in place since 1986. The number of applicants has risen steadily over the years, reaching roughly 1,400 in the 1998 cycle. Applications pass through academic, policy, and site reviews, conducted by volunteers who winnow the field down to twenty-five finalists. These twenty-five finalists then deliver presentations before a selection committee composed of public policy experts, former members of Congress, former mayors, and some influential journalists. Ten of the finalists are selected as winners, each receiving $100,000 to be used for the purposes of replicating and extending their innovations; the fifteen other finalists receive $20,000 for the same purpose. Harvard University's John F. Kennedy School of Government administers the program in partnership with the Council for Excellence in Government, based in Washington, D.C.[1]

The innovations competition spans the range of government agencies and makes no distinction between regulatory and other innovations: each is evaluated on its own merits and against the whole pool. Nor does the review process lay down policy criteria or impose particular doctrines as to what should and what should not be regarded as valuable. Site evaluators are not sent out with any particular paradigm in mind, and when considering regulatory innovations, the selection committee does not have a particular regulatory model in mind. Evaluators use their personal and collective judgment as to what is valuable and what is genuinely innovative.

In the absence of an underlying evaluative doctrine, and assuming evaluators to be drawn broadly from across the political and policy spectrum, reviewing regulatory innovations that made it to the top of this particular pile should provide some insight into what the public at large (that is, not regulatory experts) perceive as valuable in regulatory practice. Common themes, particularly those that span innovations across a range of regulatory professions, deserve close examination.

Customer Service and Related Reforms

Some themes are familiar and could have been anticipated by anyone paying attention to the political pressures for reform over the last decade: customer service, facilitation, easing of the regulatory burden, process improvements, automation, voluntary cooperative programs, and the rationalization of enforcement practice with increased fairness and transparency. Four innovations that fit this mold are described below.[2]

1. IRS: Telefile Program (1997 winner)

The IRS telefile program allows the filing of 1040EZ tax returns using a touch-tone telephone. It was introduced on a pilot basis in Ohio in 1992 and developed into a fully fledged program used by nearly 5 million taxpayers in 1997 (roughly 20 percent of those eligible to use the simplified form). Entering the necessary financial information via the telephone number pad takes about ten minutes per return, and error rates are reduced to 0.0002 percent from 6.6 percent for equivalent forms sent in by mail.

2. FDA: Reform of the U.S. Drug Approval Process (1997 winner)

FDA officials negotiated an accelerated approval process with pharmaceutical manufacturers, codified in law in 1992. Under the deal, industry agrees to pay substantial application fees, supplementing the FDA budget and cutting the average approval time from two and a half years to fifteen months. Drugs targeted at certain critical illnesses (AIDS, cystic fibrosis, and cancer) can be handled on an accelerated schedule, reaching approval in as little as six months.

3. EPA: 33/50 Program (1997 finalist)

The Environmental Protection Agency's 33/50 program was announced in 1991 by EPA administrator William K. Reilly. The program challenged industry to promise and then produce, on a voluntary basis, reductions in emissions of seventeen targeted chemicals. The chemicals, all covered by the Toxic Release Inventory (TRI, an annual compilation of emissions data reported by industry and published by the EPA), were selected as high priority by the EPA's regulatory programs. The EPA's hope was to reduce emissions of these chemicals by 33 percent before the end of 1992 and by 50 percent before the end of 1995 (using 1988 levels as the benchmark). A total of 1,300 companies made commitments and subsequently reported reductions. The TRI data for 1994, published in 1996, shows that the EPA reached its 50 percent reduction goal one year early. Any company that participated, regardless of degree (and without validation of their claims), received a certificate of appreciation signed by the administrator.

4. City of Chicago: Parking Enforcement Program (1991 finalist)

In 1990 the city of Chicago implemented an integrated and highly automated parking ticket issuance and adjudication system. The system was designed to improve customer service, deliver rapid and fair adjudication and enforcement, and increase accountability and transparency of related processes.

In these four cases, we see that the innovations evaluators and final selection panel recognize customer service, process improvements, facilitation, and the rationalization of enforcement as valuable. Clearly, these are perfectly sensible and appropriate advances for regulators to make.

Risks Reduced

However, process improvement is by no means the strongest current running through the regulatory finalists. The theme of mission accomplishment, particularly *specific risks identified and reduced,* seems to run much more powerfully, outnumbering these others by a ratio of roughly five to one. Moreover, in contrast to the reinvention rhetoric, the vast majority of these programs contain not the slightest hint of backing away from enforcement when it helps accomplish the identified purpose. They are oriented around a specific set of risks or problems rather than around processes or relationships. Although they *use* processes or relationships, or construct new ones necessary for a given purpose, the focus of the innovation is external to the regulatory agency, as the agency directs its own attention and that of its partners to specific patterns or trends. The work described here is the operational work of reducing risks—results oriented, often highly analytical in identifying risk concentrations, but open as to the means employed to accomplish the goal. I have described this shift elsewhere: "Rather than perpetuating their dependence on processes, procedures, and 'coverage,' these professions . . . are each developing new capacities for analyzing important patterns of noncompliance, prioritizing risks, and designing intelligent interventions using a much broader range of tools."[3]

Certainly, this theme runs through the regulatory innovations award winners. In fact, the eight innovations described below constitute tailor-made responses to defined patterns of noncompliance or to specific risks or risk concentrations. And a further thirteen innovations relate not to only one risk and its solution but to a *new system* for specifying risks, problems, or risk concentrations and then managing them on a continuing, dynamic basis. So we see not only risks reduced or problems solved; but also the emergence of risk control or problem solving as a continuing form of operational practice.

I first describe some specific problems, identified, addressed, and in many cases well along the way to resolution or abatement.

1. San Francisco, District Attorney: First-Offender Prostitution Program (1998 winner, 1997 finalist)

The San Francisco district attorney's first-offender prostitution program was launched in 1995 and focuses on breaking the cycle of offending, arrest, and reoffending that typifies the lives of women and girls drawn into prostitution. The methods used include counseling, treatment, life skills training, and support for girls in detention and on probation (with a view to getting them out of the criminal justice system); case management services for women trying to exit prostitution; arresting customers by using police decoys; and offering first-time offenders an eight-hour seminar on the risks and impacts of prostitution, in lieu of prosecution. The application states that the program represents "a paradigm shift from simply prosecuting prostitutes to targeting customers, addressing trafficking in girls, and building a continuum of prevention, early intervention, and rehabilitation for prostitutes and customers alike." The program, clearly multifunctional, involves law enforcement, public health, and private agencies.

2. Boston Police Department: Operation Ceasefire (1997 winner)

In Boston, between 1990 and 1994, 155 children and teenagers died as victims of homicide, most of them in the course of gang violence involving firearms. Under a grant from the National Institute of Justice, Operation Ceasefire brought together a range of criminal justice agencies and other city services to focus on the problem of youth gang violence. Extensive analysis showed that the population at risk was highly concentrated within known gangs, most of whose members (both potential offenders and potential victims) were well known to the criminal justice system.

Operation Ceasefire targeted considerable enforcement capacity on any gang whose members engaged in violence and launched a carefully articulated information campaign to warn gangs of the extreme consequences that would follow an act of violence. The authorities twice carried out their threat, acting in concert, to put an entire gang out of business, using available legal powers and sanctions. After the second such demonstration, gang-related violence dropped off dramatically. In the first year after Operation Ceasefire was implemented, the number of homicide victims in Boston aged twenty-four or younger dropped by 68 percent (from forty-one to thirteen) and continued to decline thereafter. This represented a drop of more than two-thirds from the average rate for the prior five years

3. Bureau of Alcohol, Tobacco, and Firearms: Disarming the Criminal (1997 finalist)

The Treasury Department's Bureau of Alcohol, Tobacco, and Firearms (BATF) maintains records of all firearms sold in the United States, but formerly lacked the technological capacity to convert the data into useful information. Beginning in 1994, the bureau relocated the data to a state-of-the-art computer facility, developed a new software package that could extract leads on gun traffickers, and provided on-line access into the system for its field officers. As a result of these new analytic capabilities, focused on the identification of trafficking activity, the BATF has prosecuted and incarcerated 2,230 illegal firearms traffickers for trafficking 34,491 firearms. Recently BATF extended this work to focus on illegal youth firearms markets, working with local law enforcement in seventeen pilot cities.

4. Department of Labor, Wage and Hour Division: Eradicating Sweatshops in the Garment Industry (1996 winner)

The Wage and Hour Division (WHD) of the Department of Labor is responsible for enforcing labor laws in 6.5 million workplaces but has only 800 investigators to accomplish this mission. Today's $45 billion garment industry is structured like a pyramid, with relatively few retailers at the top buying finished goods from manufacturers, who in turn contract out most of the work among roughly 22,000 sewing contractors. At the contractor level, noncompliance with minimum wage, occupational safety, and other labor laws is widespread. In an attempt to solve these systemic noncompliance problems and to gain some leverage over this massive industry, the WHD focused its efforts at the top of the pyramid. Making extensive use of existing "hot goods" provisions of the Fair Labor Standards Act, which make it illegal to ship goods in interstate commerce made in violation of the act, the WHD positioned itself to mobilize the media and public opinion against retailers and manufacturers who failed to monitor their own contractors. Concerned about their public image, more than forty manufacturers signed compliance agreements with the WHD, committing themselves to regularly monitor their contractors; more than 200 retailers committed themselves to combating violations.

5. Occupational Safety and Health Administration: Maine 200 Program (1995 winner)

OSHA's Maine 200 program focuses on effectiveness (improving worker safety), consciously rejecting the old bean counting output, or productivity, measures. The original application for the innovations award points this out: "Now, however, OSHA compliance officers in Maine are no longer supposed to 'rack up their numbers' of inspections, citations, and fines. Rather, they are supposed to focus on achieving the underlying purpose of their agency. For many, this is a radical change from the traditional regulatory mentality." The Maine 200 program also exhibits many elements of a problem-solving approach. It identifies an important concentration of risk through systematic data analysis and then focuses resources on those risks in an attempt to mitigate them. The significant concentration of risk (identified through data analysis of workdays-lost-to-injury data) lay with just two hundred employers. This group represented 1 percent of Maine's employers but employed 30 percent of the state's work force and accounted for 44 percent of compensable workplace injuries, illnesses, and fatalities.

Having identified the concentration of risk, OSHA designed a new partnership program to address it. Each employer was presented with work-site-specific injury and illness profiles and then given a choice (under the unofficial motto "Choose your OSHA"). One option for them was to conduct a comprehensive hazard survey of their own facilities, to correct all hazards identified, and to implement a comprehensive safety and health program with employee involvement. OSHA would provide information, advice, and technical assistance. Employers who did not select this option or who failed to maintain their commitment to the program were placed on the primary inspection list and targeted for a traditional comprehensive inspection. From 1991 to 1993, after the first full year of the program's operation, worker compensation claims in Maine dropped by 35 percent.[4] At least 320 safety and health committees were established at employer locations. In the first year alone, 182 participating employers identified 95,800 hazards and abated 55,200. (Compare with 36,780 hazards cited by OSHA inspectors in the state over the previous eight-year period).[5]

6. *Immigration and Naturalization Service: Operation Jobs (1995 winner)*

The Dallas field office of the Immigration and Naturalization Service developed a new approach to the enforcement of prohibitions against employing undocumented aliens, launching Operation Jobs in 1994. Previously, INS agents would make unannounced visits to employers and immediately arrest and remove illegal aliens. This practice had the effect of disrupting production schedules but was ineffective in improving compliance, as other illegal aliens quickly filled the vacancies created. The pervasive availability of fraudulent documents (especially green cards) made it extremely difficult for even well-intentioned employers to filter out illegal hires.

Operation Jobs linked enforcement actions to a new system for placing legal workers in the positions vacated. INS agents developed relationships with other public agencies and voluntary organizations to provide legal replacement workers, to stop the cycle of illegal hiring. The
Texas Employment Commission and other local human services agencies help identify unemployed workers and welfare recipients who might
be able to fill positions vacated. The Salvation Army refers homeless
people, and the Dallas Police Department has referred troubled youths.
The Refugee Services of North Texas and the International Rescue Committee have identified refugees needing jobs. In its first year, Operation
Jobs provided 2,500 jobs for unemployed U.S. workers in Texas. In
March 1995 the INS expanded the scope of the project to eighteen
states in INS's central region, making job placement referrals for 1,400
U.S. citizens and legal residents within the first two weeks.

7. City of New York, Department of Transportation: Red Light Camera Program (1995 finalist)

Traditional law enforcement methods (apprehension and prosecution)
had turned out to be ineffective in controlling widespread noncompliance with traffic signals (red light running) in New York City. After a
five-year battle to obtain enabling legislation, the Traffic Engineering
Division of the New York City Department of Transportation, supported by public advocacy groups, installed automatic cameras at
selected intersections. The cameras create digitized photographs of the
rear of any vehicle traveling above a threshold speed and in the vicinity
of the stop line while the lights are red. After reviewing the photographic
evidence, which contains the registration number, notices of liability are
issued to the registered owner of the vehicle for a $50 fine. In the first
year of operation (at just fifteen problem intersections), 170,000 sum-
monses were issued through this system (compared with a previous average of 100,000 red light violation citations per year, for the whole city).
The explicit goal of the project is to obtain stricter enforcement of traffic
violations, focused upon this particularly dangerous practice.

8. Minnesota Pollution Control Agency: Voluntary Inspection and Cleanup Program (1994 winner)

The object of the Voluntary Inspection and Cleanup Program (VIP)
was to minimize potential harm caused by hazardous waste sites already
designated under the (federal) Superfund program. Despite Superfund

designation, cleanup was excessively slow, so the Minnesota Pollution Control Agency used "partnerships under duress," with the hammer of Superfund hanging overhead, to coerce relevant industries into accelerated cleanups. By providing incentives (liability assurances) and using technical assistance as a motivator, the program spurred voluntary cleanup activities ahead of Superfund schedules, stretching public dollars much further than otherwise possible. Without the cumbersome and weighty Superfund procedures lurking in the background, the agency acknowledges that probably nothing much would have happened. They sold the program on the basis of "Either you work with us or we'll leave you to Superfund." This notion of partnerships under duress is reminiscent of the Maine 200 program's offer (threat), "Choose your OSHA." The message to regulated facilities is, "We intend to accomplish our mission, but we can do it the easy way or the hard way: you choose."

Risk Analysis and Management as Operational Practice

The other thirteen innovations—all winners or finalists—move beyond individual problems, risks, or patterns of noncompliance to establish *dynamic systems* or mechanisms for identifying high-risk areas, quantifying them, comparing them, selecting focus areas, and then managing them on a continuing basis.

In a minority of these cases, the system embodies an express preference for particular tools (for example, the Blackstone project's preference for preventive approaches to pollution control and Florida Ecosystem Management's preference for alternatives to enforcement). In other cases the choice of method is unspecified, albeit the goal remains to find artful and resource-efficient interventions that produce meaningful impacts. In nearly every case, identification and comparison of risk areas are accomplished through a specific form of analysis or inquiry (for example, the repeat-calls analysis used by the Minneapolis police and the citizen surveys employed by Baltimore's COPE teams), and it is interesting to recognize these as choices already made, during the design of the program, as to the source of relevant data and the form of analysis to be conducted.

1. New York State, Unified Court System: Center for Court Innovation (1998 winner)

The Center for Court Innovation was established by the New York court system and the Fund for the City of New York to foster innovation in New York courts. The application stated the reasons: "Unfortunately, today's court administrators are hindered by outmoded technology, scarce resources and the day-to-day responsibility of operating large public institutions with escalating caseloads. . . . As a result, they are unable to respond to changing times, emerging social problems and increased public expectations." The new center establishes "a team of independent planners who function like the research and development arm of a corporation—investigating chronic and emerging problems and formulating new programs in response."

The "problems" that the center focuses upon are external, community-based issues, not internal administrative ones. Planners from the center have conceived, developed, and implemented (among others) the Midtown Community Court, the Brooklyn Treatment Court, the Brooklyn Domestic Violence Court, and the Manhattan Family Treatment Court. These represent tailor-made responses, spanning a number of criminal justice and other social institutions, to community problems reflected in court caseloads.

2. New York City Police Department: Compstat Program (1996 winner)

Short for "computer comparison statistics," the Compstat system allows police to track crime incidents and spot emerging patterns early. Compstat produces maps illustrating where and when crime is occurring citywide. The system's outputs are used in conjunction with weekly meetings of department managers, at which local commanders are held accountable for the identification and suppression of emerging problems in their precincts. Once a pattern has been identified, the department seeks to fashion a comprehensive response involving community groups or representatives when appropriate. Ongoing monitoring assesses the impact of interventions and measures progress toward the reduction or elimination of the problems identified.

3. Florida Department of Environmental Protection: Ecosystem Management (1996 finalist)

The ecosystem management program divides Florida into twenty-four ecosystem management areas (closely corresponding to watershed areas) and establishes "grass-roots teams to identify environmental problems, devise solutions, and carry them out." At first, such a statement seems broad and all-encompassing. However this program does explicitly prefer some methods over others: "Citizens work with government to develop incentive-based voluntary alternatives that provide better environmental and economic results." It handles some problems better than others. Given that ecosystem committees are structured around watersheds, this approach can handle efficiently only those environmental problems of that shape, that is, those specific to particular watersheds or subcomponents thereof.

4. Pension Benefit Guaranty Corporation: Early Warning Program (1995 winner)

The Pension Benefit Guaranty Corporation was created in 1974 as an independent federal corporation to protect employees from catastrophic losses of retirement benefits, should their employers fail to put aside or properly manage sufficient reserves to meet their long-term pension obligations.[6] By 1995, the PBGC insured 58,000 pension benefit plans, covering 41 million American workers. The PBGC had an enforcement function too: monitoring the financial solvency of plans and permitting or prohibiting the termination of plans. The PBGC's past practice revolved around rescuing underfunded pension plans left without financial support when companies failed. The early warning system moved the emphasis from rescue (after failure, often through bankruptcy proceedings) to early monitoring and intervention, before a plan's fiscal integrity becomes seriously jeopardized. According to the evaluator's site visit report, "the Early Warning Program represents the cutting edge of innovations in enforcement. It combines an anticipatory posture (prevention of future loss), prioritization of effort with solutions tailored to each case, using methods that encourage compliance and voluntary disclosure."

The new approach involves proactively identifying pension plans at risk, identifying corporate transactions that might jeopardize retirement benefits, and negotiating protections for the plans that protect workers and retirees. At the outset the early warning program targeted pension plans underfunded by $25 million or more, utilizing financial data from an array of sources to identify them. Four hundred plans in this category represented only 2 percent of the total number of plans insured but accounted for more than 80 percent of all the workers in underfunded plans and federal insurance exposure. Having got that high-risk pool under some semblance of control, the PBGC successively lowered the underfunding threshold to bring in lesser risks. The system therefore provides a continuing, dynamic method of targeting resources and attention to the highest-risk plans and works with affected companies selected as potentially problematic (as does the Maine 200 program), negotiating solutions that preserve and protect pension plans.

5. Florida Department of Environmental Protection: Marine Spill Analysis System (1994 finalist)

Oil spills in Florida's shallow water ecosystems have disastrous consequences for wildlife, human communities, recreation, and tourism. Prompted by the Exxon Valdez disaster, the Florida Marine Research Institute and the Bureau of Emergency Response (both parts of the state's Department of Environmental Protection) have worked with other agencies to enhance the state's spill response capabilities. The marine spill analysis system, part of that enhanced response, provides a state-of-the-art computing platform for capturing, integrating, analyzing, and mapping the diverse data sets necessary to protect natural resources from spills. The system was "designed to support the entire life-cycle of oil spill management, from initial planning to post-spill damage assessment," not only supporting early coordination and response for damage minimization (including real-time oil slick tracking) but also providing the state with comprehensive information for assessment of damage and recovery of monetary compensation after the fact.

6. State of Illinois, Criminal Justice Information Authority: Spatial and Temporal Analysis of Crime (STAC) Project (1997 finalist)

This computerized crime mapping system pinpoints developing "hotspots" of criminal activity. The application for the project claims that "what puts STAC on the cutting edge of police work is that it not only produces timely, accurate, maps, but also identifies Hot Spot areas and other patterns, regardless of arbitrary ward, district, or census tract boundaries. . . . STAC's core innovation is that it organizes that information in user-friendly ways that can help community-police teams solve practical, real-time community problems." Armed with this information regarding spatial and temporal clusters, "law enforcement can now develop patrol, intervention, and prevention strategies that more precisely address the problems of their neighborhoods." Between 1982, when it began, and 1992 the STAC system had been adopted by thirteen agencies.

7. Massachusetts Department of Environmental Protection: Blackstone Project—Preventing Pollution Before it Happens (1991 winner)

The Blackstone project was designed to prevent pollution in the Upper Blackstone Water Pollution Abatement District. The key to the project's success lies in the integration of the regulatory function (a responsibility shared by federal, state, and local agencies) with the technical assistance function (the responsibility of an entirely separate Office of Technical Assistance). To make the full range of tools available for designing pollution prevention solutions, facility by facility, a great deal of interagency cooperation was required. The whole project was results oriented, as the application stated, "making reduction of wastes at the source an explicit goal of compliance assurance efforts." And the method chosen involved a clear integration of the enforcement and assistance functions: "coordinating the Commonwealth's technical assistance (carrot) and regulatory (stick) programs, without compromising the goals of either."

8. Newport News (Virginia) Police Department: Problem-Oriented Policing (1990 finalist)

Newport News, Virginia, was the first American city to adopt problem-oriented policing as an operational method to be used department-wide. The program had no budget items and no formal organizational structure, even though a Problem Analysis Advisory Committee acted as internal consultants for problem-solving projects. The Police Department learned the importance of data analysis in performing risk assessment and prioritization and learned that the pursuit of important results necessarily entails a broad range of partnerships. As the site evaluation report notes, "A review of project reports suggests that participating officers . . . have acquired significant skills in using statistical data, in identifying and digging up needed information, and in recognizing that problem-solving often requires the involvement of other government agencies and citizens."

9. City of Minneapolis Police Department: Repeat-Call Address Policing Unit (RECAP) Program (1988 finalist)

Minneapolis police also adopted a problem-solving approach, with the specific goal of eliminating the underlying conditions that produce multiple 911 calls from particular addresses. The application states that "the program is part of an innovative approach to policing called 'problem-solving,' which aims at accomplishing clear goals rather than just processing cases or answering calls." The RECAP unit rank-ordered all addresses in the city by call frequency over a one-year period and found that the top 250 addresses had generated more than 20,000 calls in 1986. The unit then devoted itself to analyzing the underlying causes and eliminating the problems through tailor-made interventions, address by address.

Like Maine 200, the RECAP unit focused on rigorous analysis of one objective data source (911 calls). The benefits of such an approach are that it avoids subjective judgments during the risk assessment stage and makes resource allocation decisions on a technical rather than a subjective basis—therefore easier to defend. (The downside, if there is one, is that focusing solely on call data excludes from attention any problems not adequately represented in the 911 data.)

10. Baltimore County Police Department: Citizen-Oriented Police Enforcement (COPE) Program (1988 finalist)

One of the earliest police programs presented to the innovations competition, Baltimore's COPE program broadened the police mission from its traditional focus on crime and safety, in this case embracing the need to address citizens' fears, whether or not they were directly linked to real risks of victimization.[7] The application also describes the program as "accomplishment oriented," adopting a range of tools, and using community partnerships and a "refined problem-solving process" involving "emphasis on accurate problem identification." The application states that "the mission of COPE is to reduce citizen fear. Corrective action is focused on both the surface problems and the root causes of the issues that generate fear. Both traditional and nontraditional police responses are used. . . . The use of participative management, interaction with the community, and a refined problem-solving process provide a fertile atmosphere for developing new and effective strategies."

11. State of Washington State Patrol: Traffic Enforcement and Management System (1987 finalist)

This system represents an "organizational approach to the reduction of traffic accidents in the State of Washington." It begins by establishing local area accident reduction goals. Local troopers, encouraged to explore the sources and causes of groups of accidents, then fashion their own action plans to meet their objectives. Accident reduction plans involve both targeted enforcement and community participation.

Innovations Ancillary to Risk Reduction

Two other regulatory innovations come from agencies already committed to broad risk-reduction strategies and techniques.

12. Consumer Product Safety Commission: Fast Track Program (1998 winner)

The Consumer Product Safety Commission has a tradition of risk assessment through analysis, calculating injury and fatality rates associated with specific commodities and products. Using analysis of data from a range of sources, the commission then hones in on specific risks and risk factors and, subsequently, works either with particular companies or with entire industries to mitigate the dangers. The commission's fast-track program overcomes one specific impediment to speedy recalls.

Once the commission determines that a product is defective or dangerous, it works with the company on a recall plan or other corrective action. Even cooperative companies do not like to recall products, in part because they fear the commission's "preliminary determination" (that there is a problem) might be used against them in product liability suits. The new program offers responsible companies an option for an expedited review that eliminates the issuance of a preliminary determination, thus reducing their exposure to suits. To use this option, companies must report the problem and simultaneously propose a satisfactory recall plan that can be implemented within twenty working days. The commission reviews the plan for adequacy and for sufficient public notification. Since the program became available, nearly half of all corrective action programs have used this route, hastening recalls (and potentially reducing liability exposure for companies involved).

13. Florida Department of Environmental Protection: Secretary's Quarterly Performance Report (1998 finalist)

Florida's Department of Environmental Protection, under the leadership of Secretary Virginia Wetherell, had moved on a number of fronts to enhance its capacity for results-oriented, data-driven, problem solving. This department appeared on the list of innovations finalists three times: for the marine spill analysis system in 1994, for ecosystem management in 1996, and for the *Secretary's Quarterly Performance Report (SQPR)* in 1998. Meanwhile, the department also adopted a formal environmental problem-solving program (never the subject of an innovations application), modeled on problem-solving techniques pioneered by the police profession. The *SQPR* provides an umbrella framework that helps all these programs identify trends, patterns, or focus areas; and it displays the department's progress (or lack of it) in addressing those concerns for the whole world to see, via the Internet.

Published quarterly since December 1997, the *SQPR* (nicknamed "Squipper" in the department) is a comprehensive summary of environmental and performance data gathered from across the six geographic districts and six program divisions of this 4,200-person department. The data is organized into three main sections, or tiers: tier 1 lays out environmental indicators; tier 2, compliance measures; and tier 3, departmental outputs and productivity measures. The September 1998 printed version of the report runs to 122 pages; it is distributed broadly within the state and beyond. The report is designed to address all the department's various reporting obligations, spanning the requirements of state-level performance-based budget statutes, the department's performance partnership agreement with the Environmental Protection Agency, and EPA's core performance measures, among others. The report is available on the department's website as soon as it is published, complete with graphs and charts showing improvements or degradations in performance.

The secretary of the department has the opportunity to review the data before publication and to designate *focus areas* (the most serious) and *watch areas* (less serious) where data reveal worrying trends, environmental degradation, or anomalies in performance. District or division directors are then responsible for identifying the source of the problem and devising a plan to correct it. Given the public availability of the data, and increasing use of it for managing the department, the integrity of the data and data collection methods is paramount. Beginning in 1999, the department's Office of Inspector General embarked on random audits of the data and data collection mechanisms to ensure their validity.

Stephen Humphrey, chair of Florida's Environmental Regulation Commission (to which the department answers) wrote in a foreword to the September 1998 edition of *SQPR*:

The quarterly report is a measuring device, a set of yardsticks. Behind this tool is an outcome-oriented philosophy of management, the Environmental Performance Management System. Together, these impose intellectual discipline and methodological rigor on the agency's programs. Like the practice of fiscal accounting, this systematic scrutiny of outcomes is intentionally revealing. It yields important information—history, lessons, and questions. It is repeatable, defensible, and adaptable. It provides a common basis for communication. It empowers observers. In particular, it identifies status and trends, successes and failures, problems and opportunities. It enables need-based priorities to be set, cost-effective methods to be chosen. It drives the agenda, by focusing on greatest needs and best means. It enables internal programs, divisions, and offices to improve by comparing past and peer performance.[8]

Summary

Humphrey's comments about Florida's *SQPR* reflect much of what emerges as valuable from this collection of regulatory innovations. Viewed as a whole, they reveal nothing soft, no compromise of law, no retreat from enforcement, and surprisingly little preoccupation with customer service.

Rather, these innovative programs seem utterly focused on their regulatory task and on the agency's ability to break it down into manageable pieces and then tackle each one. Those pieces invariably take the form of specific, well-articulated problems, risks, or risk concentrations. Where these agencies have focused on patterns of noncompliance, they have chosen forms of noncompliance perceived as particularly troubling or dangerous (such as aggressive running of red lights in New York City).

The vast majority of these programs avoid any a priori preferences for particular means, using enforcement without hesitation if necessary, and using alternatives without hesitation when they might work better. These agencies seem willing to cooperate with regulated industry whenever the problem gets fixed quicker that way—and provided the manner and terms of cooperation do no damage to their enforcement capacity, nor to broader deterrence. They proactively select whom to work with on the basis of analysis, picking the partners they need *for the job*.

All the programs have extremely strong preferences about ends, being emphatically results oriented, wanting and expecting to see risks reduced and problems mitigated. They prefer interventions that act at the earliest feasible opportunity, in order to prevent or minimize harm. They search for resource-efficient interventions, often leveraging public resources and cooperating with other agencies. And they rely on monitoring and analysis to show them, and others, what they have and have not achieved.

CHAPTER SEVEN

The Elements
of Reform

THE REVIEW OF the innovations winners and finalists points to a renewed task orientation and to the variety of methods and systems agencies have constructed to focus their attention on specific risks or patterns of noncompliance. I suspect, however, that readers may be puzzled by the fact that such an orientation can be seen as innovative. After all, did these agencies not just do their jobs? Is not risk control and problem solving precisely what the public expects from agencies of social regulation? Do those ideas not represent the core purposes for which agencies of social regulation were created? Often regulatory practitioners tell me there really is nothing innovative about any of this: that they solve problems all the time, and always have done so, and how dare anyone suggest otherwise.

Three Core Elements

To see more clearly what is new and what is not, it helps to pick apart the emerging task-oriented, risk control strategies of regulatory practice. By examining the component elements piece by piece, one may see the whole more clearly than before and be in a better position to assess how far agencies have progressed on various fronts. One would also be better equipped to identify the kinds of organizational development that separate the pioneers from the rest of the regulatory field. Three core elements—distinct but interrelated—capture the essence of the emerging strategies. In no particular order, they are

1. *A clear focus on results.* This involves an explicit rejection of a principal reliance on traditional output or productivity measures as a basis for assessing effectiveness; a recognition of the absence of meaningful measures of effect or impact (and the difficulty of developing them); perseverance in the search for more meaningful indicators of agency performance; and a growing reliance on measurable reductions achieved within specific, well-defined problem areas, as indicators of success.

2. *The adoption of a problem-solving approach.* This involves the systematic identification of important hazards, risks, or patterns of noncompliance; an emphasis on risk assessment and prioritization as a rational and publicly defensible basis for resource allocation decisions; the development of an organizational capacity for designing and implementing effective, creative, tailor-made solutions for each identified problem; the use of a range of tools for procuring compliance and eliminating risks; and the recognition of the need to retain and enhance the agency's enforcement "sting," while using enforcement actions economically and within the context of coherent compliance strategies.

3. *An investment in collaborative partnerships.* Such partnerships with industry, unions, employees, industry associations, municipalities, and other government agencies at the federal, regional, and state levels are designed to produce a sense of shared purpose through collaborative agenda setting and prioritization; more effective interventions resulting from the active engagement of multiple parties; and optimal leveraging of scarce agency resources.

Interdependence

As agencies revamp their regulatory strategies, they may focus at the outset on any one of the three elements listed above, but no matter which element first draws them in, they usually end up engaging all three. Striving to achieve measurable results (element 1) quickly leads to the use of partnerships (element 3) as a way of making public dollars go further. Likewise, focusing on risk control or risk reduction accomplishments as performance goals naturally demands a risk orientation (element 2) as a feature of organizational life.

The police profession uses different names for these elements. The label *community policing* focuses attention on a police department's partnership with the communities it serves. That partnerships serves two purposes: first, it enables joint agenda setting and prioritization (which tends to diminish the traditional police focus on serious crime and raise the level of priority given to persistent community problems). Second, community partnerships mobilize significant nonpolice resources in collaborative efforts to achieve the selected goals.

The label *problem-solving policing* focuses attention on the second element, providing methods for addressing problems in a systematic and rigorous manner. The adoption of a problem-solving strategy (or problem oriented, as Herman Goldstein calls it) stems from a conviction that police "incidents" are symptoms of underlying problems, usually soluble, and that policing is more effective when it pays attention to the problems rather than treating each incident in isolation.[1] Problem-solving policing places emphasis on the longer-term impacts and effects of police actions through the discipline of identifying patterns among the myriad calls for service and then designing interventions to deal with those patterns. Problem-solving policing allows for the identification of problems on many different scales and in many different dimensions. It encourages the use of creativity and imagination by officers of all ranks. It looks for a careful analysis of the nature of a problem, identification and weighing of all relevant interests, the careful selection of the most appropriate solutions, and the systematic monitoring of the effectiveness of the action taken. A results orientation is built into the problem-solving methodology.

Community policing and problem solving now represent the two major strands in police reformist thinking. Many police departments embrace both and understand their compatibility and synergism. The police profession is fortunate to have established a vocabulary to describe these aspects of reform. Most other regulatory professions do not enjoy the luxury of an established reform vocabulary. Many speak broadly of a results orientation but do not identify results closely with *risks reduced* or *problems solved* (indeed, there are many other kinds of results). Many speak of partnerships and partnership programs but often with a stronger sense of responsive government and customer service than of collaborative agenda setting, common purpose, and joint endeavor. Even when professions other than policing share the aspiration (for example, William Reilly's motto, "managing for environmental results"), they focus more on changes in regulations and high-level program design than on the daily operational aspects of risk control.

Assessing Progress

Putting aside the pioneers and innovators for a moment, one should consider how far the regulatory and enforcement side of government in general has progressed with respect to the three core elements of reforming regulatory practice. Of the three, the third (investment in collaborative partnerships) seems the most advanced, perhaps because of its non-confrontational nature and the way it fits the reinvention agenda. Even so, there now appears to be a gradual mutation under way (or a shift of resources from one kind of partnership to another), as regulators are forced to ask what benefits their partnership programs produce.

The next most advanced is the first element: a clear focus on results. Here the *need* for more meaningful measures of agency performance seems firmly established, yet satisfactory methods for measuring, recording, and reporting regulatory accomplishment remain elusive. The need is inescapable. At the federal level, the Government Performance and Results Act of 1993 requires agencies to design and implement more sophisticated performance measurement schemes and to emphasize outcomes rather than outputs. At the state level, many performance-based budget statutes demand the same. Nevertheless, despite several years of inquiry and experimentation, most agencies still have considerable trouble producing a convincing demonstration of their results in terms of impacts, outcomes, or effects.

Lagging considerably behind the other two, in my experience, comes the second element: development of an explicit problem-solving, compliance management, or risk control strategy. Many agencies have not yet even realized the need for this. Or, if they have, some do not regard it as in any way different from their traditional methods of operation. In other words, they think they have it already, a claim that always begs careful examination. Even the vocabulary with which to discuss this subject remains poorly formed. The Internal Revenue Service would call it *compliance management*. The police profession calls it *problem solving*. The Occupational Safety and Health Administration and the Customs Service have adopted or adapted the police profession's language of probem solving. Customs calls its program *Strategic Problem Solving*. Environmental agencies (starting with the Florida Department of Environmental

Protection) are beginning to talk about *environmental problem solving*. Other professions, particularly those safeguarding the solvency of financial plans or institutions, might more naturally use the language of *risk control*. In any case, even when an agency settles on an appropriate vocabulary, there remains a vast distance between encapsulating the aspiration in a phrase (for example, managing for environmental results) and implementing operational systems to deliver on that promise.

In the remainder of this chapter, I describe the shift under way in the portfolio of regulatory partnerships. Chapter 8 describes the *early* stages of the struggle to find performance measures that count. I put off until chapter 9 (and a number of subsequent chapters) the practical challenge of problem solving, as I believe this subject requires the most careful and detailed explication.

And I must put off the *closing* stages of the search for performance measures until the very end of the book (part 4), because I believe that the search for convincing performance measures (element 1) is tightly linked with development of an organizational capacity for problem solving (element 2); so tightly, in fact, that failure to do the second largely accounts for failure to progress on the first element. In other words, I think a regulatory agency's ability to present a convincing account of its risk control accomplishments depends utterly on its ability to *produce* those accomplishments. Or to put it yet another way, the nature of the *performance account* that regulators can deliver will be limited by the kinds of *performance* they can deliver. If they want to tell the story of risks controlled or problems solved, they must first orient themselves and their organizations to the tasks of risk control or problem solving. Otherwise, they will probably find themselves limited to a performance story built around functions and processes (which is not what they are searching for; that story they already have).

Partnerships with a Purpose

In the spring of 1995, once the need for special focus on reinventing regulation had been accepted, a White House memorandum spelled out the four themes federal regulatory executives should use to focus their reinvention efforts.[2] One item was titled "Get out of Washington and Create Grassroots Partnerships," but it did not say what purpose these partnerships would serve: "I direct you to promptly convene groups consisting of frontline regulators and the people affected by their regulations.

These conversations should take place around the country—at our cleanup sites, our factories, our ports. I further direct you to submit a schedule of your planned meetings to the NPR staff by March 30, and work with NPR in following through on those meetings." Clearly the focus was on meeting with the regulated community, presumably to expose regulatory managers to "outside the beltway" perspectives that might help them understand the plight and concerns of regulated industries and enable them to adjust their stance accordingly. Actually, the use of partnerships was already well established in reinvention efforts: forming partnerships fit well with the customer service focus, and partnerships often served as a platform for collaborative process improvements, decreasing the burden and improving the timeliness of interactions between government and the governed.

When the imperative to form partnerships landed on regulators, they had some natural and appropriate reservations about getting too close to those against whom they might some day have to take enforcement actions. In fact, getting close to industry at all opened them to accusations of betrayal from their traditional allies in the public interest and advocacy communities. To protect themselves from any appearance of compromise, they preferred to partner with respectable companies. The result was a proliferation of mentor programs, excellence in leadership programs, awards for best practice, and the issuance of green stickers and other badges of government approval, which companies could exploit for marketing purposes.

The first column of table 7-1 characterizes partnership programs driven solely or largely by a customer service mentality and a desire to demonstrate the responsiveness of government. Such partnership arrangements would tend to provide services to those segments of the regulated community that ask for it (reactive service provision). These partnerships would deal predominantly with responsible and well-motivated entities (ones the government is not embarrassed to be seen partnering with), and the principal purposes correspond to the expressed needs of the regulated community, oftentimes burden reduction. Of course, the thorny problems of enforcement need not be discussed, as the parties at the table were all "good guys." These partnerships tend to make the regulated community look good in the eyes of the community and make regulators appear responsive and service oriented.

By 1995, regulators were beginning to question just how much partnership was enough. Once the word spread that regulators were now in

Table 7-1. Characteristics of Partnerships with the Regulated Community

Characteristic	Customer service focus	Compliance focus
Whom partnerships are formed with	Whoever asks for help	Whoever needs to be involved or has something to offer
Who partners tend to be	Good actors, responsible mentors, and leaders	Bad actors, locus of significant problems
Stance of regulatory agency	Reactive, responsive	Proactive, seeking out appropriate partners
Objective of partnership	Response to citizen/ industry's requests; meeting their needs	Compliance with regulations, collaborative risk reduction
Method of avoiding public embarrassment	Dealing only with responsible parties	Limited use of immunity and amnesty in partnership design
Motivation for forming partnership	Mutual advantage	Formed under duress

the partnership business, all kinds of industries and industry associations came calling—many of them, regulators feared, looking for some privilege or amnesty or some form of immunity from either inspection or prosecution. Regulators, with their resources already stretched to the limit, began to resent the many hours they were required to spend each week attending meetings, offering educational sessions, and listening to the viewpoints of those they regulated. Traditional enforcement activities dropped off, not just because of the political pressure to deemphasize coercive methods but also because resources were being diverted into partnership activities.

There is nothing wrong with such partnerships per se, provided regulators do not compromise their ability to take a firm stance when necessary. Rewarding best practices and praising socially responsible companies in public are all perfectly reasonable activities for regulators. But regulators' ability to accomplish their core missions might be jeopardized if their portfolio of outreach activities consisted *only* of such warm, positive, engagements. In that case regulators, by focusing so much of their time and effort on good actors, would be tiptoeing around the edges of their serious noncompliance problems.

The regulatory innovations discussed previously suggest a rather different kind of partnership: one oriented around a specific hazard or risk area and focusing on actors central to that problem. In the case of OSHA's Maine 200 program, the partnership offer was made to 200 companies that accounted for a major portion of the state's workdays lost to injury. Some of these companies were definitely bad actors, with a history of problems; others were simply large corporations. (The analysis used total number of incidents rather than rates per worker.) In either case, OSHA chose the companies based upon the results of analysis. The companies did not step forward as volunteers, nor had they come requesting a service. Likewise, the Pension Benefit Guaranty Corporation certainly preferred to work *with* troubled pension plans, but the corporation selected the plans based on their own risk assessment models. Likewise, the Minnesota Pollution Control Agency's voluntary inspection and cleanup program sought out and focused upon sites already designated for cleanup under the federal Superfund program; and the Boston Police Department's Operation Ceasefire worked closely with those gangs and gang members most likely to kill or be killed, forcing them into cooperation through well-communicated threats of concerted enforcement. (The latter was not exactly a partnership with the gangs, in the cooperative sense of the word, but was a much closer engagement than normal.)

These programs show the value of partnerships in achieving the central purposes of the agency. In the examples above, the partnerships are not driven by a customer service motivation nor by a politically inspired desire to please, to make government popular, or to transform regulatory agencies from enforcers into service providers. Rather, they are driven by a clearly articulated goal and the realization that close engagements with other parties, some good and some bad, can produce more effective, resource-efficient solutions.

Regulatory *partnerships with a purpose* are often formed under duress. Certainly the enforcement option is never far away. In OSHA's case the choice for companies was to either join a partnership agreement with OSHA to construct a comprehensive safety and health program or face a traditional inspection and consequent enforcement action. In PBGC's case, the agency used its sanction of termination to reinforce negotiations. Under Operation Ceasefire, the Boston police threatened the decimation of a gang, with most members facing incarceration if any member engaged in violence. Each of these agencies negotiated their partnerships from a position of strength, with no hint of turning a blind eye for the sake of creating or preserving cozy relationships.

The second column of table 7-1 characterizes the partnerships that focus on regulatory effectiveness, which are becoming more common. These partnerships seek out companies or industries where intervention is needed (a proactive, analytical, and compliance-oriented focus). They tend to concentrate on those with substantial problems or histories of irresponsibility (often bad actors, or the locus of significant problems). They use amnesty or immunity rarely, cautiously, and only in the very short term (so as not to compromise enforcement capacity); and these partnerships are evaluated not in terms of customer satisfaction but in terms of whether the program produces the desired regulatory outcomes.

Regulators have begun to shift their resource allocations from the partnerships described in the left column of table 7-1 toward those in the right column. As pressure for results continue to drive regulators to evaluate activities in terms of measurable contributions to mission accomplishment, these allocations will surely shift further. When regulators are approached by the regulated asking to form a partnership, regulators are learning to ask, What is this partnership for? What common purpose, within the mission, would be better served by acting together than apart? If such purpose is not clear, or not central to the mission, then regulators will begin to hold back. For the time being, holding back is extremely difficult. Political pressure for better customer service from regulators has created expectations among regulated industries that they are entitled to a special deal—and that they only have to ask.

Other Forms of Partnership

Table 7-1 focuses only on partnerships with the regulated community and not on interagency cooperative endeavors, which should not be ignored. Innovations finalists repeatedly demonstrate the benefits of collaboration between agencies and with other nongovernmental groups when focused on a specific problem, goal, or regulatory objective. For example, the Immigration and Naturalization Service's Operation Jobs, in Texas, brought INS agents into working relationships with an extraordinary range of public, private, and nonprofit groups. These other groups helped place legal workers into the positions made vacant through INS enforcement actions against illegal workers, thus ending the cycle of illegal hires. The New York City police project on red light runners was launched in conjunction with a neighborhood traffic safety advocacy group called STOP (Stop Traffic Offense Program), started by a mother whose eighteen-month-old daughter had been dragged thirteen blocks in her stroller by a red light runner. Operation Ceasefire, in Boston, brought together a coalition of city, state, and federal criminal justice agencies, which pooled their resources and coordinated their actions under a single integrated intervention plan.

I revisit the issue of interagency cooperation later in the book, when I review the curiously awkward task of defining problems at the right level, noting how real life risks, risk concentrations, and noncompliance patterns generally fail to respect the jurisdictional boundaries that define agencies and how solutions that are sufficiently holistic or systemic often require interagency cooperation.

CHAPTER EIGHT

The Search for Results That Count

PRESIDENT CLINTON'S MARCH 4, 1995, memo describing his regulatory reinvention initiative provided heads of regulatory agencies at the federal level unambiguous direction on the subject of performance measurement:

> *Reward Results, not Red Tape:* I direct you to change the way you measure the performance of both your agency and your frontline regulators so as to focus on results, not process and punishment. For example, Occupational Safety and Health Administration (OSHA) inspectors should not be evaluated by the number of citations they write, nor should officials of the Consumer Product Safety Commission be judged by the number of boxes of consumer goods that are detained in shipment. . . .
>
> You should identify appropriate performance measures and prepare a draft in clear, understandable terms, of the results you are seeking to achieve through your regulatory program. . . .
>
> You should evaluate and reward employees based on the realization of those measures/goals.
>
> By no later than June 1, I direct you to (a) eliminate all internal personnel performance measures based on process (number of visits made, etc.) and punishment (number of violations found, amount of fines levied, etc.), and (b) provide to the National Performance

Review (NPR) staff a catalogue of the changes that you are making in existing internal performance evaluations to reward employees.[1]

The President's memo is startlingly clear about what not to do and what not to measure, dismissing a tradition among regulators of describing their performance principally in terms of enforcement-related activity counts. The use of such systems, particularly when accompanied by internal managerial use of enforcement quotas, might easily push frontline regulators into unreasonable and unwarranted enforcement actions. These effects played into the hands of congressional critics, so some urgency attached to the abandonment of such practices even before anyone knew what would replace them. The memo simply orders the abandonment and offers no guidance on what to measure and report instead. The Government Performance and Results Act of 1993 provides the background pressure for regulators to figure out, when preparing their five-year strategic plans, what goals to set, what kind of results to measure, and how to report their achievements.

In May 1995, President Bill Clinton, Vice President Al Gore, and Secretary of Labor Robert Reich publicly celebrated the Occupational Safety and Health Administration's innovative Maine 200 program at an event in Washington, D.C. The Democratic administration had been desperately searching for an example of commonsense regulatory practice with demonstrable results to blunt continuing Republican assaults. Maine 200 (despite the fact that it was instigated during the Bush administration) served the administration's political purposes reasonably well, provided the coercive aspects of the program were not emphasized. In his speech at the celebration, President Clinton briefly addressed the performance measurement issue:

> I'm interested in results, not red tape. The vice president says that all the time; we're determined to make that the rule of the land—in worker safety, the environment, in every other area that we can possibly extend it to. We're interested in prevention, not punishment. It would suit me if we had a year in this country where OSHA did not levy a single fine, because if that happened, we'd have safer workplaces, more productive businesses, we'd be making more money with happier people going to work every day.[2]

Of course, low levels of enforcement may well result *from* greater workplace safety (no doubt, the president's point); but low levels of enforcement are unlikely to result *in* greater workplace safety. Nor, from a performance measurement standpoint, would low levels of enforcement reveal much about OSHA's contributions to worker safety. The trap for OSHA—or for any other regulatory agency—would be to allow enforcement levels to drop off before it had learned to give a compelling account of how, using a wider variety of approaches, it had achieved real risk reductions. Doing so would leave OSHA vulnerable to the accusation that it had simply slowed down or gone soft on violators. In 1996 OSHA, having survived the worst of the congressional assaults, faced exactly such criticism from organized labor unions (its traditional allies), particularly the AFL-CIO. OSHA's "redesign" program, incorporating a broader range of approaches to improving workplace safety, contributed to a significant decline in their enforcement numbers.

The Environmental Protection Agency experienced a similar drop in enforcement outputs in 1995. In fiscal year 1994, the EPA referred 430 civil violations to the U.S. Department of Justice. In 1995, partly as a result of EPA's emphasis on new voluntary compliance programs, that figure dropped to 214. In the absence of measurable environmental results, environmental groups complained the agency had gone soft and abandoned its public responsibilities.

Noting that the drop in inspection statistics had been steepest in the New England region (EPA's Region 1) the *Boston Globe* in April 1996 questioned that office's commitment to enforcement.[3] Reporting a 59 percent reduction in inspections and fines over the preceding six-month period, the *Globe* blamed the decision of the regional administrator John DeVillars to transfer staff from enforcement to new programs promoting voluntary environmental improvements. DeVillars responded— as have so many other regulatory agency executives—that they had not backed off enforcement but had become more sophisticated in their choice of tools and more selective in targeting the worst offenders for enforcement, while finding more efficient and reasonable methods for dealing with lesser violators.

George Hawkins, a senior EPA official from the New England region, recognized that sudden declines in activity counts created a vulnerability for his agency: "Society would be crazy to judge the success of an enforcement enterprise on its ability to maintain levels of violations. Yet this is exactly how EPA's enforcement program is judged. Each year, the numbers of inspections, fines, and civil and criminal actions are counted. Any drop in the numbers is considered not to reflect a reduction of violators, but a lack of effort [on behalf of] the EPA."[4]

State agencies have had similar experiences. Florida's Department of Environmental Protection's enforcement statistics declined during 1993 and 1994, leading external critics and even some internal staff to ascribe the lack of cases to improper political meddling coupled with a lack of senior managerial will to resist. At the time, the department was beginning to formulate its new compliance strategy, investing in a range of new initiatives. For the Wisconsin Department of Natural Resources, the sudden drop came in 1996, when the number of criminal referrals to the state Department of Justice dropped by two-thirds from a level that had been roughly constant for the previous three years. An article in the *Wisconsin State Journal* typifies external reaction to such trends: "Is the state Department of Natural Resources, once the most feared and tenacious of regulatory bulldogs, losing its bite? Some close observers of the massive agency think so. They fear a three-year reorganization, which actually got under way last year after two years of study, has left the environmental regulatory giant kinder and gentler and more responsive to the public but less effective at protecting the Wisconsin landscape."[5]

The story cites agency employees who shared outsiders' concerns and who placed the blame squarely on the agency's undifferentiated adoption of the customer service mind-set:

> [The employees] worry that the reorganization, probably the most sweeping ever by a state agency, will result in less enforcement and more coddling of violators. At the heart of the reorganization is a philosophy that makes everyone who deals with the agency— from anglers seeking licenses to polluters seeking permits— "customers". . . .
>
> It's a philosophy, critics say, that may be fine for a grocery store but wrong-headed and possibly dangerous for an agency charged with upholding the state's environmental laws.
>
> "They're into compliance hand-holding now," says Caryl Terrell, the Sierra Club's legislative coordinator, of the agency's enforcement approach. "Instead of saying, 'Here's your obligation and if you haven't done it in a week, we'll be back and start enforcement.' We think it's a slippery slope."

George Meyer, the Wisconsin Department of Natural Resources secretary, fiercely defended his agency's record and his belief in the value of working with industry rather than "taking an antagonistic attitude toward everyone." Asked to account for the fact that the number of hazardous waste referrals dropped from nineteen in 1993 to just two in 1996, Meyer and his staff responded that "referrals have dropped because hazardous waste programs are working, with companies coming into compliance."

The Measurement Dilemma

These arguments have been repeated around the country, in numerous regulatory settings. To prove his point, Meyer would need to be able to produce statistically valid compliance rates (based on random or representative sampling) to support his contention that compliance had improved. In the absence of such measures, the ambiguity persists: maybe compliance improved. Or maybe the department got distracted or captured. No one can tell which, so observers remain free to choose whichever explanation suits their purpose.

A similar issue arose with respect to the Customs Service passenger processing statistics. The *Washington Post* reported that one issue of concern to newly appointed customs commissioner Raymond Kelly was a decline in the percentage of passenger searches that resulted in arrests or seizures.[6] Fiscal year 1998 data showed that of 2,076 passengers who had to take off part or all of their clothing for a customs inspection, only 21 percent were found to be carrying illegal drugs. Ten to fifteen years before, these rates approached 100 percent. Referring to such a development as a "public relations nightmare," both Kelly and the *Washington Post* (and a host of congressional overseers) sought valid explanations. Several are possible. Perhaps the targeting mechanism that used to work so well fell apart. Perhaps a decade ago there was so much drug smuggling that finding "mules" among the crowd was easy. Or perhaps drug cartels have better schooled their mules in how to dress and act, reducing the effectiveness of behavioral profiling and monitoring as a selection tool.

How can it be determined which explanation is true? By measuring the noncompliance rate systematically, drawing a random sample of passengers, and conducting rigorous searches of each one, in order to produce definitive compliance measures. With a clearer sense of the underlying smuggling rate, the agency could calculate the effectiveness of customs' targeting mechanisms by comparing the hit rate among passengers selected with the noncompliance rate in the general passenger population (extrapolated from the sample). With information about the underlying smuggling rate and the selectivity of search procedures, executives could make better informed decisions about the appropriate levels of inspection and about which inspection mechanisms need enhancement. Ironically, the notion of strip searches applied randomly (for the purposes of measurement) presents even worse public relations problems than targeted, but unfruitful, searches—hit rates would be even lower in a random sample. Nevertheless, without reliable mechanisms for measuring the seriousness, frequency, or prevalence of the underlying noncompliance problem, customs officials and the agency's overseers cannot tell how well inspection programs are operating, nor can they interpret trends in enforcement outputs or hit rates.

Many regulatory agencies lack systematic compliance measurement systems and cannot prove, therefore, that declines in enforcement numbers reflect better compliance rather than softer attitudes. The EPA and OSHA, among others, believe that their own sudden reductions in enforcement levels resulted from reinvestment of resources in a broader range of compliance programs and from increased use of partnerships, collaborative efforts, and negotiated agreements. When these reductions occur, however (usually early in the development of compliance management techniques), agencies generally lack the measurement, recording, or reporting systems necessary to dethrone enforcement statistics in the minds of their audience. Unable to produce convincing evidence that compliance has increased, they find themselves held hostage by their own reporting traditions and face enormous pressure to get the numbers back up.

Unfortunately, but perhaps predictably, the EPA and other agencies are tempted to return to the enforcement numbers game, partly because it seems the only game their audience understands and partly because counting enforcement actions is so much simpler than dealing with the complexities of measuring compliance rates, outcomes, or impacts. Not that they necessarily give up on the development of such measures, but progress is so painfully slow that, to satisfy their critics, they are forced to deliver a traditional performance meanwhile.

Having to *keep the numbers up*, at least until a more sophisticated performance account becomes available, in turn slows progress in agency reforms. In 1989 a senior EPA manager (who describes himself as an "arch bean counter") explained how this pressure could easily thwart administrator William Reilly's commitment to managing for environmental results:

We have a new administrator who talks much more about whether or not the environment is cleaner, but, PR-wise, he's not going to be able to stand the media pressure if at the end of this fiscal year they detect that our number of judicial referrals to the Department of Justice has dropped by 20 to 40 percent from what it was the last year Lee Thomas was here. The chances are that he'll become as much a hostage to bean counting in certain respects as people think I am.[7]

EPA Region I was forced into an interim response in order to fend off the criticism over its enforcement decline. As the *Boston Globe* reported it, "DeVillars' own chief enforcement attorney, Harley Laing, sent a memo to his staff last month expressing concern over the pace of enforcement in recent months. 'I am particularly concerned about our enforcement program. We need to maintain our baseline enforcement program activities,' wrote Laing, urging staff to aim for '75% of the enforcement output we had last year.'"[8] Others in similar situations talk of the need to maintain a credible deterrent, which can so easily provide an excuse to revert to business as usual, justifying every and any enforcement action. The need to continue delivering the old kind of performance (in the absence of a satisfactory replacement) can be a stumbling block to reform. Usually, executives intend such backtracking (instructing staff to get the numbers back up) as a pragmatic and temporary response to external pressures, useful in tiding them over until the agency can work out what it really wants to measure and how to do it. The unfortunate appearance, from outside the agency and sometimes even from within, is that the agency has given up on its reform agenda and has fallen back into the old enforcement mode. Needless to say, these make for painful and confusing times.

The Internal Revenue Service provides the most recent and embarrassing failure to dethrone or displace the use of enforcement statistics. The IRS too received the president's March 1993 memo prohibiting the use of enforcement statistics as a method of evaluating staff, particularly the use of quotas as an internal management device. For all practical purposes, the agency ignored the directive (as did many others) because it lacked an alternative method of holding staff accountable. In testimony before the National Commission on Restructuring the IRS, a senior IRS official declared the results of recent IRS collections efforts:

In conclusion, I want to share the significant accomplishments that we have achieved in collection over the past three years. In FY 1996, we collected $29.8 billion—the most ever by the IRS. In fact, for the past three years our collection yield has increased. In FY 1994, collection yield increased 3 percent; in FY 1995, an increase of more than 7 percent; and in FY 1996, an increase of over 18 percent. That's a 30 percent increase since FY 1993.[9]

Members of the bipartisan commission did not object to this use of enforcement statistics. To them it seemed perfectly ordinary; such statistics demonstrated that government agents had been industrious and productive. Commission members probably would have had no more idea than IRS managers how else to report performance. Anyway, Congress was accustomed to hearing such reports not only from the IRS but also from most federal regulatory agencies. The way Congress normally justified marginal allocations to the IRS budget was to have the IRS specify the enforcement revenues that would result. In other words, Congress itself had for many years been colluding in the business of negotiating, sanctioning, and monitoring IRS enforcement quotas.

Only ten months later, in December 1997, IRS's bean-counting practice turned into a major public embarrassment. Three days of hearings, held by the Senate Finance Committee and focusing on the Arkansas-Oklahoma IRS district office, revealed that the use of enforcement quotas (particularly for collections and seizures) had led to unduly harsh treatment of taxpayers, particularly the seizure of taxpayers' houses.[10] IRS employees testified that supervisors' emphasis on collection statistics created the impression that their job performance was being measured by the amount of money collected or the value of assets seized. An IRS internal audit report, delivered to the same committee in December 1997, confirmed the findings.[11] In October 1997, Deputy Commissioner Mike Dolan (as acting commissioner) formally suspended the use of dollar goals and quotas to rank the thirty-three district offices.[12] As part of incoming Commissioner Charles Rossotti's plan for modernization, the IRS would seek to develop a more "balanced system for measuring organizational and individual performance" that incorporates measures of customer and employee satisfaction as well as business results.[13]

Rossotti is not the first IRS commissioner, and may not be the last, to vow to counteract the distorting efforts of production quotas. As long ago as 1973 the Senate Finance Committee questioned Commissioner

Alexander during his confirmation hearings as to his views on production quotas.[14] He responded that he was completely opposed to their use. Later in 1973, he instructed his staff, in a "Special Message to all Enforcement Personnel," that "individual case or dollar goals—formal, informal, or implied—are not permitted and will not be tolerated." In November 1973, the IRS adopted a (still current) policy statement prohibiting absolutely the use of enforcement statistics to evaluate the performance of enforcement personnel. Twenty-four years later, the IRS had apparently still not escaped the power of such measures.

The power of enforcement statistics across the regulatory spectrum arises partly from their long-established tradition of use. Regulatory agencies, their overseers, their critics, the public, and the media have all been conditioned to evaluate regulatory and enforcement performance in terms of enforcement productivity, efficiency, and return on investment. Furthermore, these measures are all delightfully objective, numerical, easy to aggregate, and easy to compare across regions, between agencies, and over time. Hence their appeal—and the difficulty of displacing them.

In 1995, when I visited a Customs Service port on the southern U.S. border, members of the staff informed me that their port topped the charts year after year in drug seizures and arrests and that no other port in the United States even came close to their figures. As their guest, I felt constrained to congratulate them, but the question I wanted to ask was, Why do drug runners keep using *your* port? Presumably, the effective tax on the drug runners' business, represented by the probability of detection, must have been lower at that port than at alternative points of entry. (I sensed that these folk would not have responded well to an academic poking holes in the source of their greatest professional pride.)

These traditional measures demonstrate convincingly that inspectors, agents, auditors, collectors, or other enforcement personnel are working hard and getting results (of a certain kind). For that, taxpayers should be thankful. What they will never be able to show, though, is whether these same personnel are working on the right things, or in smart ways, using the best methods, or actually influencing external behaviors or conditions.

Designing Measurement Instruments

The experiences of the last few years reveals the extraordinary staying power of the old methods of demonstrating regulatory results and the elusiveness of satisfactory replacements.[15]

The IRS's recent struggles, and the language it has now adopted, point to the need to balance *customer satisfaction, employee satisfaction,* and *business results.* Note that the need to shift this balance in the direction of increased customer satisfaction arises most acutely when business results continue to take the form of enforcement statistics. The use of that type of business result, as the IRS experience in the Arkansas-Oklahoma district shows, generates internal pressures for heavy-handed regulatory action.

Recognizing the importance of customer service, many agencies have begun surveying their customers (and a few also survey their employees), using questionnaires distributed shortly after an encounter. Given the complexities of the term *customer* in the regulatory environment and the wide range of parties to regulatory encounters, most agencies have also learned to separate out different categories of customer, each of which brings its own distinctive set of expectations and entitlements. While the experiences of those arrested do count and should be monitored, it makes little sense to mix their opinions with those of crime victims, witnesses, permit applicants, or inquirers. In the regulatory context, customer satisfaction necessarily carries a more variegated set of meanings. Without a clear differentiation among categories of encounter, and of parties encountered, aggregate measures of satisfaction would be almost impossible to interpret in any useful way.

Business Results

For performance measurement, the major impediments that remain, however, lie not so much with measuring customer satisfaction as with defining and measuring business results (or mission accomplishments). This area presents formidable intellectual challenges that have never been solved in a way that provides clear guidance to practitioners.

Table 8-1 introduces a simple classification scheme for major categories of business results, or regulatory accomplishments, that can be useful in mapping out the pressures for change in measurement and reporting practices. Such classification schemes are familiar to environmental scientists but are less familiar to other regulatory professions.[16] Tier 1 measures represent the ultimate goals of most forms of social regulation and would include measures of public safety, indicators of environmental quality, rates of worker injuries and illness, and indicators of

Table 8-1. Classification of Business Results

Tier 1. Effects, impacts, and outcomes (environmental results, health effects, decline in injury and accident rates)

Tier 2. Behavioral outcomes
   a. Compliance or noncompliance rates (significance . . .)
   b. Other behavioral changes (adoption of best practices, other risk reduction activities, "beyond compliance," voluntary actions, and so on)

Tier 3. Agency activities and outputs
   a. Enforcement actions (number, seriousness, case dispositions, penalties, and so on)
   b. Inspections (number, nature, findings, and so on)
   c. Education and outreach
   d. Collaborative partnerships (number established, nature, and so on)
   e. Administration of voluntary programs
   f. Other compliance-generating or behavioral change-inducing activities

Tier 4. Resource efficiency, with respect to use of
   a. Agency resources
   b. Regulated community's resources
   c. State authority

---

health and welfare. Tier 2 measures describe behaviors of parties external to the agency. Tier 3 contains the more familiar measures of regulatory output and productivity. Tier 4 captures notions of efficiency, noting the obligation of regulatory agencies (whatever they achieve in tiers 1, 2, or 3) to make efficient use of public resources; to minimize the burden on the regulated community; and to be sparing with the use of that precious commodity, the coercive power of the state.

In the field of tax administration, tier 1 may not be relevant. Broad taxpayer compliance (in tier 2), bringing with it equitable distribution of the tax burden, may be the primary business result desired. Thus the separation of tier 1 from tier 2 may be less meaningful for tax administrators. Tier 2 refers to behavioral changes beyond mere compliance with regulations, which regulators have learned can have great significance. These changes can be voluntary (as in EPA's 33/50 program), or coerced (for example, the use of supplemental environmental projects as part of an enforcement settlement). Regulators also recognize a range of problems with no noncompliance component. Examples include such environmental problems as radon gas in homes and the cumulative air quality effects of domestic barbecues. Similarly, OSHA could hardly ignore repetitive strain (ergonomic) injuries, now a major cause of workplace injury, despite the fact that Congress has not yet authorized any relevant regulations or standards.

The precise contents of the four tiers are less important than the table's overall shape, which reveals the aspirations of regulatory agencies with respect to reporting their accomplishments. Traditional reporting practices focus heavily on levels of enforcement and inspection activity, clearly a narrow subset of the available spectrum. Performance reporting for regulatory and enforcement agencies has traditionally focused on aggregate activity counts, or outputs (numbers of inspections, enforcement actions, judicial referrals) and case disposition statistics (convictions, jail terms, financial penalties) as demonstrations of effective enforcement. These belong in categories 3a and 3b in the table.

Effective enforcement was assumed to lead, through the mechanism of deterrence, to broad compliance; and broad compliance was assumed to lead, in turn, to the achievement of the overarching regulatory goals (public health and safety, environmental quality, worker safety). Reform pressures now oblige regulators to question both the link between traditional enforcement bean counts and compliance rates and the sufficiency or relevance of raising compliance levels as a method of addressing higher-level (tier 1) goals. As regulatory agencies seek to identify important results and to embrace a broader range of tools, their performance focus changes in various ways.

A Broader Tool Kit: Tier 3 Extended

First, the range of agency activities that the agency values expands, so tier 3 needs to be extended to include measures relevant to a broader class of activities. Otherwise, if an agency continues to count enforcement activities with great precision and rigor but does not pay equal attention to newer methods, the imbalance will produce an internal bias toward enforcement. Hence the need to capture the degree of effort and the level of resources devoted to other activities, such as outreach, partnership programs, and customer service.

A Different Perspective on Compliance Levels: Tier 2a

Second, management shifts its perspective on compliance levels. Under a traditional enforcement-oriented approach, compliance levels are often used as a demonstration of good targeting. For that purpose, a *low* compliance rate in a targeted group is considered good news, because it shows that scarce inspectional resources are being successfully directed to high-risk areas. The same is true for the adjustment rate per audit used by the IRS and the hit rate per passenger searched used by the Customs Service.

But an agency that wants to demonstrate its ability to improve compliance in an entire industry or industry segment will hope to observe compliance rates *rising* over time. Moreover, for measured compliance rates to be statistically valid, they must result from random, representative, or comprehensive samples of the relevant industry, industry segment, or population. Few agencies can produce such valid compliance measures, because most compliance data result from inspection programs focused on known or suspected risks—and that therefore produce biased (low) estimates of underlying compliance rates. Dealing with this problem necessitates the diversion of some resources from focused inspection programs into random sampling for the sake of measurement, which is notoriously difficult. Nevertheless the emergence of compliance management as a plank of regulatory strategy will require a new emphasis on compliance measurement, inevitably involving representative sampling, and with higher compliance rates as the objective.

The Search for Convincing Measures

Third (a much more profound change), as regulators seek to demonstrate their accomplishments in controlling or mitigating particular risks, they shift more emphasis to tier 1. What regulatory executives really wish they could find (some refer to it as the Holy Grail of performance measurement) would be a set of tier 1 indicators that represent improvement in conditions, for which agencies could unambiguously claim credit and which they could connect directly to specific agency activities. Regulators would also like to be able to prove that the links are causal rather than merely correlated, and they would like to be able to present this outcome data in the same neat, unambiguous, objective, statistical tables that agencies formerly used to present enforcement numbers.

Part of regulators' frustration when this Holy Grail remains elusive arises from the undiminished and unreasonable expectations of their overseers and legislatures, who—having demanded, but not joined in, the search for such measures—cannot understand why agencies should not provide them measures as simple and straightforward as the old bean count, yet relating to outcomes rather than outputs. Regulators protest that such outcomes (tier 1) depend on many factors outside their control—the weather, demographic changes, technological developments—and therefore that they dare not declare themselves responsible in that way. Agencies that deal with long-term risks or natural systems (ecosystems, endangered species, exposure to carcinogens) argue that solving such problems or demonstrating positive health effects could take ten or twenty years and that outcomes may also be affected by external factors. They regard as dysfunctional the requirement to break down such longer-term strategies to fit the requirements of annual budgets and reporting cycles. And how, they ask, can they be expected to provide compelling measures of success in the area of *prevention* (upon which so many of the newer programs concentrate)? How does one count the accidents that did not happen, the spills avoided, the crimes prevented?

Regulators generally lack good answers to these questions, as do legislatures and oversight agencies—and as do academics (except those who believe that every aspect of regulatory operations can be subjected to rigorous and definitive program evaluations). The absence of feasible, operational, practical answers results in an intellectual impasse, followed by pragmatic accommodation that reduces strategic planning and reporting to a superficial or paper exercise, with the old reporting traditions surviving intact and not far beneath the surface.

If true value in regulatory performance involves problems solved, compliance rates improved, risks mitigated, then regulators must persevere in the search for performance measurement and reporting techniques to match that kind of performance. They cannot give up on the obligation to develop a clearly articulated and broadly shared understanding of what that account should look like.

If risk control *counts,* then we must learn how to count it. But for now, we have to put off the counting long enough to tease out the underlying nature of the performance we seek to measure and report. When we really understand the *business* of risk control, perhaps the nature of the corresponding *business results* will become less opaque.

CHAPTER NINE

Problem Solving:
A Different Kind of Work

ALL REGULATORY AGENCIES have their problem-solving successes in which persistent issues have been identified, isolated for special attention, and solved through the implementation of creative, tailor-made solutions. Not all agencies, however, recognize the patterns of organizational behavior associated with such work as distinctive, central to the agency's ability to produce demonstrable results, and worth extending. Very few agencies establish and operate a formal apparatus serving to institutionalize such behavior as a routine component of operations.

The Internal Revenue Service has produced some remarkably effective solutions to specific noncompliance problems. For example, in the mid-1980s many taxpayers were claiming fictitious dependents. In 1986 the agency reduced the problem substantially simply by redesigning form 1040 to require a social security number (SSN) for each dependent claimed.[1] At the time, the IRS had no capacity to match or validate the SSN data. Nevertheless, the following year the number of dependents claimed dropped by 7 million. More recently, the IRS addressed the problem of undeclared tip income for wait staff in restaurants. Beginning in 1994, the agency implemented a tailor-made solution involving special tip determination and reporting agreements, by which conservative estimates of tip income are developed from business volume, not from counting the tips. Tax liabilities are clearly established, and employees benefit from increased social security benefits, unemployment benefits, retirement plan contributions, and worker's compensation benefits. By December 1996, the IRS had established agreements covering more than 22,000 establishments, resulting in reported tip income increases of more than $2 billion.[2] Despite these successes, the IRS has not yet finished the task of devising and constructing the organizational infrastructure necessary to turn the concept of a coherent compliance strategy into an operational reality.

The Customs Service, one of the few agencies to have progressed far toward agencywide implementation, has an established strategic problem-solving program, initiated during the early months of 1996 and then ratcheted up with a significant injection of funds in July 1996. The agency's discovery of problem solving stemmed largely from the difficulties it encountered in applying the tools of process management to narcotics interdiction. But the agency also learned a great deal, and at just the right time, from its efforts to control one particularly offensive form of drug smuggling. These efforts in due course constituted the agency's prototype problem-solving project.

The Port-Running Problem

The project involved *port running,* a particularly violent method of smuggling drugs across the U.S. border with Mexico. Port runners would load up to 500 pounds of drugs in cars or small trucks, making little attempt to disguise or conceal it, and then drive up to the inspection booth at selected border crossing points. The driver would be uncooperative, essentially challenging the inspector. If the inspector asked for identification, or took too long, or asked to look in the trunk, or attempted to pull the vehicle over for secondary examination, the driver would accelerate away agressively, smashing other vehicles out of the way if necessary and running down the inspector or anyone else foolish enough to get in the way—never mind the damage to the vehicle, the *load* was much more valuable. Port runners picked crossing points where, within half a mile of clearing the border, they could be lost in the backstreets of a densely populated urban area, making pursuit and arrest virtually impossible.

During 1994 customs logged 827 incidents of port running along the southwest border, peaking at 94 in December.[3] In more than a dozen of these incidents, gunfire was exchanged between the smugglers and customs officials. In two cases, the port runners were shot dead. Obviously, such flagrant violation of U.S. sovereignty at the borders, especially with the potential for such violence in crowded public spaces, could not be tolerated. Growing public alarm and pressure from Congress demanded that a solution be found, since traditional operational and enforcement responses of inspections, seizures, and apprehension were not working. There was no shortage of resources, for Congress provided funds through a special appropriation. Rather there was a shortage of ideas and of relevant methods.

In January 1995, Deputy Commissioner Mike Lane formed a team to tackle the problem. Until then it had not been clear whose job it was, for the *size* and *shape* of the problem did not align with anyone's job description or role. Port running occurred at many ports, with port directors responsible only for what transpired at their ports. So the problem did not really belong with any one port director.. Nor did the problem fit customs' regional structure, as it affected crossings all the way from Brownsville, Texas, to the California coast, straddling two federal regions. Nor was the problem national, as it was confined geographically to land border crossings in the Southwest. Nor did it fit specific functional responsibilities, as tackling it would involve inspectors, enforcement agents, and intelligence staff. Recognizing the problem as multiport, multifunctional, biregional, but not national, Lane pulled together a multiport, multifunctional, biregional team, consisting of roughly fifteen core personnel, to match the size and shape of the problem.

The team had plenty of ideas about what to do. Enforcement agents preferred pursuit, arrest, and seizures; inspectors focused more naturally on changing inspection procedures; the intelligence group wanted to study the smuggling organizations and take them down. But most of that they had been doing already, and it was not enough. Besides, their charge was not to make arrests or break down smuggling organizations (although they were allowed to do those things if it helped); they had been charged with *eliminating the problem of port running*. Before working on an action plan, the team set out to determine how it would measure success. How would it know if it was making progress, if not by numbers of arrests and seizures? Obviously a decline in the number of port-running incidents would be good, but even that would be open to different interpretations. Some inspectors, faced with the potential for such violence, were beginning to lose heart and might just wave port runners through rather than risk a confrontation. If they did that, those incidents would not be counted, and nobody would know it had happened. (Even the inspector might only have a suspicion that he was dealing with a port run-ner.) So a decline in the number of *recorded* incidents (which necessarily involve a confrontation) would not necessarily constitute good news.

Because of the ambiguity, the project team identified two other indi-cators to supplement the incident count. First, they would monitor the number of "returns to Mexico" (RTMs), in which a driver approaching an inspection point suddenly changes his mind, does a U-turn, and drives back to Mexico. RTMs were often observed by inspectors. These incidents were captured on the port's video surveillance cameras, so they could be counted. Sometimes RTMs occurred when the smuggling orga-nization's spotters (co-conspirators on the Mexican side who studied customs' physical and staffing arrangements through binoculars) saw something that made them uneasy and radioed the drivers. Sometimes the port runners themselves would make the decision. If the project team succeeded in making ports less attractive to port runners (a con-cept it referred to as hardening the ports), it expected to see the number of RTMs rise at first and then fall off as the smuggling organizations abandoned the practice.

Even with the RTM measure added in, however, the team felt they would not have conclusive indicators. Given customs' traditions of per-formance measurement, the *rise* in RTMs would likely be interpreted as a sign that the team was on the right track. But the subsequent *decline* would as likely be interpreted as a sign the project had faltered as that it had succeeded. (Field agents often experienced this form of ambiguity with respect to seizure rates. Correctly identifying a specific smuggling pattern would produce a flurry of seizures, applauded by management. But field agents complained that when they forced smugglers away from one route or technique, and the associated seizure rate dropped off, the message from headquarters all too often was, Whatever happened to that project on [x]?)

Eventually the project team devised a third, and more reliable, indica-tor. They asked intelligence agents to find the price smuggling organiza-tions paid port runners to run a load; it was determined to be $5,000 per load at the outset. If that price rose significantly, they figured, it would mean that customs had made it more difficult or more dangerous to run a load. With this portfolio of indicators in place, and each of them benchmarked (that is, starting levels determined), the team felt it could tell whether its interventions worked. If over time the number of incidents fell, the number of RTMs peaked and then dropped off significantly, and the price paid to port runners rose, then they would know they were on the right track.

With what to measure settled, the team turned its attention to what to do. First it tried pursuit, which required Customs Service or state police cars ready to give chase at a moment's notice. If the pursuit vehicles were visible from the Mexican side, spotters warned off the runners, so the cars were stationed away from the port and out of sight. Still the runners seemed to be warned off, as the smugglers would send through a "clean" vehicle first, to reconnoiter. For a while, the team tried using Customs Service Black Hawk helicopters, but keeping them ready to go at a moment's notice was expensive and of limited value without supporting ground vehicles. Next the team considered hydraulic or pneumatic bollards built into the road surface, which would leap up at the flick of a switch, stopping the vehicle and trapping the port runners. However, bollards were expensive to install (one bridge at the port of Brownsville in Texas has thirty-two lanes) and immobile once installed. Besides, with the potential for gunfights, trapping port runners right at the port (in a crowded public area) seemed too dangerous.

At last the team began to make some real progress. It developed the tactic of closing down enough lanes, depending on traffic volume, to ensure that queue lengths exceeded five or six vehicles. If enough cars were in front of a port runner when he first joined the queue, he could not "run" from that point. Then customs deployed *primary rovers* (dog handlers with drug-sniffing dogs) to work the queues in front of the inspection booths. The dogs could smell these huge drug loads across many lanes of traffic, enabling Customs Service officers to surround the vehicle while it was stuck in the queue. This approach, while more successful than anything else tried up to that point, suffered from being manpower (and dogpower) intensive and highly visible from the Mexican side. Also, the dog handlers were reluctant to make their dogs work for protracted periods during the heat of the day, when the road surface was scorching hot and the air choked with exhaust fumes.

Eventually, and at about the fifth attempt, the team came up with a sustainable solution. They arranged Jersey barriers (concrete barriers used to protect highway construction sites) in a zigzig pattern *behind* the ports. Once cleared at the primary inspection point, vehicles had to carefully maneuver left and right through a chicane of barriers before they could drive away. With barriers in this configuration, port runners were denied rapid escape. If they tried to run, they could be easily confined away from the crowd. Very few port runners would attempt any port with such arrangements. Best of all, this solution required minimal long-term commitment of human resources. Using a variety of methods, and with increasing deployment of the Jersey barriers, the team began to see their selected indicators move the way they hoped. The number of RTMs peaked and then fell off. In the first six months of 1995 the number of recorded incidents declined by 30 percent from the previous six months. By June, the rate of incidents (per month) had dropped by more than half from its December peak. And intelligence agents discovered that the prevailing price for running a load had risen to $7,500. Much to the relief of everyone involved, it finally looked as if the problem could be brought under control.

A Few Observations

Although this was not the first time Customs Service personnel had fashioned a creative responsive to a specific problem, the high-profile nature of this exercise made it a potent learning experience, driving home basic truths about problem solving and how it differs from work oriented around functions or processes. To define or prescribe the practice of problem solving more generally, consider the following observations about this specific project, which illuminate the nature of problem solving and reveal the absence of the machinery necessary to produce such behavior as a matter of course. (These same observations apply to the majority of the regulatory innovations in chapter 6, classified as examples of problem solving.)

— The problem to be addressed was external to the agency rather than a part of the agency's inner workings.

— Responsibility for solving the problem did not naturally lie with any one official and had to be assigned.

— Neither the specific components of the problem nor the solution were conceived in customs' authorizing legislation.

— Attention to the problem would have remained diffuse, uncoordinated, and probably ineffective had senior management not made a conscious decision to organize resources around it.

— The relevant performance measures (indicators of success) were selected *before* (and independent from) the selection of an action plan.

— The particular set of performance measures selected was special to this project and had no broader relevance. There was probably no other project under way at customs (not even another drug interdiction project) for which this set of measures would have been appropriate.

— Inventing the right set of performance measures for the project took as much creativity and imagination as inventing the action plans.

— The best solutions were not the first ones tried. The team needed the flexibility to experiment with a number of approaches and to quickly abandon those that did not work. The team could not have predicted in advance what would work or how much it would cost (as contemplated by some performance-based budgeting requirements).

— The solution of the problem required neither a change in legislation nor any change in customs' general policies.

— The problem was identified, managed, and solved below the level of strategic planning. Although customs' mission statement, authorizing legislation, and strategic plans specified the agency's responsibilities for narcotics interdiction, this project addressed only a particular subcomponent of that overall responsibility.

— All personnel engaged on the problem solving team had other duties.

— The solutions were qualitatively new, not merely a different mixture of existing methods and tactics. These solutions could never have been found by adjusting the balance of resource allocation among existing functional responses.

— Once the problem was solved, the project team ceased to exist. Neither the team's creation nor its dissolution affected the organizational chart.

The Three Competencies

With the benefit of such experiences, regulatory agencies begin to recognize how their capacity for problem solving or risk control differs from their other existing capacities. In particular, they learn to distinguish among three important competencies: the first focuses on *functions*, the second on *processes*, and the third on significant *risks, risk concentrations*, or *problems*. Table 9-1 summarizes the distinction.

Functional Expertise (Form 1)

Being functionally organized, an obvious form of competence or professionalism for regulatory agencies involves functional expertise. Most of the IRS's resources, for example, fall within designated functional

Table 9-1. Distinguishing Regulatory Competencies

Regulatory competency	Form	Focus
Functional expertise	Specialist enclaves, state of their art.	Productivity and efficiency; quality defined in function-specific terms.
Process management and improvement	Organized around core, high-volume processes; cross-functional teams; "quality circles."	Process improvement, redesign, reengineering. Efficiency, timeliness, customer satisfaction.
Compliance management and problem solving	Organized around specific identified risks (problems, patterns, trends); temporary project teams.	Measurable impact on specific risks; elimination or substantial mitigation.

areas: returns processing, taxpayer services, examination, collections, and criminal investigation. Functionally specific improvements might be achieved through raising the quality of recruits, improving training, or making other investments in functional expertise. Such investments might increase the productivity and efficiency of each functional unit and improve the quality of the work done by each one. Each function would develop its own sense of what constitutes quality: inspectors, a high-quality inspection; investigators, a high-quality investigation; educators, a high-quality education program. Measures of quality would be specific to each function.

Process Management (Form 2)

The second form of competence recognizes that citizens frequently have to deal with multiple functional units of a regulatory agency. Consider the experience of a taxpayer dealing with the IRS: a tax return passes first through tax returns processing but may then move to examinations, collections, or even criminal investigation. Meanwhile, taxpayer services (functionally separate) may be handling related phone calls and queries. In the absence of effective coordination across functions, taxpayers may still have an unnecessarily miserable experience dealing with the bureaucracy and may encounter the agency as inept, regardless of how well each of the separate functions performs in isolation.

The second form of competency recognizes this basic truth and seeks to identify and improve an agency's core operational processes. Recognizing the cross-functional nature of these processes, this model emphasizes a systems view and brings together cross-functional teams to smooth the handoffs, eliminate bottlenecks, provide seamless handling of clients' business, and reduce the administrative burden on the regulated community. A plethora of managerial tools, imported from the private sector, support investments in this second form of competency, such as quality management, continuous process improvement, business process redesign, or the more radical process reengineering.

Problem Solving, Compliance Management, or Risk Control (Form 3)

The third form of competency adds a distinctively different organizational capacity for regulators, much less well established in most regulatory agencies than the other two: the capacity to identify significant risks, problems, or patterns of noncompliance and to design solutions that eliminate or mitigate those problems. The essential elements of such a capacity have become sufficiently clear that one can now lay them out. A problem-solving strategy would typically involve each of the following elements:

— a systematic identification of important hazards, risks, or patterns of noncompliance;

— an emphasis on risk assessment and prioritization as a rational and publicly defensible basis for selecting among identified risks;

— a project-based approach, offering the opportunity to design and implement creative, tailor-made solutions for each selected risk;

— the utilization of a broad range of tools (including, but not limited to, enforcement) in fashioning tailor-made responses to specific risks;

— a periodic evaluation of the outcomes or impacts of the designed intervention; and

—flexible resource allocation, enabling the agency to open and close projects in response to changing conditions and priorities.

In a nutshell, what regulatory agencies would want from this third form of competency is the capacity to identify, prioritize, and fix significant risks, problems, and patterns of noncompliance. A problem-solving strategy picks the most important tasks and then selects appropriate tools in each case, rather than deciding on the important tools and picking the tasks to fit. A problem-solving operation organizes the tools around the work, rather than organizing the work around the tools.

Historical Order of Acquisition

In U.S. government agencies the first form of competency, functional expertise, is the longest established of the three competencies. Organizational charts usually emphasize functional units, budgets are divided and subdivided along functional lines, and productivity of functional units forms the core of traditional measurement and accountability systems. Substantial advances have also been made with respect to process management; federal and state agencies have adopted a range of process improvement strategies and can demonstrate significant accomplishments in reducing waste, increasing timeliness, smoothing cross-functional handoffs, and increasing efficiency. The National Performance Review and the reinvention movement, by placing significant emphasis on customer service and process improvement, have added momentum to this learning.

The traditional assumption of regulatory agencies is that functional expertise, coupled with process management, automatically takes care of compliance. Recent experiences across the regulatory spectrum show this assumption to be false (examples are the experiences of the IRS with the nonfiler problem, of customs with drug trafficking, and of environmental agencies as they contend with emerging environmental problems). The tools of process improvement, useful as they have been in improving high-volume core operational processes, offer little help to regulators trying to manage compliance or mitigate risks. Regulators have discovered that compliance does not automatically follow from the first two forms of competency and, worse still, that a regulatory agency can perform well in functional and process management terms, yet miss the point entirely when it comes to recognizing and addressing important risks or problems. Hence the emerging focus in the Customs Service, the IRS, OSHA, and other agencies on developing a formal organizational capacity for problem solving, not just as a high-level approach to strategic planning but also as an operational methodology that infuses the entire management structure.

Pick Important Problems and Fix Them

Picking important problems and fixing them is such a beguilingly simple idea, and appealingly nonpartisan. Yet it turns out to be such a bugaboo to implement.

Working with a range of regulatory agencies, I have found this simple phrase extremely useful in communicating the essence of the problem-solving challenge. Its usefulness arises from two quite predictable, and quite contradictory, responses that the phrase evokes. When regulators first encounter the idea they tend to scoff, as if I have insulted their intelligence: *Of course* that is what they already do. Nothing new about *that*. They point to recent examples where their agency has solved a problem or two.

Most of these examples, however, are either at the highest levels or at the lowest levels of the organization, the two levels at which the method occurs most naturally. It happens at the agencywide level when public concern and legislative pressure push an agency into designing a new program; it happens at the field level when entrepreneurial individuals, acting alone or in a small unit, spot an issue and solve it themselves, with little or no formal support from the agency. Most of the problems that agencies ought to be dealing with, however, fall between these levels, at midmanagement, and come in shapes that do not fit the organizational structure (like the port-running problem).

Then we talk a little about the meaning of these few simple words: What is a *problem*? What forms (shapes and sizes) do problems come in? Through what avenues do they arrive? Which ones can the organization accommodate?

Next, the alternatively technocratic or intensely value-laden (depending on your point of view) word *important*. When is a problem important? Who decides, and through what mechanisms? What set of criteria does the agency employ in determining importance? Does the agency consult others on the question of importance? If so, who? And on what basis? Do other parties have a vote or a veto in the decision, or simply an opportunity to express their views?

Then we come to that alarmingly discretion-laden word *pick*. If an agency really does *pick important problems and fix them* as a matter of routine, they should be able to tell me whose job it is to do the picking and in what forum they do it. How often? Where do they get their list of candidate problems? Where do they write down their decisions? How are those decisions communicated within and beyond the agency? Once a problem is picked, what procedures are used to allocate personnel and resources to the problem? What recording and reporting mechanisms track the project's progress? What role does management play in overseeing the progress of the project? What happens to the problems that are not picked?

In the course of such discussion, most practitioners who initially protested, "That's not new, that's what we do already," switch tack: "That's impossible, we could never do that here" (particularly in large functionally specialized agencies). A notion that appears to be ordinary common sense turns out, upon reflection, to be enormously complex and judgment laden at every stage.

While the OSHA redesign team was struggling to define their problem-solving approach to hazard mitigation in the workplace, Joe Dear, the assistant secretary heading OSHA at the time, told me one day that he wished this competency was not called problem solving. He felt the simplicity of the label was misleading and that some more complex, sophisticated-sounding name would prevent his staff from assuming it was all simple, straightforward, or familiar. I have resisted the temptation to invent new language, or even to settle on any specific vocabulary. All the currently available options have drawbacks or work better in some regulatory professions than in others. Besides, critics of management theory love nothing more than to show how management fads bearing fanciful names lack substance. One recent commentary described management theory as "an apology for an academic subject, methodologically sloppy and slave to fashion," and its practitioners as "charlatans of the worst sort, charging gargantuan fees for nothing more useful than translating common sense into grotesque jargon."[4] So for now, I have stuck with simple language.

Different Types of Problem Solving

The term *problem solving* (perhaps more than *risk control* or *compliance management*) has such broad usage that agencies that choose this label have to distinguish this kind of problem solving from some other kinds already familiar in different managerial contexts. The language of problem solving has been used

— In the context of team building, management of cooperative partnerships, negotiations, and conflict resolution. For some reason the team or partnership breaks down, because one party has given or taken offense. The purpose of the problem solving is to cure the resulting dysfunction and restore the team or partnership to healthy functioning.

— Under quality management (or TQM), where quality circles or other teams examine internal agency processes with a view to improvement, redesign, or reengineering. The teams are usually cross-functional in composition, as important agency processes span multiple functions. However, the focus here is internal and the problems being solved are glitches or inefficiencies within existing processes.

— As an operational methodology. This is the version under discussion here. It differs from the first two in that the problems are external to the agency, rather than part of the agency's internal workings. Unless these three forms of problem solving are carefully distinguished, agencies tend to invest in the first two (internal) forms rather than in problem solving as an operational methodology. The agency remains introspective and focused on its own process machinery rather than looking outside for risks or patterns of noncompliance worthy of focused, creative attention.

At the outset, practitioners may find process improvement and (external) problem solving difficult to distinguish, given the similarity in the logical procedures (problem definition, search for solutions, monitoring) associated with the two ideas. They correctly point out that solutions to problems sometimes involve changes in processes. In fact, problem-solving interventions and an agency's routine processes interact in many ways.[5] Unfortunately, many disciples of the process management philosophy, and some masters of it, think that process management has all of this covered provided one addresses processes in a sufficiently systemic fashion. They are wrong. Just because processes and problem-solving interventions interact, this does not mean they are the same thing. Practitioners, with a little guidance and some experience, learn to distinguish them easily. Table 9-2 lays out a framework for telling which is which.

Formal or Informal?

The following chapters describe a formal methodology for problem-solving, and then a formal set of apparatus—the organizational infrastructure—necessary to sustain this type of work. Some colleagues have questioned whether such elaborate prescriptions are really necessary, or even helpful. Much of progressive management theory emphasizes the merits of empowering employees and relying upon their own self-motivation and initiative, liberating them from stifling and constraining systems. So why, they ask, would I want to weigh down this emerging and exciting new competence with all kinds of formal baggage?

Bitter experience, I'm afraid. Without some reasonable degree of imposed methodological rigor, regulators tend to slip back into old habits, built on old assumptions. And without formal supporting

Table 9-2. Distinguishing Characteristics of Process Improvement and Problem Solving

Characteristic	Process improvement	Problem solving
Work addressed	Existing core operational high-volume processes	External risks, threats, or noncompliance problems
Objective	Improve agency machinery or processes	Eliminate or mitigate external problems
Focus	Internal; efficiency	External; effectiveness
Scope	Broad, long-term changes in agency-wide procedures	Context specific, tailor-made solutions, sometimes temporary.
Staff responsible	Process owners and multifunctional process improvement teams	Project teams formed around specific external problem
Definition of success	Greater productivity, timeliness, efficiency in routine processes	Specific external risk or patterns of noncompliance mitigated or eliminated
Nature of tool	Management method	Operational method

machinery, problem solving happens only occasionally, being adopted by some as a matter of personal style, and remaining the preserve of a few entrepreneurial individuals. Educating and motivating—to the point where everyone understands what problem solving is, how it is different, and why it might be valuable—turns out never to be enough. Unless the organization requires it, drives it, manages it, records it, reports it and rewards it, everything else takes precedence; so it does not happen. That is why a number of regulatory agencies (but still a minority) have sought to define and establish more systematic approaches.

Problem solving is not totally new. But for most large government agencies such behavior remains the exception rather than the rule. What *is* new is the organizational commitment to institutionalize problem solving as an operational methodology. The following chapters tease out the practical details of this challenge. As I hope they will make clear, there really is nothing difficult or complicated about problem solving—except *doing it*.

CHAPTER TEN

The Stages of Problem Solving

IN AN ERA WHEN we celebrate public sector creativity and the cutting of red tape, we should take care not to bury the emerging business of problem solving under a mass of procedural requirements. Yet problem-solving teams, given tasks they really care about and want to succeed in, come back time and time again asking for procedural guidance. Without some discernible structure to the process and a sense of orderly transition from phase to phase, they feel totally at sea, and their meetings tend to dissolve into confusion. All questions remain open. Nothing is ever settled. Decisions already taken are constantly revisited. Plans are devised and then not fully implemented, sometimes because the team is divided and collectively lacks conviction about its own proposals and sometimes because the team lacks the resources or authority to make it happen. Progress is hard to discern, because no one is clear how to discern it. Eventually, staff begin to lose their initial enthusiasm, and projects just peter out. Practical experience shows that staff need some guidance. But how much?

In *Problem-Oriented Policing*, Professor Herman Goldstein lays out eleven "basic elements" of problem solving.[1] Not all of these eleven elements are procedural stages, as the list includes some broader features of a problem-oriented strategy:

— A focus on substantive problems.

— Effectiveness as the ultimate goal.
— The need for systematic enquiry.
— Adopting a proactive stance.
— Strengthening the decisionmaking processes and increasing accountability.

Goldstein's remaining six elements, with "implementing the response" added in, could easily have been adopted by the police profession as a procedural recipe to be followed for each problem-solving project:

— Grouping incidents as problems.
— Disaggregating and accurately labeling problems.
— Analyzing the multiple interests in problems.
— Capturing and critiquing the current response.
— Uninhibited searching for a tailor-made response.
— Implementing the response.
— Evaluating results of newly implemented responses.

Many police departments that embraced Goldstein's message, both within the United States and abroad, chose to implement a slightly simpler framework called the SARA model (for *scanning, analysis, response, assessment*), partly because Goldstein did not specify an explicit procedural protocol. The SARA model was developed by John Eck and William Spelman working in collaboration with the Police Department in Newport News, Virginia—work that they reported in 1987.[2] (The Newport News police's problem-solving initiative won the department a spot as a finalist in the 1990 Innovations in American Government" competition; see chapter 6 for details). Police departments have welcomed the SARA model as "a major conceptual vehicle for helping officers to think POP [problem-oriented policing] in a structured and disciplined way."[3] The four stages of SARA are *scanning,* or problem detection and identification; *analysis,* or learning the problem's causes and consequences; *response,* or designing and implementing a solution; and *assessment,* or evaluating the effectiveness of the solution.[4]

Eck and Spelman's conception of the problem-solving process is insightful and rigorous. Yet Goldstein finds cause to lament the reduction of problem-oriented policing "to a simplistic four-step process for dealing with problems." Addressing a 1995 conference on crime control in England, he described what he regarded as widespread trivialization of the problem-oriented policing concept by American police departments:

This narrow interpretation [the SARA model, as applied by police] roughly captures a central element of the concept. But lost in the translation is the potential and the richness contemplated in the concept as originally set forth. The value of problem-oriented policing is in its breadth—in its comprehensive nature as an integrated plan.[5]

Now, was the "potential and the richness contemplated" in his original concept lost because the SARA model has only four stages, rather than the seven that Goldstein envisages? Or because police interpreted and applied those four in a careless and superficial manner? Or because the problem-solving *procedure* had become detached from the deeper philosophical and strategic realignment of which it was supposed to be just one part?

Presumably, if police or other regulators were inclined for whatever reason to trivialize a four-step procedure, then it would not be much harder or take much longer for them to trivialize a seven- or ten-step procedure. At some point we must decide on the right level of granularity for any procedural specifications; and in the spirit of avoiding unnecessary bureaucracy, we should probably choose the level that imposes only essential disciplines. But no one should imagine that laying out an abbreviated template, however helpful, will produce proficiency in problem solving. Whether there be four major stages or seven, or fifteen, several of them will constitute art forms and will demand mastery. Goldstein's frustration with the police profession's implementation of problem solving stems more from police failure to acknowledge the complexity and subtlety of the problem-solving business than from a choice of one particular template over another.

The broader literature on practical aspects of *risk control,* just like the largely police-specific literature on problem solving, relies upon relatively few procedural stages—typically four or five. And each template follows the same basic structure: identify the problem, design solutions, select one and implement it, monitor the effect.

For example, Herb Appenzeller's volume, *Risk Management in Sport,* considers a broad range of risks and risk management issues related to administration of college sports programs, including sudden death in competitive athletes, emergency medical preparedness, events crowd management, vehicle safety, blood-borne pathogens, defamation suits, and cheerleading. Despite the extraordinary range of risks considered, Appenzeller confidently imports a generic risk management process consisting of five steps, which he asserts can properly be applied to each one:

— Identifying exposures to accidental loss that may interfere with an organization's basic objectives.

— Examining feasible alternative risk management techniques for dealing with these exposures.

— Selecting the apparently best risk management technique(s).

— Implementing the chosen risk management technique(s).

— Monitoring the results of the chosen techniques to ensure that the risk management program remains effective.[6]

Another practical guide to risk management addresses the range of risks encountered by dentists and others responsible for operating or managing dental clinics. The author, J. B. R. Matthews, lays out for clinic administrators a slightly more formal decision process, entitled the risk management cycle. The decision cycle involves four major steps: risk identification, risk assessment (as significant or insignificant), risk control (prevent risk, avoid risk, or accept and reduce risk), and risk financing (assume risk or transfer risk).[7]

After a while, all such templates begin to look much alike, and very straightforward, despite the fact that they are drawn from such diverse professions. In fact, Matthews (for dentistry) regards risk control techniques as little more than perfectly ordinary managerial decisionmaking processes, applied consciously to a range of risks. Those perfectly ordinary managerial decisionmaking processes, he says, consist of defining the problem, evaluating possible solutions, selecting and implementing the optimal solution, and monitoring the performance of the solution.[8] Just a perfectly ordinary, commonsense, pattern of thought—yet still worth writing books about, apparently, whether the field be dentistry, sports administration, or highway safety. Whatever the field, the books about risk control are filled with facts, figures, research, and analysis; and they lay out a lot of residual uncertainties, value judgments, and choices. Risk control, it turns out, is a data-intensive, analytically demanding, and very messy business.

Matthews does not assume that conceptual simplicity of frame makes for simplicity of operation. As a physician, he knows that much of medical practice (where so high a premium is placed on training, knowledge, and experience) follows the rather simple three phase sequence: diagnosis, treatment, then monitoring. By analogy with medicine, Matthews presents risk control as a substantial professional discipline, worthy of serious study.

> The [risk management decision process] may appear to be self-evidently pedantic and time-consuming. Consider it, however, in the daily context of diagnosis and treatment planning. As a student or newly qualified professional, it is essential that these activities are carried out in accordance with a rigorous "template": medical, social and dental histories, presenting complaints, full examinations, special tests, different diagnoses and so on. Inevitably, as experience is gained, a dentist acquires the ability to focus on significant signs and symptoms. Indeed, patient care would grind to a halt were the full diagnostic net applied to every consultation.
>
> In effect, dentists are not in any sense abandoning the rigors of diagnosis, and the prudent clinician appreciates that to do so would incur its own risks—those of missed or faulty diagnosis. Instead, there is acquired the ability to apply the principles without the pursuit of irrelevant or confusing detail, and it is towards the acquisition of the skill, amongst others, of determining what is or what is not relevant that the lengthy path of medical training leads.[9]

This viewpoint seems especially valuable, as it acknowledges the complexity and subtlety of the problem-solving art yet permits the use of rather simple frameworks to emphasize fundamental principles. Viewing problem solving as a professional skill, which may take years to master, dispels the misleading notion that anyone who has learned the procedure has necessarily mastered the art.

The Essential Disciplines

Practical experimentation with various problem-solving templates or frameworks (mostly in OSHA, the Customs Service, and Florida's Department of Environmental Protection) reveals several core principles worth building into any formal problem-solving procedural template. The following six-stage framework incorporates all of these core principles with no other extraneous detail. OSHA and the Florida Department of Environmental Protection now use precisely this framework. Customs has varied it slightly. It differs from Goldstein's elements and from the eight-stage version presented in my own volume, *Imposing Duties*, in a few material points.[10] The six stages are

1. Nominate potential problem for attention.
2. Define the problem precisely.
3. Determine how to measure impact.
4. Develop solutions or interventions.
5(a). Implement the plan, with
5(b). Periodic monitoring, review, and adjustment.
6. Close project, allowing for long-term monitoring and maintenance.

The lessons learned through practical experience, and incorporated into this framework, are as follows. First, the project life cycle should be distinguished from the supporting organizational infrastructure. We need to distinguish the life cycle of a particular problem-solving project from the organizational infrastructure that supports problem solving in general. The first is a project team responsibility; the second is an organizational and managerial responsibility. They interact (at various stages of the project) but are not the same thing. Teams come and go, along with their projects, but the infrastructure for managing a problem-solving strategy should be a permanent feature of the organization. Note that Goldstein's basic elements cover project-specific procedure as well as organizational philosophy and strategy. The six-stage sequence above specifies only the life cycle of an individual project. The next chapter describes the supporting organizational infrastructure.

Second, different levels of detail are needed for different levels of skill. We should recognize that beginners need much more detailed guidance than experts (Matthews's point, above). At the same time, we should strive to keep an uncluttered template in the hope that it will sink deep into people's professional consciousness. Provision of supplementary materials for those less experienced serves these ends. OSHA and the Florida Department of Environmental Protection both make available to problem-solving teams a much more detailed template (running roughly twelve pages), which lays out many of the issues and considerations relevant to each of the six stages.[11] For instance, note that Goldstein emphasizes the importance of first *grouping incidents as problems* and then *disaggregating and accurately labeling these problems*. These two are subsumed under "describe the problem precisely," with practical guidance regarding aggregation and disaggregation to the right level transferred to the detailed guidance documents.

Third, problem nomination is a separate stage. Problem nomination needs to stand alone from the rest of the procedure, for the simple administrative reason that problems may be nominated by different people from those who subsequently take responsibility for solving them. In fact, between problem nomination (stage 1) and any subsequent work on that problem comes the operation of the organizational infrastructure in *selecting* this problem and *assigning responsibility* for it. Separating problem nomination as a stage makes for administrative clarity.

Fourth, performance measures should be independent of action plans. Selecting relevant measures of success (stage 3) should *precede* design of an action plan (stage 4). This helps guarantee a results orientation, with the focus on impacts and outcomes rather than on faithful execution of a plan. Most common risk control models, by contrast, place monitoring or assessment at the last stage, with the consequent danger that measurement becomes an afterthought. If measurement comes after action planning, teams face a powerful and natural temptation to monitor implementation of their plan, rather than abatement of the problem. Requiring attention to measurement issues before action planning obliges a project team to work out what success would look like (that is, what indicators would move in what directions, or what intelligence reports they might expect to receive), before they craft solutions. Subsequently, that allows for a more honest assessment of whether a plan has actually achieved the desired result and provides a proper basis for management to determine when the project is finished.

Fifth, managerial review is required. Management should oversee problem-solving projects, just as they oversee all other important work of the agency. Hence they should review each active project periodically. Problem-solving projects frequently stall, fizzle out, or go off track. Sometimes they produce action plans that are illegal, impractical, or too expensive. More often, by failing to define problems precisely or by paying insufficient attention to measurement, project teams embark on a course of action with no possible way of determining its value. Requiring periodic review ensures that course corrections can be made before a team goes too far down an inappropriate path. (Once every two months, for each project open, seems to be about the right frequency.) The challenge for management, explored in the next chapter, is to provide the necessary guidance and oversight without stifling the creativity and initiative upon which such work depends.

Sixth, there should be a formal closure mechanism. Opening projects always seems easier than closing them. In the absence of a formal closure mechanism, projects tend to run on forever without any rigorous evaluation, or they just fizzle out as staff lose interest and turn to something newer. Including closure as the final stage (stage 6) and requiring all projects to undergo managerial review every two months until they are closed prevents stalled projects from festering and communicates the expectation that all projects are temporary whether they succeed or not. The essential discipline here—so easily neglected if not formally required—is that projects should either be pursued energetically or unambiguously closed; that projects should be abandoned through decision rather than through neglect; and that no project should be allowed to consume resources indefinitely unless the organization decides that continued suppression of a particular risk warrants a permanent program. In the long-term steady state, one would expect an organization to be closing projects at roughly the same rate as it opened them. However, regulatory executives find opening them much more attractive and easier to defend publicly than closing them, hence the need to force the issue. Otherwise agencies that jump into problem solving quickly open hundreds of projects but never finish any of them.

The Specific Issues Associated with Each Stage

Just as the physician's art lies within the substance of diagnosis and treatment, so the problem-solving art lies within the substance of these stages. None of them are straightforward. Some of them, particularly the selection of measures (stage 3) and the design of action plans (stage 4) demand a great deal of creativity. Most of them involve judgments and choices.[12]

In the remainder of this chapter, I summarize those practical issues associated with each stage that appear to have significance across a broad range of regulatory professions.

Stage 1: Nominate a Potential Problem for Attention

Problems are different from incidents or cases. Goldstein provides a number of candidate definitions for problems, including "a cluster of similar, related, or recurring incidents rather than a single incident"; a "substantive community concern"; and as a new "unit of police business."[13] The object of problem solving is not to describe routine duties in new terms but to conceive of the work, refashion it, and address it in terms that routine processes neither suggest nor support.

Note that the Internal Revenue Service, as part of its enhanced customer service initiative, has recently taken to holding "problem-solving sessions" in its district offices around the country, wherein taxpayers can bring their unresolved issues and have them all resolved in one session. Such sessions usefully enhance taxpayer service and may constitute substantial improvements in the process of resolving taxpayer issues, but the associated problem solving is individual and specific. If and when IRS officials stand back from the process, analyze the issues common across many taxpayers, and devise solutions to prevent recurrence, then they enter the realm of operational problem solving as discussed here. Analysis of process loads (for example, complaints, reports, requests for assistance) may reveal important problems. However, some problems may not be adequately represented in the agency's existing workload (for example, the IRS' nonfiler problem) and may be revealed only through other outreach and proactive scanning mechanisms.

Problem nomination should be open to anyone, inside or outside the agency. Field-level staff often discover patterns or trends. Data analysis may uncover important patterns or trends but is only one way of discovering them. Political processes may nominate problems for attention, as may customers, constituents, communities, the media, other agencies or advocacy groups. With respect to problem nomination, "Anyone, anytime, anywhere" seems to be a useful motto.

Agencies should avoid dressing up old work in new clothes, and problem nominations should be filtered accordingly. The Florida Department of Environmental Protection's environmental problem-solving program makes a simple one-page problem nomination form available inside and outside the department (although the department will accept for review nominations presented in any format, via any medium, from anyone). The nomination form presents an invitation from the secretary herself to direct the department to issues requiring attention.[14] The form has a guidance section that reads:

Guidance: DEP welcomes anyone inside or outside the department to nominate problems for attention. In making this invitation DEP seeks to identify environmental problems, human health problems, or significant patterns of non-compliance:

— which are not currently being addressed by existing programs
— which represent significant patterns or trends (i.e. not just isolated or individual instances)
— and which fall within the agency's role and jurisdiction.

Initial descriptions of problems need only be brief (no more than three or four sentences) but should be reasonably specific. The most useful ones represent some insight into patterns or trends and usefully decompose broader strategic foci into actionable projects.

Stage 2: Define the Problem Precisely

Many problems nominated will not make it past stage 1, due to limits on available resources. Stage 2 offers the opportunity to examine a nominated problem more carefully and more rigorously before committing substantial resources to it and to refine the scope and definition of the project. Data analysis or other evidence collection should confirm or deny the existence of the problem and estimate its seriousness.

Discussion with other parties affected or potentially affected should introduce a range of perspectives on the problem, its origins, potential goals for the project, and potential solutions. Conversation with other parties sooner (at the problem definition stage) rather than later (at action plan implementation stage) helps to minimize backtracking and maximize the involvement and contributions of external parties. Consultation with the regulated community should not offer them a vote in, or veto over, any action plan, for such plans may involve enforcement action against them. Regulators should be genuinely concerned to understand the perspectives of those they regulate, without giving up the prerogative to make (potentially unpopular) regulatory decisions.

Problems come in different shapes and sizes, and a considerable degree of skill is required to define the problem in the right dimensions and at the right level. Police traditionally define problems in terms of time and space, identifying "hot spots" and directing patrols to the relevant area at the relevant time. But many crime problems are more naturally defined in different terms. A crime problem might involve a repeat offender (who roams the whole city), a repeat victim, a class of victims (convenience stores being robbed at night), a class of offenders (school children burglarizing houses on the way home from school), a particular offense (carjacking), or a particular method of committing an offense (modus operandi).

Many regulatory and enforcement professions other than policing also have their own traditions and preferences regarding ways to slice and dice the universe. Tax administrators use industry segmentation, identifying issues peculiar to specific trades or industries. But tax compliance problems might equally be concentrated geographically, or by income range, family composition, type of abusive tax shelter, method of return submission, or type of return preparer. Or they might be specific to one particular credit or deduction, to one tax form, or to one line on a form (such as the invention of fictitious dependents).

Environmental agencies have worked hard to break out of traditional media-specific conceptions of their work and to broaden the number of dimensions in which they can conceive and analyze their work. Ecosystem management enables more holistic understanding of issues contained within a watershed area. Place-based management considers issues specific to communities. The Environmental Protection Agency's Common Sense Initiative orients staff to the environmental issues surrounding specific industries. Environmental problems might also be defined in terms of specific chemicals, specific industrial processes, particular commercial products, household threats (radon gas, lead paint, asbestos insulation), endangered species, endangered habitat, natural resources (aquifers, lakes, streams, a stretch of river). No one dimension is any better than any other. The point is they are many and different. The trick is to define the problem in the most natural and insightful terms, resisting the temptation to force problems into the mold of existing programs or bureaucratic structures. Ecosystem management structures (watershed-based committees) can tackle ecosystem-shaped problems, but they are the wrong apparatus for solving industry problems that straddle multiple watershed areas or for addressing household threats. Forcing problems of one shape into apparatus designed for another inevitably produces inefficiencies (duplication and redundancy) as well as likely ineffectiveness. The goal is to define the problem in the most natural terms and then to organize the right mix of resources around it.

Another artful choice involves selecting the right level of aggregation, or size. Should the project tackle the whole river or just one stretch? All chemicals or just one subset? Drug dealing, or just *street* drug dealing? Many problems, as originally nominated for attention, are so big, so general, and so vague as to be completely overwhelming: drug smuggling, wetlands loss, violent crime. Hence the need for what Goldstein terms *disaggregation*—breaking down complex and overwhelming tasks into discrete, actionable projects. The resulting problem definitions usually grow a little longer as they are made more precise:

— "Lacerations to hands and forearms for production line workers in the poultry industry at the five major plants in the Atlanta area" (an

Occupational Safety and Health Administration hazard mitigation project).

— "Drug smuggling across the Mexican border involving concealment between the double-skins of refrigerated trucks" (a Customs Service Strategic Problem-Solving project).

— "Undeclared tip income for waiters and waitresses in restaurants" (an Internal Revenue Service initiative).

— "Deaths and serious injuries resulting from construction site workers falling down open and unprotected elevator shafts" (OSHA).

— "High blood-lead concentrations in New Jersey bridge painting contractors" (one of OSHA's earliest successful projects, run by the Parsippany Area Office in New Jersey).

— "Aggressive running of red lights within New York City" (1995 Innovations in American Government finalist).

— "Export of stolen high-value vehicles through the port of New Orleans" (Customs Service Strategic Problem-Solving project)

— "Municipal wastewater spills and discharges within the Orlando metropolitan area" (Florida Department of Environmental Protection environmental problem-solving project).

While problems must be defined at sufficiently low level to be feasible and actionable, they must also be defined at sufficiently high level to be worth doing. Success, if it comes, should represent a worthwhile achievement. If quashing one problem merely produces another, then the original problem may not have been defined at a high enough level. Stopping port running at one bridge when there is another bridge half a mile down the street may not matter much. Eliminating port running altogether, even though there may be some displacement to other methods (many of them less dangerous and less offensive than port running) may well be a significant accomplishment.

Many commentators use the term *holism* to capture the merits of taking a broad enough view. In setting the right level for a project, problem solving should consider the interconnectedness of systems, the possibility and costs of displacement, the need for inter-agency cooperation. One of Britain's more progressive police chiefs described problem-oriented policing as the "adoption of a longer-term, more holistic, approach. . . . Put simply, it involves putting policing problems into their wider context so as to understand them more clearly, and then taking more appropriate action (which may not be police action at all) to get to the root of the problem. . . . The idea of problem-oriented policing is to cure the disease."[15]

A holistic or systemic approach, in public policy, seems quite fashionable these days. One analysis of the Innovations in American Government award program, which examined 217 applications that had reached semifinalist status between 1984 and 1992 (not just regulatory innovations), found the theme of holism represented in 61 percent of them.[16] Eugene Bardach, in his 1998 book about interagency cooperation, relates a historic lack of holism to the artificiality or obsolescence of administrative structures:

> Institutional divisions also serve as barriers to thinking creatively—some critics would say thinking realistically—about the systemic, or holistic, nature of certain problems and appropriately systemic solutions. Policies are fragmented by outmoded thinking enshrined in outmoded programs, say the critics, our attention misdirected, and our resources deployed inefficiently and sometimes ineffectively. It often takes heroic efforts to overcome such fragmentation.[17]

Problem-solving teams themselves may not always understand the broader implications of the problem they solve or the solution they use. In *The Fifth Discipline,* Peter Senge points out that "solutions that merely shift problems from one part of a system to another often go undetected because . . . those who 'solved' the first problem are different from those who inherit the new problem."[18] A collection of highly localized successes might not, in the aggregate, amount to much. Hence the obligation rests with management and the project management infrastructure to ensure that individual projects are conceived and tackled at high enough levels to be worthwhile and that portfolios of projects are constructed in such a way that aggregate success really counts.

Problem definition, it turns out, is not so straightforward. Problem definitions must be at sufficiently low level of aggregation not to be vague or overwhelming; at a high enough level to be worthwhile; short enough to galvanize attention; detailed enough to be precise; and expressed in terms or dimensions natural to the problem, irrespective of available apparatus. In other words, artfully.

Stage 3: Determine How to Measure Impact

Relevant measures should be as specific as possible to the problem definition but not at all specific to one action plan. Usually a portfolio of indicators serves better than just one indicator, and portfolios may include qualitative as well as quantitative indicators. In law enforcement contexts, indicators may include intelligence reports that one might expect to receive if the project were successful. Generating an appropriate set of measures usually takes some time and often demands at least as much imagination and inventiveness (brainstorming) as devising action plans. The question to ask is, How would we recognize success if it happened? The answers may be closely related to, How did we know this was a problem in the first place?—and may draw upon similar data sources.

Relevant data may not always be available and may have to be deliberately collected (customs intelligence officers being asked to find out the price being paid to the port runners to run a load). Even when data are available, they may have to be filtered to make them fit the precision of a problem definition. For instance, one of customs' problem-solving projects aims to control the export of stolen high-value vehicles through the port of New Orleans. A relevant measure might be the rate of vehicle theft in the city (readily available from the city police), which is certainly related to the export problem. But more than half of the vehicle theft rate concerns local joyriding, where vehicles are subsequently recovered. A more useful measure, cognizant of the details of the problem being addressed and filtered to suit, might be "the number of vehicles stolen within the city and not subsequently recovered, valued over $10,000, and less than two years old." Performance indicators should match problem definitions in size and scope as closely as possible.

To preserve a results orientation, the portfolio of measures must include sufficient indicators of impact, outcome, or effect (tier 1 in chapter 8's discussion of performance measures). When the desired effects may take many years to show up, tier 2 measures should be used to track relevant behavioral changes (where trends can be measured and interpreted more quickly), provided the project has established a compelling account of the connection between specific behavioral changes and the desired goal. Too much emphasis on tier 3 measures (outputs and productivity) tends to hitch the measurement scheme too closely to a particular mode of intervention and obfuscates the underlying issues of success or failure. For example, if customs' interdiction projects measure their successes only or principally in terms of arrests or seizures (tier 3), then real success (reducing the traffic) would look like failure (declining seizure rates); and real failure (increased traffic) might produce the appearance of success (record seizure rates).

In the practice of problem solving, one discipline turns out to be more important and valuable than any other: pick the measures, and benchmark them, *before* launching any intervention. Stage 3 before stages 4 and 5. "No action until the measures are in place." Otherwise no one can tell what works and what does not.

Stage 4: Develop Interventions

Practitioners find stage 4 more comfortable than stages 2 and 3. They are more accustomed to brainstorming in the context of action planning than in the process of problem definition and indicator selection. The most common failures in problem solving stem from the tendency to leap straight to action, without taking sufficient care over the earlier stages. When that happens, the resulting action plans consist largely of familiar tactics—more of what we already know how to do—and lack any reliable mechanism for determining efficacy.

Design of truly effective and resource efficient solutions arises from a clear sense of the desired end state, coupled with a recognition that everything the agency did before so far failed to produce it. Discussions during stage 4 should cover the following steps:

— Enumeration of the methods previously used to address the problem.

— Honest appraisal of what works, what does not, and how one knows.

— Open-minded search for new responses (generating a long list of ideas), including discussions with affected parties, potential partners, and other constituencies.

— Consideration of the pros and cons of each option, assessing legality, feasibility, cost, side effects, and so on.

— Selection of the best available remedy or combination of remedies.

Before settling on a particular intervention plan, project teams must generate some notion of how resources might eventually be withdrawn from the solution without the problem reappearing. Focusing significant resources on a problem area, in the spirit of directed patrol or blitzes, may be useful for initial suppression (usually there are better ways) but can never suffice as long-term solutions. Solutions that require substantial resource investment in perpetuity are inadequate and should be rejected. Just a few of them could tie up agency resources forever, bring-ing the ongoing, dynamic business of risk control to a halt. Long-term monitoring and maintenance (stage 6) may require some level of resources and attention over the long term but one hopes much less than the level devoted during the design and implementation of the original intervention.

Senge echoes this point in a discussion about government interven-tions more generally (not only regulatory ones):

> The long-term, most insidious consequence of applying non-sys-temic solutions is increased need for more and more of the solu-tion. This is why ill-conceived government interventions are not just ineffective, they are "addictive" in the sense of fostering increased dependency and lessened abilities of local people to solve their own problems. The phenomenon of short-term improve-ments leading to long-term dependency is so common, it has its own name among systems thinkers—it's called "Shifting the Bur-den to the Intervenor."[19]

Notice the importance of permanence in the particular solutions fash-ioned by the innovations finalists: in San Francisco, a program that *breaks the cycle* of prostitution; in Texas, the Immigration and Natural-ization Service plan that *breaks the cycle* of illegal alien hiring by filling vacancies created with legal workers (see chapter 6).

Stage 5: Implement the Plan, with Periodic Monitoring, Review, and Adjustment

In many ways, implementing the plan and monitoring its progress now seems the most straightforward of all the stages. The judgment-laden, cre-ative, and cognitive work has mostly been done, and the analytic and monitoring methods necessary to track progress have all been put in place. Now the agency just has to carry through with its plan, pausing often enough to consider what it learned along the way and whether any of the decisions made earlier need to be revisited or the framework for action and evaluation adjusted. The supporting infrastructure should pro-vide systematic review on a periodic basis (see next chapter), with project plans permitted to hold a steady course between times. Thus team mem-bers can be spared the debilitating misery of second-guessing all their prior decisions every time the team meets. Solutions must be given time to work, and management has to decide how much time.

Stage 6: Close Project, Allowing for Long-Term Monitoring and Maintenance

A project might be terminated because it succeeded (the risk was mitigated to the point that it no longer required dedicated attention), because it failed (the problem turned out to be intractable, and resources would therefore be better used elsewhere), or because it was no longer a priority. On occasion, a project might be suspended, if it remains valuable but some crisis overrides it on a temporary basis. A major accident at an industrial facility, for example, consumes virtually all available resources from whichever of OSHA's area offices covers the facility, at least during the early stages of an investigation. In such circumstances suspending less time-critical projects is perfectly reasonable, provided some kind of tickler system prevents suspended projects from being forgotten.

Deciding to terminate a project because it succeeded requires awkward judgments about degrees of abatement. Perhaps ten victims per week justified special focus and the creation of a dedicated project. Now the rate is down to two per week. What story might the agency give to the next two victims after the project had been closed? Perhaps such victims might be comforted to know that ordinary process channels remain open for them to report the harm and that routine responses (whatever they may be) would still be delivered. But the story about why no more special project—if it has to be told in public—would be a story about competing priorities, emerging risks elsewhere, shifting priorities, managerial choices, and artful resource allocation. Closing projects always suggests explicit acceptance of some level of residual harm, which perhaps explains why projects are formally closed so rarely. Agencies will have a slightly easier time explaining such decisions if they are routinely in the business of making such decisions, they present such choices as the inescapable obligation to allocate resources responsibly, and, for each project closed, they have a sensible long-term monitoring and maintenance plan that prevents observers from assuming that they have lost interest.

The Problem-Solving Art

This brief commentary no more does justice to the art of problem solving than any five-page summary of diagnosis and treatment would do justice to the practice of medicine. But I hope these few observations suffice to demonstrate why such a simple idea turns out to be so complicated in practice. And so far I have only described the life cycle of one project. I have yet to describe how a regulatory organization might manage and track a portfolio of such projects (the work of the next chapter). I have also to describe how such work fits with all the other work (functional responsibilities, process management, crisis response) that regulatory agencies have to do. Eventually we have to connect this apparently ad hoc and miscellaneous collection of activities to the central mission, to strategic plans, and to the aggregate performance account that regulatory agencies want to deliver. Only then will we really have understood what it takes for an organization, as a matter of operational routine, *to pick important problems and fix them.*

CHAPTER ELEVEN

The Problem-Solving Infrastructure

The challenge we face is how to ensure that problem-solving—or our preferred terminology of an "integrated risk based approach to compliance
and enforcement"—becomes the organizational framework and not just an
add-on activity. . . . It is a much more difficult task to seek to adopt this as
an overall whole-of-organization approach.
                AUSTRALIAN SECURITIES AND INVESTMENT COMMISSION

WHETHER EXECUTIVES NEED apparatus for managing problem-solving or risk control operations depends on how they answer these questions: Is problem solving for individual employees or is it for the organization? Is it just a matter of personal style for regulators or is it a
pattern of organizational behavior? A problem orientation can be
taught to individuals and left to them as a matter of personal professional style, without significantly altering any of the major administrative systems of the agency. If executives choose this path, then they may
preach problem solving and the associated results orientation, they may
teach relevant techniques to new or existing staff members, they may
include "problem-solving ability" within the criteria for individual
assessments, and they may commission the production of some handy
little guide for field-level staff to carry around with them (called the
"Beat Officer's Guide to Problem Solving," or something like that).

Under such conditions the internal fabric of the organization (middle
management) need only pay scant attention to the concept and remains
free to assign personnel, allocate work, and measure performance along
traditional lines. Field-level staff may jump at the chance to engage in
this form of work, glad that sensible, creative ideas at the front lines
might finally be appreciated. However, they will soon discover that they
can only take on projects that cost the organization nothing, that

require no managerial engagement, that involve no other parts of the agency or any other agencies, and that they can handle in their spare time without dropping any of their other obligations. For these are the natural limitations for problem solving if taken up only as a question of style.

At the opposite extreme, executives might conceive of problem-solving as the work of major agencywide programs, each with full-time staffing. In that case one would expect to see a relatively small number of very large programs, each one approved by the legislature, budgeted separately, and highly visible publicly. The 1995 study by the National Academy of Public Administration, *Setting Priorities, Getting Results,* in proposing "problem-oriented action strategies" focuses on this level, perhaps influenced by the Environmental Protection Agency's earlier experience with a small number of major projects, such as the Great Lakes program, the Chesapeake Bay program, and the industrywide partnership programs of the Common Sense Initiative:

> The administrator would announce each project with significant fanfare and assign a senior career executive or political appointee to manage it. Staff would be assembled from around the agency, from other federal agencies, and from state and local agencies, in numbers sufficient to accomplish the tasks involved. Depending on the environmental problem selected, several hundred employees might be freed up from their traditional duties and offices and reassigned to the project. Within a year, each team would develop proposals and begin the work of securing any necessary congressional support or public authorization. At the conclusion of each team's work, the agency would evaluate the project's effectiveness.[1]

Remember, problems come in all shapes and sizes. Some can adequately be dealt with by individuals in an afternoon (in which case, not much formal support is required). Others genuinely warrant massive programs, with legislative approval, separate budgets, and hundreds of full-time staff. But most fall somewhere in between. Bear in mind that none of the problem-solving projects described so far in these pages, nor any of those that appear as finalists in the Innovations in American Government competition, was conceived and operated either at the agencywide level or at the level of individual field officers. Virtually all of them (port running, red light running, hiring of illegal workers in Texas, prostitution in San Francisco) fall somewhere below the realm of agencywide programs and above the realm of individual field-level initiative—in the awkward in-between realm where resources have to be allocated and plans approved or denied, but without accompanying changes in legislation, policy, or budgetary structure. That troublesome reality lands the problem-solving and risk control business firmly in the lap of middle management and makes it the stuff of administrative systems.

If an organization (as an entity distinct from its employees) were in the business of picking important problems and fixing them, then one would expect it to have—just as a matter of ordinary logic—apparatus for nominating, assessing, and selecting problems; for appointing project teams and allocating tasks; for overseeing and administering projects; and for recording and reporting the progress of problem-solving projects. One would expect managers to be able to present an inventory of projects under way, and to describe the criteria used for problem selection. One would expect managers to know who did the picking, and how often. And if the organization truly took this kind of work seriously, one would expect such projects to feature prominently in the broader accounts of agency performance.

When regulators tell me that their agency routinely identifies important problems and solves them, but they cannot name a single project that has been closed, or tell me how many are open, or enumerate their recent risk reduction achievements—then I remain skeptical of their claim. Usually they are quite genuine in wishing their agency acted this way, but the practical reality fails to match up.

The Minimal Requirements for a Problem-Solving Infrastructure

In laying out the stages of problem solving in the previous chapter, I tried to incorporate only essential disciplines and avoid cluttering up or weighing down the procedure with unnecessary detail. I try to show similar restraint with respect to the supporting infrastructure, pointing out only those features of organizational apparatus that seem central or crucial. At a minimum, the enabling infrastructure should surely include the following seven features:

— A nomination system for generating and funneling candidate issues to some selection point.

— A selection system for comparative assessment and selection of projects to move forward.

— A system for assigning responsibility and allocating resources (human and financial) to projects, where necessary relieving staff of other duties.

— Project records or project files (paper or electronic) to track discussions, decisions, actions, and progress.

— Managerial oversight and periodic review for monitoring and adjusting the course of a project, where necessary.

— A reporting system for channeling an account of project accomplishments into the agency's routine performance accounts, both internal and external.

— A support system for teams and managers to provide access to consultants or specialists in the problem-solving art (for staff and managers less familiar with it).

Two other features, while perhaps not absolutely essential, seem highly desirable:

— A system for learning, to provide broader access to the knowledge the organization acquires with respect to what works, what does not, what resources are available inside and outside the agency, and whom to call for advice with respect to particular types of problems.

— A reward system to provide recognition for project teams that achieve important results.

A Nomination System

Nominations may come from many sources. Data analysis may reveal important patterns. Questionnaires or public meetings may reveal new concerns. Staff at any level of the organization might nominate problems through their own insightful observation. Other agencies might forward work that came first to them. Given the multiplicity of channels through which nominations could arrive, one cannot help notice how the pioneers of problem solving (for example, the innovations finalists described in chapter 6) usually alight on *one* method. Perhaps they analyze the log of 911 calls for repeat addresses. Or they canvass the public through questionnaires. Or they build a risk based model and rely on its rank-ordered output. Or they plot reported crimes on a map and look for geographic patterns. Or they obtain some other kind of data from some other data source and do just one kind of analysis. Looking forward, as the art of problem solving matures, we should expect to see agencies embracing multiple channels and funneling their miscellaneous insights toward a common destination.

One simple point, sometimes overlooked: people inside and outside the organization have to know where to send their nominations—which, in the absence of a central clearinghouse, can become a rather complex question. The right destination may depend on the size and shape of the problem being nominated, and nominators may not always have a clear sense of these parameters. Nominations should be acknowledged within a reasonable time and nominators kept informed of subsequent decisions regarding their problem, lest it appear that their suggestions have disappeared into a black hole.

Problem nomination should be quick and simple. Florida's Department of Environmental Protection designed a problem nomination form that takes only a minute or two to complete. Problem nominators are asked to provide basic contact information and a brief statement of the problem as they see it, and to note relevant evidence or data of which they are aware. The simple one-page form (also available electronically throughout the department and on its website) carries on its reverse side a list of geographic districts or program offices where nominators can send it or fax it if they know roughly where it belongs, and the address of a central clearinghouse at headquarters if they are not sure.

A Selection System

Whereas nomination seems straightforward and mechanical, selection seems infinitely textured and nuanced. With limited resources to allocate, a manager or group of managers now have to decide whether to launch a project on some aspect of wetlands loss, or to focus instead on an emerging threat to an already endangered species of bird, or to address a sudden rash of deformed frogs, or to pick any one of seventeen equally unlike problems. A police commander has to decide whether to launch a project on domestic violence, or one on traffic congestion, or one that responds to an outbreak of glue sniffing in the area junior schools. The best experts in the emerging risk sciences, even after years of dedicated study, struggle to provide rational frameworks for such decisions. Yet here the complexities and subtleties of comparative risk assessment (the very issues that infuse the regulatory reform debate at the national level) land in the laps of operational managers.

At this point the technical science of risk assessment and the operational practice of risk control may diverge. Operations cannot wait for definitive study or complete information and cannot—except for the largest projects—commission comprehensive cost-benefit analyses.

Operations must consider political priorities and public concerns, whether or not they properly reflect underlying risks. As public officials, managers who sit on problem selection panels engage as much in the democratic business of *valuing* projects as in the more technocratic business of *prioritization* based on hazard and exposure rates.[2] They must take account of the fact that the layperson's perceptions and valuations differ from those of experts and statisticians. Ordinary people tend to focus less on the numerical aspects of risk, which are difficult for them to fathom, and more on the qualitative aspects of risk, which have intuitive, emotional, and ethical significance.[3] With such a range of factors to consider, as NAPA's discussion of environmental problems suggests,

> deciding what problems are most serious or pressing is a difficult, subjective task. The task requires decisions not only about scientific evidence of risks to human health and the environment, but also about basic political and human values. . . .
>
> The ranking process is inherently subjective and value-laden, requiring individuals or the team as a whole to compare problems along many different dimensions at once. . . . The question is complicated by the range of possible effects, the number of people affected, how they are exposed, and the steps that individuals can take to reduce their exposures. Technical analysis can provide some of the raw material for making these judgments, but ultimately the decisions are of a type that some would call policy decisions.[4]

I prefer to call them *operational* decisions rather than *policy* decisions, to avoid the presumption that such decisions rest only with legislatures or senior executives. Lower-level problems (the majority) rest with lower-level management. As in the case of the Customs Service's port-running project, the majority of problems may be solved through sequences of operational decisions, none of which amounts to broader changes in policy. Operational managers, using their judgment and the best information available, need to pick the important problems—and problems may be important to many different people for many different reasons. As a practical matter, when operational managers meet together over the task of problem selection, not only do they lack definitive information or precise criteria, they might only have an hour or so to decide!

Why do I think that middle-level managers should be taking such weighty decisions, and in such a hurry? And why should anyone trust them with such responsibility? Because—if we really want regulatory agencies to engage in risk reduction, compliance management, and problem solving—then managers have to play these roles. If operational managers cannot decide these questions, if they refuse to do so, or if they keep sending every problem back for more and more analysis ("paralysis through analysis"), then their agencies will never be able to run a risk control operation.

One might derive some comfort from the knowledge that operational managers make equally demanding resource allocation decisions all the time and from the hope that a clearly articulated problem-solving strategy codifies expectations and provides them a more rational framework, a clearer sense of purpose, and more predictable patterns of accountability than they may have had in the past. One might also derive some comfort from the knowledge that operational managers have shown themselves quite capable of making such complex decisions in the past. According to NAPA's commentary on the ranking of EPA's "unfinished business": "the projects have shown that participants with many points of view and levels of technical expertise can evaluate a large amount of technical, risk-related information and reach a consensus on which problems are the most serious and which the least."[5]

Even if regulators lack the scientific sophistication of academic theorists, the public may nevertheless trust their motivations more. Risk analysis as set forth in the context of the regulatory reform debate is often perceived by advocacy groups as a tool to legitimize decisions harmful to public health or the environment.[6] Some fear that a risk management approach, as structured by academics and then filtered through legislatures, would render rule making so slow and raise so many evidentiary hurdles that it would cause social regulatory policy to change too slowly in the face of real opportunities for better protection. Interest groups may regard analytic approaches as elitist and technocratic, or as ethically or morally suspect; some view the science itself as not yet mature enough. But in the context of operations, surely risk analysis (or even practitioners' best attempts at it) forms a better basis for practical resource allocation decisions than anything else. A problem-solving strategy merely requires that managers do their best with respect to risk assessment and problem selection and not shy away from making these choices. Even if regulators take up this practical challenge, society might still pursue more exhaustive risk-based reassessments at the national level as a way of reordering its macrolevel regulatory priorities. But we do not need to wait for such high-level changes, or rely upon them, in order to obtain more effective regulatory protection.

In *picking important problems*, managers not only have to assess individual risks as candidates for selection but also have to think in terms of portfolio management. They want neither too many projects nor too few. This kind of work has to be balanced with other kinds. They should avoid choosing only huge, overwhelming projects with very long time lines. They need some projects likely to produce quick wins, else the whole strategy may founder for lack of demonstrable results. They need to involve enough staff, yet they may prefer to give this work only to volunteers, at least to begin with. While problem solving remains relatively new, managers may choose a portfolio of smaller, tightly contained projects, deliberately selecting those that do not require extensive interagency cooperation. Such pragmatic choices may accelerate the learning process and increase the chances of overall success. Later, staff may be ready for bigger, more complex challenges.

A System for Assigning Responsibility and Allocating Resources

The goodwill and enthusiasm of a few volunteer staff, given no relief from other duties, can only take an agency so far. Important problem-solving projects take time and cost money. So the management apparatus has to be able to assign staff or staff time to a project, grant relief from other duties when appropriate, and provide access to necessary resources. As projects unfold, their action plans may affect the focus of inspections or investigations, and they may impose additional burdens on processes, either for the purpose of supplementary data collection or to administer experimental responses. Project teams generally have no line authority over *any* resources (other than their own time), nor control over any processes, so the managerial infrastructure has to assess each project's resource implications, make sure they are commensurate with the significance of the problem, and procure the requisite access to other agency resources.

It is usually impossible to tell, when a project is first opened, how much it will cost or how long it will last. It is usually a mistake to open a project for which an action plan has already been devised and priced, because that suggests inadequate consideration has been given to problem definition, measurement, and searching for newer, less familiar, solutions. Given the initial uncertainty over cost and duration, managers need to reexamine staffing and resource levels from time to time, checking that they are adequate and appropriate, and making sure no more resource-efficient alternative has been overlooked.

Project Records

During the summer of 1996, at the invitation of the Customs Service, I spent three weeks touring the southern border ports of the United States, meeting with project teams under customs' fledgling Strategic Problem-Solving program. One meeting, at the Miami Seaport (which handles shipping containers), centered on ramp conspiracies at that port. Ramp conspiracies, as a general category of smuggling, involve collusion between workers responsible for loading vessels (ships or planes) at the point of departure and workers responsible for unloading them within the United States. Such collaboration can introduce drugs or other contraband into perfectly legitimate cargo at the point of departure (for example, Colombia), and have it removed in the United States by dockyard or airport workers before the load clears customs examination. Miami Seaport had been plagued by ramp conspiracies for years, and more than half of the dockyard workers (members of the Longshoremen's Union) had criminal convictions, mostly for drug-related offenses. During their period of duty at the Miami Seaport, dockyard workers were permitted to drive their private vehicles into the dock area and park them on the wharf, only yards from the ships and from shipping containers stacked on the dock.

The Miami Seaport customs management team had designated ramp conspiracies, particularly involving containers shipped from Colombia, as a Strategic Problem-Solving project. Containers carrying coffee were choice targets for ramp conspirators, because the smell of the load overcame the scent of drugs, rendering drug-sniffing dogs ineffective. I was introduced to the team leaders, and asked what they had tried so far. They had tried many different approaches. They had considered and experimented with physical alteration of container-stacking configurations. They had tried several forms of surveillance. They had used frogmen to patrol the waters around the ships, aware that contraband loads often left the port by water rather than by road. As they described initiative after initiative, slowly the room began to fill up as they called in other staff. Each new person had a piece of the story to tell: their idea and their contribution to a succession of plans. Eventually there were eighteen customs officers in the room, all involved in some way. (There was also more than $1.5 million in the room—small-denomination currency packed into cardboard boxes and lining the walls—the fruits of an outbound currency seizure.) But the project had stalled. "Washington" (headquarters) apparently did not appreciate all the fine work they were doing and had not approved their latest equipment request for a new batch of night-vision surveillance gear. They were stuck. I asked why "Washington" did not appreciate all the fine work. Had they not seen the project file?

There was no project file. The team had never created one. They had not kept minutes of their meetings or records of their actions. Why not? Because there were *no forms* for that. When they made arrests or seizures, there were forms for that. When they worked overtime, there were forms for that. If they damaged their uniforms or lost a flashlight, there were forms for that. But there were no forms, and hence no files, for projects. Hence no record of all this team's creative work, except their collective recollections. In which case, how could senior management possibly review the progress of the project? On what basis could significant expenditures be justified? And how would the agency ever be able to report this work if it first failed to record it. I asked how long it would take them to create a file and get it up to date. "About two hours," the team leaders estimated, including time to write out brief minutes from all their past meetings. Time well spent, one would think; if the work is important, then it should surely be recorded. Project files are essential. Yet the need for them is not obvious to people, even when they engage in fabulously creative work.

Managerial Oversight and Periodic Review

As managers from time to time review the progress of projects, they have to balance the notions of *empowerment* and *accountability*.[7] They must avoid the temptation to summarily dismiss ideas that a team has generated, even if those ideas appear on their face to be infeasible, illegal, unwise, or excessively expensive. As fellow academicians have pointed out to me, the difference between gibberish and genius is usually about thirteen drafts. Many of the most effective solutions start out looking silly but emerge as something quite brilliant and creative through a process of refinement. Managerial oversight forms a part of that refinement process. Problem solving depends upon the generation of new ideas, so management must avoid killing them.

Another major piece of the managerial oversight responsibility involves learning to recognize the pitfalls and traps that surround this style of work, many of which can be avoided by enforcing a modicum of methodological rigor. For example, managers should watch for the "jump to action" syndrome, in which teams neglect the issues of problem definition and performance measurement, embarking immediately on action without much thought. They should watch for broad, vague, problem definitions and press for more insightful identification of specific subcomponents or concentrations. They should ensure that the indicators selected include valid measures of impact or outcome, so that the team can monitor mitigation of the problem as well as implementation of the plan. They should insist that project teams benchmark their performance indicators before implementing an intervention; otherwise subsequent improvements cannot be evaluated.

Overseers should also watch for any signs that teams have become dysfunctional and should know how to restore them; or that teams lack the requisite analytical skills, in which case they must provide them. At a minimum, management reviews should address the following four central questions. First, should the project be continued? Normally the answer will be yes. Too much scrapping of projects, once they have begun, will create a sense of uncertainty and transience about the project approach and will remove the incentive for teams to persevere in the search for solutions that actually work. But a project might be discontinued for a number of reasons, including that it is finished and the goals have been sufficiently achieved; the problem is intractable, and the resources would be better used elsewhere; or some other priority demands these resources.

Second, should staffing and resources devoted to the project be adjusted? As problem definitions are refined (that is, the size and scope of projects clarified), and as action plans take shape, overseers should check that staffing and resource levels remain reasonable given the relative importance of the problem. Projects may grind to a halt because of inadequate staffing or inadequate access to relevant resources. The management system must either provide adequate resources or terminate the project. Another important function of the managerial apparatus is to procure the necessary cooperation and commitment from other agencies, when necessary. Field-level staff often form their own informal alliances across agency boundaries, but these may fail to produce sustained commitments over time. Collaborative work involving multiple agencies is unsustainable without managerial commitments all around, and these commitments need to be negotiated and agreed. For projects involving significant commitments from multiple agencies, project oversight might become a *joint* managerial endeavor.

Third, does the problem definition or the portfolio of indicators require adjustment? As projects progress, each of these may be revisited from time to time. Too often would be debilitating; not often enough produces inflexibility. If the problem definition changes, then the portfolio of relevant indicators ought to change also, to match.

Fourth, does the action plan still make sense, or does it need refinement or adjustment? Very few action plans work the first time. The third or fourth idea might be better than the first. Most plans that finally succeed pass through a sequence of adjustments along the way. Project teams have not failed when their plans do not work. An important role for managerial review is to help them judge when it is time to hold fast and when to change tack.

A Reporting System

The nature of the report that stems from problem-solving derives logically from the nature of the work itself. A completed project report will therefore show a statement of the problem (the problem definition); a summary of the initial evidence that it was a problem (data, intelligence); a description of the indicators selected to track progress, with a note of their starting (benchmarked) values; an account of the interventions implemented, with a note of resources expended; a summary of results achieved, focusing on the movement of the selected indicators; and an explanation of the longer term plan for maintaining suppression.

Part 4 of this book contains a detailed discussion of how such reports fit into the aggregate performance account regulatory agencies seek to provide. At this stage, though, we should note that project-specific accounts of success, as detailed above, would not normally establish a causal connection between interventions and results achieved. These project stories merely describe the existence of the problem, the evidence of mitigation, and the chronology of intervening actions. Note also that the results achieved across multiple projects depend upon differing sets of indicators and thus may be difficult to aggregate in a meaningful way. In fact, the degree to which such accounts can be usefully aggregated or summarized depends to a large extent upon the nature of different regulatory professions, hinging on the existence of a broader common currency into which disparate results can be converted.

A Support System for Teams and Managers

Problem-solving teams, and managers overseeing their work, may none of them be experts in the art. Each organization that I have seen create a structured system for problem solving has also selected and trained a set of in-house consultants, responding to the needs of staff thrust into the midst of work they perceive as unfamiliar and potentially chaotic. These consultants offer services internally, helping to facilitate team meetings (until they are able to withdraw), and sitting in on management meetings (as advisers to management on methodological issues) whenever problem nominations are reviewed for selection or projects under way are reviewed.

A System for Learning

Desirable, if not essential, is some method for regulatory agencies to organize the lessons they learn and to make the accumulated knowledge readily available, internally and externally. In seeking to explain why problem solving has not taken off in American policing in the way he hoped, Herman Goldstein points to a culture that does not regard acquired knowledge as a valued asset:

> The entire police establishment in the United States has developed without benefit of a careful, systematic building of knowledge regarding the multitude of different problems that the police are called upon to handle. We do not know, with any confidence, what works and what doesn't in responding to them. . . .
>
> No . . . investment has been made in understanding the business of policing—the substantive problems the police are expected to handle on a daily basis. I have reference, for example, to such common problems as residential burglaries, street robberies, thefts from cars, complaints about noise, and disorderly conduct in bars. . . .
>
> In most occupations—and especially in those that are characterized as professions—some component is committed to inquiry, to analysis, to research on the problems routinely handled or the products produced. And procedures are in place to dispense this knowledge to practitioners in ways that are useful to them. Policing has a critical need to develop a similar capacity. . . . The absence of this intellectual dimension in policing has stunted the growth of the field.[8]

Recognizing the need to capture and then disseminate the lessons learned during different projects, the Customs Service has built a learning support system into their Strategic Problem-Solving program. An automated team tracking system provides employees anywhere in the nation electronic access to summaries of all past and current projects (which now number over 200). Project teams can look up projects similar or related to their own, identify personnel with expertise in particular areas, and identify resources and contacts in other agencies. Their system now has a keyword search capability, by subject.

Of course one should beware of careless replication. Each problem may be unique and may require tailor-made interventions. Nothing kills problem solving as quickly as the assumption that what worked in one place will automatically work elsewhere. A review of similar or related projects to find out what worked and what did not, however, surely expands a team's ability to generate ideas, speeds its search for the right kind of tactics, and may reveal external resources of which it was unaware. Like any other art (or science, whichever concept applies better), problem solving, if taken seriously, will generate its own literature and knowledge sources over time.

A Reward System

Desirable also are reward systems that celebrate problem-solving successes. In law enforcement, rewards and commendations traditionally emphasize acts of heroism, major arrests or seizures, or exemplary investigations. Shifting emphasis onto thoughtful analysis and problem resolution requires realignment of reward systems, just as it requires realignment of performance measurement systems. The Police Executive Research Forum (a not-for-profit research group based in Washington, D.C.) now runs an annual problem-solving awards competition for the police profession. Customs, in 1998, instituted an annual awards ceremony (held during its annual Strategic Problem-Solving conference), recognizing ten project teams per year for their problem-solving projects. Florida's Department of Environmental Protection launched its environmental problem-solving awards program in 1999.

A System for Innovation

Some readers, free spirited by nature or worried about "good people trapped in bad systems," might be a little concerned by the last chapter's specification of procedures. Now, with all this managerial infrastructure to boot, they may be questioning my sanity, wondering whatever happened to personal motivation, initiative, and empowerment. In response, I can only offer that I come to these systems reluctantly and would prefer that they were not necessary. Indeed, if any agency can produce a risk control operation without any of these systems, that would be terrific. In my early work with regulatory agencies, I did not emphasize procedures or infrastructure, but watching projects go awry has taught me the value of procedural disciplines; and sitting in too many "why isn't it happening?" meetings has taught me the need for supporting organizational infrastructure. Problem solving as a matter of personal style cannot address important problems. Problem solving as a pattern of organizational behavior relies on organizational fabric for support. In this chapter I have simply presented a realistic view of what that supporting fabric might look like.

I am interested (and somewhat relieved, being out on a bureaucratic limb) to see that many aspects of managerial behavior, supported or encouraged by the problem-solving infrastructure, are also prescribed independently by others, from quite different vantage points. Robert Behn at Duke University—one of the keenest observers of public sector innovation—articulates features of managerial behavior that promote not just *an innovation* but *innovativeness* in public sector organizations. In a summary article he presents ten practical hints for managers wanting to involve frontline workers in creating innovative organizations.[9] These hints arise not from a focus on regulatory work, nor from a concern for the technicalities of risk control or compliance management, but from a more general desire to produce innovativeness as a feature of organizational behavior. Looking down his list of ten hints, five of them in particular relate closely to aspects of the infrastructure described above:

— Support mistakes (or sit next to the first honest innovator who is called before a legislative committee). [*Relates to fact that many action plans tried may not work.*]

— Create an explicit mission and related performance measures (or give people a reason to be innovative). [*Relates to picking the indicators and setting goals before designing the action plan.*]

— Broaden job categories (or do not let each individual do only one narrow task). [*Relates to allocating staff to project-based interdisciplinary teams.*]

— Reward teams, not individuals (or find ways to beat the formal performance appraisal and promotion systems). [*Relates to rewards and recognition for problem-solving project teams.*]

— Tell everyone what innovations are working (or have frontline workers report their successes to their colleagues). [*Relates to learning systems and knowledge sharing.*]

Behn and many others who study innovations per se focus more on managerial style and organizational culture than they do on formal systems, but the symbiosis between their styles and these systems seems plain enough. In regulatory agencies at least, the systems created to support problem solving and risk reduction may be the very systems required to generate innovations as a matter of course. And not just *any* innovations, serendipitous and miscellaneous; but *the right ones*, centered on important priorities.

CHAPTER TWELVE

The Boston Gun Project

MANY REGULATORY EXECUTIVES have watched with alarm as pressures for regulatory reform produce schisms within their own agencies. Failure to understand the real challenges of regulatory craftsmanship, coupled with adoption of overly simplistic customer service ideas, have split their agencies into camps. The enforcement-minded "dinosaurs" complain that the agency is going soft, that violators are not customers, and that nothing works like enforcement. The "voluntary compliance" camp, meanwhile, proclaims that successful prevention renders enforcement unnecessary, that enforcement creates unnecessary hostility, and that facilitating voluntary compliance produces greater gains than focusing on enforcement.

Within this dichotomous strategic landscape, practitioners—if they discuss problem solving at all—tend to place it on the soft side, along with education, outreach, and partnerships. They associate problem solving with a search for systemic and preventive alternatives to enforcement. Historically (and for a variety of reasons) problem-solving teams have often been explicitly instructed to find systemic solutions not involving enforcement.

To understand the breadth and importance of the approach, the notion that problem solving constitutes a tactical alternative to enforcement, or that problem-solving strategies exclude enforcement methods, must be dismissed. The Boston gun project (an Innovations in American Government winner in 1997) provides a compelling counterexample to the theory that problem solving is soft or that it cannot be applied to problems of serious crime. The project also provides a wonderful demonstration of how a well-crafted, tailor-made, compliance management strategy can substantially mitigate risks—in this case, youth homicide—otherwise pessimistically viewed as chronic conditions of American life. In the five years prior to the project's inception, the city of Boston experienced 155 youth homicides involving guns or knives. Most involved guns, and most of the victims were young black men.[1] The National Institute of Justice funded the work, explicitly conceived as a problem-solving project, the purpose of which was to devise and implement strategic interventions in an attempt to control youth violence.

Three researchers from the John F. Kennedy School of Government's program on criminal justice policy and management—David M. Kennedy, Anthony A. Braga, and Anne M. Piehl—led the project, pulling in a large interagency group to study the problem and coordinate a response.[2] Agencies involved included the Boston Police Department; the Bureau of Alcohol, Tobacco and Firearms; the U.S. attorney for the Commonwealth of Massachusetts; the Suffolk County district attorney; the Massachusetts Department of Probation; city of Boston youth outreach workers; the Massachusetts Department of Parole; the city of Boston School Police; and gang outreach and mediation specialists employed by the city of Boston, known as "street workers." Working Group participants started meeting in early 1995 and continued to meet biweekly for several years.

The researchers' analysis concentrated first on the 155 prior homicides. What was happening on the streets? Who were the offenders? Who were the victims? And where did the guns come from? At the outset, the project was labeled the Boston gun project, and the team focused on uncovering the nature of the illicit gun market that supplied juveniles. Working group members initially assumed that gun supply routes originated in states such as Virginia, Georgia, Tennessee and Mississippi, and arrived in Boston through the I-95 corridor. But when the researchers examined traces of weapons recovered from city youth, a different pattern emerged. Over a third of the weapons had been purchased originally in Massachusetts. Many were rather new (less than two years from first purchase), semiautomatic, and had obliterated serial numbers, a profile that suggests that guns were being diverted into the illicit market very close to the point of first sale. The working group continued inquiries back through the chain of possession to get to the roots of the initial diversion. They hoped to show that people who diverted guns into the juvenile market could be brought to book.

The project's analysis also explored the demand side of the equation, examining the characteristics of the killers and the killed. It turned out that the profiles of the killers and the killed looked remarkably similar. The problem of youth homicide was concentrated among a small number of serially offending youths involved in gangs, most of them very well known to the criminal justice system. Only 1,300 gang members—less than 1 percent of their age group citywide—were responsible for at least 60 percent, and probably more, of all the youth homicide in the city. Three-fourths of both homicide offenders and victims had been arraigned at least once before. Of those who had been arraigned at least once, the average number of times arraigned was 9.7 for offenders, and 9.5 for victims. One-fourth of the offenders were on probation when they committed murder, and 14 percent of the victims were on probation when they died. These statistics translate into a roughly one-in-seven chance of being killed at some point during an average nine-year gang membership spell, an observation that lent some credence to the idea that much gun carrying was at least partially self-protective.[3] And an observation that also pointed to a specific feature of the compliance management challenge: that it would be hard to get any one gang to disarm unless their enemies did so at the same time.

Pooling the street-level knowledge of the working group participants, the project identified sixty-one active gangs and mapped their territories, and their "beefs" (which gangs fought with which other gangs). Most of the violence, it turned out, happened within the context of these beefs. This observation in particular helped shape the intervention plan. If the violence was largely confined to gangs, most of whose members were well known to authorities, and most of it happened in the context of intergang rivalries, then the strategy should be designed to focus upon and take advantage of these concentrations. As project director David Kennedy puts it, the strategy was designed to take advantage of what is normally regarded as extremely bad news: the fact that the offenders were "persistent, manifoldly deviant, and tightly networked."[4] Gang members were relatively few, and news would travel fast throughout the gang networks. So the working group devised what came to be known as the Ceasefire strategy, which involved artfully crafting news that the working group wanted to travel over the gang network—and then deliberately communicating it to the gang members.

Operation Ceasefire's communications campaign, designed to reach all sixty-one gangs, involved a sequence of meetings between project personnel and gang members, brokered by probation officers, youth workers, community workers—and whoever else could persuade or coerce gang members to come to the meetings. At the meetings, a threat (or "promise") was made, to the effect that any violent offenses would be immediately met by a coordinated interagency action to "pull every lever," not just against the individual offender but against his whole gang. In other words, the threat was to sanction the whole gang by any and all means available, through the coordinated actions of the wide range of federal, state, and local law enforcement agencies that were party to the plan. Warrants would be served, existing probation restrictions rigorously enforced, arrests made for minor offenses, resulting cases pushed through higher level courts, and more serious penalties sought. The threat was that law enforcement, by pooling its resources and focusing on one gang, could invariably impose serious sanctions on that gang.

This threat was far more credible than the fashionable rhetoric of zero tolerance. The normal experience of gang members taught them that the limited capacities of enforcement agencies and the constraints on courts and prisons meant that punishment, even for violent crimes, was neither swift, serious, nor sure. The dissipation of law enforcement attention across many offenders and offenses routinely rendered it ineffective against chronic offenders. These meetings, by contrast, were a decidedly abnormal experience. Here were representatives of all the major enforcement agencies, and prosecutors, pledging their collective commitment to produce a singularly unpleasant experience for any gang that engaged in violence and thereby came into their sights. These officials explained during the meetings that the new regime applied specifically to offenses involving violence and that other offenses would receive ordinary "baseline" criminal justice attention. Thus no "permissions" were granted, nor any deals struck—just a very special promise for these very special crimes. Part of the communications strategy emphasized that the project was designed to protect gang members from gang members. The overriding object was to keep them alive. The message in summary: "The violence is going to stop."

This message was delivered after an initial crackdown had been crafted and fully carried out, to demonstrate to gang offenders that the authorities were serious. An internal struggle within one gang—the Vamp Hill Kings—led to three homicides during the first few months of 1996. The working group's coordinated intervention, which followed, included heavy police presence on the streets within the Kings' area, disruption of their drug markets, heavy probation enforcement, Department of Youth Services surrenders, warrant service, and a small number of federal indictments.[5] In May 1996, the meetings, called "forums," began, in which the working group publicized the fate of the Vamp Hill Kings. They also publicized, with posters and flyers, the case of Freddy Cardoza, an active member of another gang, who had been sentenced to nineteen years and seven months in prison with no possibility of parole when caught in possession of a single bullet (and prosecuted under federal law as an "armed career criminal"). The message essentially was, "Look what enforcement agencies can do to you if they focus on you," coupled with "The Kings didn't listen. Look what happened to them. You do violence, and you can be next." Shortly thereafter, a different gang sent a message to the working group through a street worker: "We got the message, we're not doing anything, leave us alone."[6]

The second coordinated and gang-specific intervention focused on one of Boston's most violent gangs, the Intervale Posse. Despite the warnings, it had continued its reign of terror in Roxbury. On the morning of August 29, 1996, the Boston police and the Drug Enforcement Agency arrested fifteen members of that gang on federal drug charges. New forums explained the enforcement operation to the other gangs: "It was because they did *violence*; who wants to be next?"

At that point, the rate of youth homicides in the rest of Boston's gang network dropped off abruptly. In the first year after Operation Ceasefire was implemented, the number of homicide victims in Boston aged twenty-four or younger dropped by 68 percent (from forty-one in 1995 to thirteen) and continued to decline thereafter. This represented a drop of more than two-thirds from the average rate for the prior five years. Since older offenders were involved in gangs, and gang members often hurt older victims, impact was also felt in older age groups as well. From a yearly average of about 100 homicides before Operation Ceasefire, citywide homicide totals (covering all age groups) fell to forty-three in 1997 and thirty-five in 1998.

The gang officer for the Boston Police Department—whose beeper would go off every time a gang homicide was discovered—sent his beeper in to be checked. It had stopped going off. In subsequent months,

the Boston Police gang unit was able to turn its attention to lesser problems, such as street drug activity and disorder, for which it would not
have had time before. As a result of the dramatic decline in youth and
juvenile homicide rates (and as a result of selection as an Innovations in
American Government winner) the project has received national attention, and many other cities have sought to emulate the program.

Lessons Learned

Quite apart from the project's obvious value to the city of Boston, to its
communities, and especially to its youth, this project is also valuable for
what it can teach regarding the art of compliance management. Most
obviously, it demonstrates the leveraging of limited enforcement
resources through careful planning, coordination, and targeting. But it
reveals some other basic truths about the problem-solving process and
suggests specific additions to the regulatory and enforcement professions' knowledge base or repertoire for managing compliance.

Openness to Problem Redefinition

The project's initial emphasis on unraveling the gun supply markets
was eventually displaced to some extent by a later emphasis on intergang violence. Early problem definitions focused on illicit gun supply to
juveniles, whereas attention expanded later to the sixty-one enumerated
gangs and what it took to control their collective behaviors. The expansion of the problem definition resulted directly from what the team
found out about the problem through analysis. Open-minded and rigorous inquiry produced new perspectives, as it often does, and problem
solving should be sufficiently flexible to capitalize upon them.

Finding Concentrations and Vulnerabilities

This strategy's success stems in part from the researchers' success in
identifying a core concentration within the more general problem and
on finding resource-efficient methods of applying pressure to that identified concentration. Ultimately, the concentration of most value (within
the broader area of youth homicide) was the narrow context of intergang rivalry. The opportunity for resource-efficient intervention arose in
part because the criminal justice system already had access to, and some
power over, most gang members.

Note that a variety of forms of analysis preceded the discovery of this concentration. Analysis of homicide locations showed that they fit almost perfectly the gang territories but offered less resource-efficient intervention possibilities (the gang territories were collectively too large for area-specific tactics such as directed patrol, or "street sweeps," to be applied to them all). Offending was similarly concentrated among chronic offenders, who were still too numerous—and too caught up in powerful street dynamics—to be dealt with one by one. The insight regarding gang membership, gang conflicts, and gang communication networks provided the basis for the intervention strategy. Finding an intervention opportunity and intervention mechanisms depended first on artfully choosing the right dimensions in which to define the problem, to describe it, and then to dissect it.

Principled Intimacy

The Operation Ceasefire strategy demanded clear and frequent communication with offenders. Such intimacy with offenders—dubbed "principled intimacy" by David Kennedy—contrasts starkly with the principled distance and mistrust that accompanies the regulatory style of legalistic enforcement. It also contrasts with the unprincipled intimacy associated either with forms of law enforcement corruption or with the "capture" of a regulatory agency by its regulated community. Operation Ceasefire involved no partnership in the vogue sense of the term, nor was any immunity or amnesty granted for any offense. Rather, the strategy was designed to act upon the minds of the gangs and to transform their behavior. That demanded frequent and effective communication, with absolutely no compromise or diminution of determination to enforce relevant laws.

Well-Publicized Change Dates

The first gang to disarm would place themselves at risk. Other regulatory fields present analogous compliance problems, in which noncompliance of particular types has become systemic, and the first party to comply places itself at a competitive disadvantage. Suppose, for example, that an industry has collectively opposed a requirement to install a new, environmentally friendly technology that is more expensive than existing systems. Whoever goes first in the industry suffers increased costs and may lose business or market position to laggards. Their incentives push them to go last, if at all. Or suppose, as the nation's major hospitals bill Medicare for services provided, that certain abusive billing practices have become widespread throughout the industry, to the point at which an attempt to enforce existing regulations would be met with concerted opposition and the predictable protest, "Why me, and why now, when for all these years this seemed to be accepted as ordinary practice?" Whichever hospital complies first not only places itself at a financial disadvantage vis-à-vis its competitors but may be regarded as breaking the ranks of professional or industrial associations.

The distinctive characteristic such compliance problems share with the gun project is that regulators need to procure widespread change in behavior across a range of violators, all at the same time, and with never enough enforcement resources to go around. The message of Operation Ceasefire, applied to fraudulent or abusive Medicare billings by hospitals, might come out something like this:

> Good morning, friends. We know, and you know, that certain abusive billing practices have become systemic within this industry. We are here today to name five of them and to announce that all five will cease as of the end of this month. This gives you three weeks to examine your own billing practices and systems and correct them if necessary. In the first week of next month, having only limited audit and claims review resources, we will monitor incoming claims particularly for any signs that these particular billing practices persist, and the first ten hospitals that we find will be subjected to a rigorous and comprehensive audit of *all* their billings. In the course of those ten audits we will pursue enforcement and recoveries of amounts due, to the full extent permitted by law. To find yourself on that list of ten, all you need to do is carry on as you are now. We advise you to correct these problems.
>
> By the way, next month we will identify five further billing practices and notify you of the dates by which they too should be eliminated.

Then one might sit back and watch the billing practices change across the industry. Regulators have to deliver on the promise, just so the audience knows they are serious. That would mean nailing the first ten hospitals that show up in the analysis and publicizing their fate throughout the industry in the same deliberate and demonstrative manner in which the working group publicized the fate of the Vamp Hill Kings and the

Intervale Posse. Or maybe such tactics might not be appropriate in these other areas. That would be for the relevant compliance management project teams to decide in their own time, based on their own analysis of those other problems. The point is, such tactics exist, and many other equally sophisticated tactics might be conceived.

Progressive Strategies

The Operation Ceasefire strategy also demonstrates the possibility of focusing on particular behaviors and eliminating them one by one (but across the board), successively moving to less and less serious behaviors in what Kennedy calls a "strategically serial fashion."[7] Traditionally, law enforcement focuses on the most serious offenders, not offenses. For this project, there were too many serious offenders, and focusing on one category of serious offenses (those involving violence) offered greater promise of real results within a short time.

The related resource allocation questions are quite interesting. Trying to suppress everything results in scarce enforcement resources being scattered all across the board, dissipating risks to offenders, and resulting in suppression of nothing. Trying to suppress something in particular therefore is more effective than trying to suppress everything, even if this way of focusing attention looks ethically peculiar at first. Provided the focused effort is successful in eliminating the particular, then—in theory—the strategy can cover the general through serial progression. In the case of Boston's Operation Ceasefire, it is still too early to tell whether the same basic strategy can be extended to suppress drug dealing and lesser offenses in the same way that it has suppressed homicide.

Spreading the Pain

Another noteworthy aspect of the intervention plan was the deliberate extension of consequences beyond the individual, to the gang. The threat was, If any one of you engages in violence, then the whole gang suffers. Note that the other gang members would suffer, not for that offense (in which they may have played no role) but for other things they had done or were doing, which means that law enforcement conditioned its enforcement discretion relating to one offense upon the commission of other offenses, even other offenses committed by other people. Here the *structuring of discretion* is taken to a whole new level of sophistication and opens a panoply of more complex, game-theoretic, multiparty enforcement and compliance strategies. (Wherein we should attend carefully to the legal and ethical questions such practices may raise.)

The effect of spreading the pain, in this case, was to mobilize peer pressure in support of compliance. A killer who might otherwise have been regarded as a hero by his peers becomes the instrument of downfall.

Not Soft

Problem solving is not an alternative to enforcement, nor does any mature problem-solving strategy eschew enforcement. Those are the simplest lessons of this project. More profound, though, is the realization that qualitative changes in societal conditions can be wrought, and quickly, when relevant resources come together with a clear purpose. But dogma and tradition have to be put aside, so analysis can lead to insight, and insight can be combined with creativity to produce interventions that work.

The first two of the six lessons drawn above—openness to redefining the problem and the importance of identifying concentrations or vulnerabilities of an enterprise—are standard elements of risk control artistry. The other four are specific strategic and tactical ideas, each more sophisticated than the ways in which regulators normally think about allocating their resources and structuring their discretion. In due course, as the practical art of risk control develops, regulators will need four *thousand* such ideas to discuss, not four, and a structure to the body of professional knowledge that would make it all accessible.

CHAPTER THIRTEEN

Of Strategies Reactive, Preventive, and Proactive

I HOPE THE LAST CHAPTER succeeded in dismissing the misleading notion that problem solving represents an alternative to enforcement. I hope this chapter succeeds in dismissing the equally misleading notion that enlightened regulatory practice necessarily rejects reactive tactics and embraces prevention. The two ideas—rejecting enforcement and rejecting reactive tactics—are related, of course, because of the strong association between enforcement methods and a reactive stance; so when regulators turn their backs on one, they most likely turn their backs on the other.

The shortcomings of reactive strategies are well established and have been much written of. The introduction of my 1994 volume states:

> The traditional cultures of environmental protection, policing, and tax collection incorporate a classic enforcement mentality, built upon the fundamental assumption that a ruthless and efficient investigation and enforcement capability will produce compliance through the mechanism of deterrence. . . . In each of these three fields the traditional enforcement approach is under stress. There are too many violators, too many laws to be enforced, and not enough resources to get the job done.[1]

Later, in introducing the notion of problem solving more formally, I point out:

There is a certain foolishness in traditional enforcement approaches. They wait until the damage has been done, and then they react, case by case, incident by incident, failure by failure. Enforcement agencies accept the work *in the form and the order in which it arrives*, and, therefore, have tended to organize their activities around failures rather than around opportunities for intervention.[2]

The Deficiencies of Reactive Strategies

To encourage enforcement and regulatory agencies to turn away from their traditional reactive strategies, scholars and practitioners point to the following perceived deficiencies:

Wrong tools. Reactive strategies appear too enforcement oriented and therefore rely too heavily on the use of state authority. Helping people comply up front is less adversarial and more economical with respect to the use of authority and therefore ought, as a matter of policy, to be preferred.

Wrong unit of work. Processing the failures, one by one, does not encourage, nor leave time for, higher level thinking and analysis and therefore misses out on the opportunity to conceive systemic or lasting solutions.

Intervenes too late. By waiting until the offense has been committed or the harm done, reactive strategies fail to capitalize upon earlier opportunities for harm reduction.

Limited scope of operation. By focusing on the incidents that present themselves (accepting the work in the form and in the order in which it arrives), reactive strategies allow the scope of existing law to limit the scope of agency operations. Other concerns or issues, perhaps unregulated, might be equally important. Also, a preoccupation with incoming workloads fails to reveal problems not properly or adequately represented by the contents of the agency's in basket (for example, the Internal Revenue Service's nonfiler problem and a broad range of other "invisible" problems).

Emphasis on the wrong kind of results. Counting success in terms of enforcement statistics may produce an internal bias against solving problems. Enforcement statistics by themselves reveal nothing about an agency's achievements in solving problems and reducing harm.

Unsustainable strategy. Proliferation of regulations and of violations, coupled with static or diminishing regulatory resources and clogged justice systems, mean that punishment is by no means certain, swift, or serious. Faced with declining impact in the area of deterrence, the regulators' traditional lament, "All we need is more of what we do already," is an inadequate and impractical response to the accumulating pressures on regulatory systems.

The Hard-Soft Dilemma and Its Surrogates

What I did not realize in 1994 was how quickly and easily rejection of reactive *strategies* leads to the decimation of reactive *capabilities*. The flawed logic that connects the two goes like this:

> We recognize the limitations of a reactive strategy, with its too-late, incident-specific, heavy-handed enforcement orientation. We therefore *replace the reactive strategy with a preventive strategy*, moving resources from the back end to the front end, replacing investigators with educators and consultants to encourage and facilitate compliance. If prevention succeeds, we will need much less response and enforcement capacity, and we will be able to deemphasize those aspects of our work. This will come as an enormous relief given the thorny nature of enforcement, which does not sit well with our public commitment to customer service.

The reinvention movement has certainly signed onto this doctrine. David Osborne and Ted Gaebler include as one of their core reinvention themes, "Anticipatory government: prevention rather than cure."[3] The National Performance Review's prescription for reform of the Internal Revenue Service states, as an underlying assumption, that compliance efforts should be "moved upstream," because prevention is cheaper per case and imposes less burden on taxpayers; whereas enforcement is more expensive per case and more intrusive.[4]

In fact, regulatory life is not quite that simple. Even if prevention is cheaper per case, preventive methods may involve a thousand times as many cases as those that would otherwise end up in enforcement. On the question of enforcement being more intrusive, scholars point out that the opposite is generally true, because preventive and proactive strategies involve engagement before any precipitating event has occurred. A desire to minimize intrusiveness normally pushes back the other way: "This reactive approach has some important advantages. It ensures that [regulators] do not intrude too deeply into social life, and that when they do intrude, there is an important reason for it."[5] The reinvention movement has certainly played a part in shaking regulators loose from their traditional, purely reactive, approaches. But as time progresses, and as the search for genuinely effective regulatory techniques matures, the regulatory field has to move beyond the simple idea that one simply switches everything from reaction to prevention.

The majority of the regulatory innovations described in chapter 6 belie that idea, for they do not fit the pure prevention mold, and many of them include enforcement as a key part of their strategy. The Boston gun project was aimed at youth homicide prevention, but the project's Operation Ceasefire strategy employed many tools, ranging from vigorous after-the-crime enforcement to carefully crafted outreach and communication. It might be more accurate to say that the goal was youth homicide reduction and that the reduction strategy employed both reactive and preventive tactics.

Another reason for making sure regulatory policy transcends these simplistic and misleading dichotomies—hard versus soft, reaction versus prevention, enforcement versus compliance—is the practical damage that those dichotomies have wrought over the last ten years. These dichotomies split agencies in two, rendering them dysfunctional. This is how it happens. Investigators and enforcement officers perceive the singular emphasis on prevention as a threat to their own role and status. They remain skeptical about the language and tools of voluntary compliance, mindful of the bad actors with whom they deal. Squander the enforcement capacity, they say, and lawbreaking will run rampant. Besides, however good the prevention programs, accidents will still happen, people will still cheat, industries will still pollute—because it is in their own short-term economic or selfish interests to do so. Human nature will not be transformed. Therefore it is as foolish to invest everything in prevention or up-front education as it is to invest everything in enforcement. Realizing that, executives resolve to do *some of each*. There follows a bitter and destructive internal battle, manifesting as an ideological conflict. Staff join either the "hard equals reactive equals enforcement" camp or the "soft equals preventive equals voluntary compliance" camp, depending on their functional loyalties. The different functions fight for resources, attention, and status.

Comparatively few agencies have so far found their way out of this uncomfortable predicament. Those whose reforms do progress pass this point discover that the internal battle is actually a battle over tools, not ideologies, nor goals. Both camps can eventually be persuaded that their common goal is broad compliance; the remaining argument is about the comparative effectiveness of different tools.

A clear focus on the task of risk reduction, problem solving, or compliance management provides the escape route from these destructive tensions. The risk reduction mindset dismisses the inward-looking focus on tools and replaces it with an outward-looking focus on important risks. By picking important problems and organizing resources around each one, these strategies demand that the complete range of tools be available and considered with respect to each problem. The objective is to fashion an intervention that works, preferably for good, without any a priori preference over tools, style, or time of intervention. In designing a solution for a particular problem, enforcement tools should always be available but should never be assumed to be the most effective or the most resource efficient. Problem solving, recognizing the scarcity of the enforcement resource, will use enforcement surgically, incisively, and in the context of coherent control strategies.

Risk Reduction in Other Fields

A genuine regulatory craftsmanship quiets the functional, tool-centered arguments, replacing the tool orientation with a task orientation and bringing forward a more sophisticated understanding of when and how certain tools work best and in what combinations. What that means with respect to a choice between reactive and preventive methods we can learn from some other fields.

One risk-reduction discipline of growing significance calls itself the injury prevention field. Even though the name explicitly emphasizes prevention, the field's experts choose a mission statement that immediately broadens the scope to emphasize reduction and to encompass a range of opportunities to achieve that reduction: they define their mission as "the prevention, amelioration, and treatment of injury and the reduction of injury-related disability and death."[6] They use the term *prevention* to refer to efforts to "reduce the risk or severity of injury."[7] The importance of the injury prevention field stems in part from the fact that it merges complementary perspectives from medicine, public health, engineering, and criminal justice; in part, from the fact that unintentional injuries are the leading cause of death for Americans in the age range of one through thirty-four years old (at age thirty-five, HIV takes over as the leading cause; then malignancies for ages forty-five through sixty-four; heart disease for those aged sixty-five and over).[8]

Given that the injury prevention field covers every conceivable kind of injury, its analysts immediately face the problem of deciding how to break this huge subject down into manageable parts. They could classify causes of injury, or victims, or injuries, or places, or circumstances. One obvious way is to use the chronology of an injury event and split it into temporal phases. Noting how prior work identified injuries as resulting from uncontrolled release of one of five kinds of energy—kinetic, chemical, thermal, electrical, and radiation—the Committee on Injury Prevention and Control (in the Institute of Medicine) specifies the chronological split thus:

> From a preventive or ameliorative standpoint, interventions can be made during three temporal phases in relation to an injury event: (1) a pre-event phase, during which the energy becomes uncontrolled; (2) a brief event phase during which the uncontrolled energy is transferred to the individual, resulting in injury if the energy transfer exceeds the tolerance of the body to absorb it; and (3) a post-event phase, during which attempts can be made to restore homeostasis and repair the damage.[9]

The chronological split is useful precisely because differing sets of ameliorative tools and techniques are relevant to each phase. Using road accidents as an example, phase 1 interventions include junction redesign, driver education, and vehicle engineering relevant to maintaining control; phase 2 covers the brief period surrounding a crash and brings such remedies as safety belts, air bags, roll bars, safety cages, and energy absorbing crumple zones; and phase 3 relates to emergency medical response and subsequent treatment of trauma. The field of injury prevention, despite its name, embraces all these intervention opportunities and all their relevant technologies.

Where prevention ends and response begins is not always clear. Smoke alarms are normally counted a part of fire prevention, although they are clearly supposed to achieve injury and death prevention through early fire detection. In seeking to reduce fire-related casualties, policymakers look across all stages of a fire event and hope to identify several efficient opportunities to achieve significant risk reductions. Those opportunities might not all be concentrated at the earliest stage. Smoke alarms, despite their activation relatively late in the history of a fire event, are a cheap and effective way of reducing harm. Smoke alarm giveaway programs, focused on geographic areas suffering unusually high concentrations of residential fire-related injuries, appear to be quite successful in reducing fire-related injury rates. A giveaway program focused on South Central Oklahoma City—an area with lower median household incomes, lower property values, and poorer quality of housing than city averages—reduced injuries by as much as 80 percent over a four-year period.[10]

In the area of fire-related injuries, changing from prevention to early detection and response might result from having to focus on attainable, or feasible, objectives. As a 1974 treatise on risk management (written for the insurance industry) points out, goals such as no fires in a nursing home or no interruptions in power may not be attainable, whereas objectives refined to offer a realistic hope of achievement, such as no fires that remain undetected for more than two minutes or no interruptions in excess of two hours, might be attainable and present many more relevant technologies and techniques.[11] In making the objectives operable, the focus (in this case) tips away from pure prevention toward detection and containment.

In terms of semantics, it may be more helpful to emphasize *control* strategies, rather than reactive or preventive strategies. A strategy oriented around risk control or harm reduction would, like the injury prevention field, embrace interventions operating at any stage, provided they presented resource-efficient opportunities for gain. Getting the language right, though, is apparently not so easy. The Institute of Medicine's panel of experts on injury reduction eschewed use of the word *control*, finding it almost offensive:

> The committee can see no use for the term "control," borrowed from the vocabulary of infectious diseases, which has been deployed in the injury field to refer mainly to the idea of ameliorating the consequences of injury-causing events. Prevention and treatment . . . appear to express these ideas adequately, and adding the term "control" can only sow confusion because it implies a preference for coercive interventions.[12]

If the word *control* seems inappropriately coercive, perhaps *risk reduction strategy* or *harm reduction strategy* will do instead. Whatever we choose to call it, a control strategy leaves wide open the analytic questions of how to divide big risks, so they can be conquered. Chronology, with its arguments over prevention and reaction, may be one way of dividing them. Others may be equally useful, while causing less ideological division. The Injury Prevention Committee (appointed in 1997 and publishing its findings in 1999) decided eventually to divide interventions into four groups: interventions for changing individual behavior; interventions for modifying products or agents of injury; interventions for modifying the physical environment; and interventions for modifying the sociocultural and economic environment. In evaluating many possible interventions, the committee lists as factors to be considered feasibility; potential mortality and morbidity reduction; economic impact; ethical, social, and political considerations; and likely acceptance by the target population.[13]

Is Risk Eradication Possible?

Where possible, we might still prefer to eradicate risks once and for all. Those would be very special victories. Some risks, like some diseases, lend themselves to total eradication. Others never will.

In 1967 the World Health Organization launched an effort to eradicate smallpox throughout the world. The characteristics of smallpox that rendered it susceptible to eradication were these: victims become infectious only shortly before a distinctive rash becomes visible, making early detection possible; no animal carries the disease; and an effective, stable vaccine existed.[14] The ensuing eradication strategy relied heavily on mass vaccination campaigns. In 1980 the World Health Assembly declared eradication complete on the basis that no cases had been discovered for more than two years.[15]

Early Detection and Suppression

For many kinds of problems, early detection and effective suppression may present a more realistic harm control approach than prevention in its most absolute sense. The Pension Benefit Guaranty Corporation's system for identifying pension plans headed for insolvency (but long before they got past the point of rescue) could be regarded as an early detection and treatment model. Elsewhere I argue that early detection of emerging fraud problems, followed by rapid suppression using whatever means are available, represent the best hopes for effective fraud control strategy.[16]

Early detection forms the core of strategies to control outbreaks of infectious diseases, such as the Ebola virus. Since 1980 more than thirty new diseases have appeared, and a variety of familiar diseases (including pneumonia, malaria, and tuberculosis) have spawned variants resistant to antimicrobial drugs.[17] Disease control experts at the World Health Organization, the Centers for Disease Control, and the Institute of Medicine accept that ecological changes in the tropics will continue to cause viruses to spread to the human population from their normal hosts—often monkeys and rodents—and that global patterns of travel and commerce can now spread an outbreak far and wide before the pattern can be spotted and understood. Outbreaks, they assume, cannot be prevented. So attention shifts to the earliest feasible intervention opportunity—early detection and containment—and the construction of systems and protocols to support this control strategy. Hence the newly identified imperative, according to these experts, of developing global surveillance systems, with technology used to link together a broad range of health and disease databases around the world, so that emerging patterns representing new infectious agents can be spotted at the earliest possible moment.[18] In the absence of such surveillance systems, it took four months to confirm the 1995 Ebola outbreak in Kikwit, Zaire, and another four months to bring it under control—this despite the early evidence of hemorrhagic fever, which is a very rare symptom and would almost certainly have triggered the alarm if entered into a surveillance data system.[19] Fortunately, Kikwit is not a hub of international travel, and the outbreak was containable even after relatively late detection.

Many common diseases, also, are controlled through early screening and treatment rather than through outright prevention. In the terminology of public health, vaccination is *primary prevention*, screening is *secondary prevention*, treatment and mitigation of consequences is *tertiary prevention*. For early screening to work, a disease must have a recognizable early stage and there must be a reasonably cheap and effective way to diagnose it and an effective therapy once the condition is detected.[20] Even when diseases display these characteristics, choosing when and where to apply screening involves a complex calculus. Setting screening frequencies and defining appropriate target populations involves careful weighing of the costs involved (including the risk of false positives and the consequences of the broader intrusiveness of preventive medical practice) against the benefits of early discovery.

Within the disease control framework, the choice between prevention and early detection is far from straightforward, involving examination of the relative feasibility of different intervention methods, weighing the relative costs, and picking the most resource-efficient intervention points. On balance, we might prefer that diseases be prevented rather than treated, but for some diseases, the costs of prevention are high.[21] Preventive measures must be applied broadly, consuming time and attention as well as funds (especially if there is no effective way of targeting the preventive program on segments of the population most at risk). Vaccines or other preventive treatments may have their own side effects, which, while the probability is low, might cause significant harm when applied across millions of people.

John Graham, one of the leading proponents of the risk sciences, points out the cost disparity between different cancer control strategies. Prevention does not always come out ahead. Hillary Clinton's task force on health care reform proposed a health security package that included preventive screening every two to three years for breast and cervical cancer. According to Graham, the marginal cost per life year saved using such methods lies between $1,000 and $10,000. By contrast, Graham calculates the cost of a set of new Environmental Protection Agency regulations aimed at controlling benzene emissions (a known carcinogen) as between $200,000 and $50 million per life year saved.[22] Cancer prevention by reducing the emissions is much more costly to society than early detection and treatment. Of course, the public would prefer not to have tumors develop in the first place, but Graham says the fiftyfold increase in price (at minimum) might be grounds for preferring early detection and treatment over up-front prevention.

Such calculations, and the weighing of different control strategies, are clearly complicated. More important, they are also risk specific. The basic lesson from the field of disease control is that whether primary, secondary, or tertiary prevention offers the best hope for harm reduction depends on the properties of the disease in question and the nature of its distribution within the population. In her book examining the central question (in medicine), *Is Prevention Better than a Cure?*, Louise Russell comes to a perhaps unsurprising conclusion, which regulators will have no trouble translating to their own field:

Choosing investments in health is more difficult than some of the claims for prevention would suggest. Sometimes prevention buys more health for the money; sometimes cure does. And indeed, since the choice must usually include some of both, the issue most often is what mix of prevention and therapy is best. It is a rare preventive measure that, like smallpox vaccine, eradicates the condition altogether.[23]

Reinterpreting Reaction and Prevention in the Context of Risk Control

Most regulators understand the limitations of reactive strategies. Indeed, most regulatory agencies have already made significant investments in methods designed to avert or minimize the need for detection, reaction, and enforcement. Having diversified their tool kits, those agencies now seek some rational strategic framework to make sense of their broader repertoire and to help staff understand what each tool is good for and how to use tools in combination. The temptation regulators face now is to switch from a reactive strategy (whose failings we know) to a preventive strategy (whose failings we have only recently begun to discover). Both are limiting, because both emphasize one set of tools at the expense of the other.

The strategic focus that regulators need is risk control (or risk reduction). A control strategy embraces all the tools and considers each stage in the chronology of any harm as a potential intervention point. Thus a control strategy brings no ideological or a priori preference for preventive or reactive tactics. Rather, per the art of problem solving, a control strategy respects the individual characteristics of each problem; seeks to identify its precursors, vital components, and methods of contagion; and from that analysis, picks the right points and moments to intervene.

Proactive Strategies

Some confuse proactive with preventive strategies or even use the terms interchangeably. Both appear in the regulatory lexicon as antidotes to the failings of a reactive strategy. But I think they address different failings. The choice between reactive or preventive stances has to do with the chronology of a harm and choosing the right point to intervene. It relates (in the list of reactive failings at the start of this chapter) to wrong tools and intervention that is too late. The choice between reactive or proactive stances has to do with passivity and with taking the world as it presents itself rather than determining how it really is. It relates to the idea that purely reactive strategies focus on the incidents that present themselves and assume the contents of the agency's collective in-baskets to represent all the important problems.

According to Chamber's *Twentieth Century Dictionary*, to be *proactive* means to act "*forward* or *forth* or *publicly*." Risk control, done well, will require regulators to become consciously and deliberately proactive in a number of senses, as follows.

Identifying Invisible or Underrepresented Problems

Regulators need to extend their view. To identify all the important problems, they have to look beyond existing workloads to uncover those problems represented only partially or not at all. That means investing deliberately in mechanisms for searching out issues that might not otherwise come to light, or that might not come to light soon enough for effective intervention.

The crime control field uses the term *invisible offenses* to refer to crimes that do not reveal themselves or that have extremely low reporting rates. They include extortion, gambling, prostitution, drug dealing, date rape, fraud, many other forms of white-collar crime, and crimes within the family such as incest and sexual or physical abuse.

To obtain the broader view, regulatory agencies need to create, or pay more attention to, techniques and systems for making the invisible visible and for spotting emerging problems early, before much harm is done. Relevant tools and techniques include proactive intelligence gathering, establishing information networks with related agencies, creative and exploratory data mining (using both internal and external data sources and cross matches), focus groups, questionnaires, victimization surveys, and canvassing external stakeholders. It is also important to include a random component in any inspection or audit program to reveal the true scope and nature of different risks. Inclusion of a random component reveals problems unlikely to be revealed by targeted activities, because the targeting is done based upon what the agency already thinks are the main problem areas. (Further discussion of these proactive information gathering methods appears in chapter 18.)

Giving Voice

Regulators also need to adopt a proactive stance in terms of teasing out opinions and perspectives that might not normally be heard and by giving voice to groups or interests that might otherwise remain voiceless. When defining or addressing problems, persisting in a reactive passivity might incline regulators to pay too much attention to the noisiest stakeholders, who often have very clear opinions about what the problem is and how it ought to be solved.

Engaging Others in Analysis and Decisionmaking

Regulators also need to engage others quite deliberately during the analytic stages of problem solving or risk assessment. They need to present draft analyses and options outside the agency, engaging communities in weighing the pros and cons of each, and ferreting out potential contributors to a solution. Regulators should be able to gather and test ideas and perspectives from outsiders without offering them a veto or vote, without suffering the paralysis that results from trying to find unanimous consensus, and without negotiating away their capacity to take adverse actions against those they regulate.

CHAPTER FOURTEEN

Balanced versus Integrated Compliance Strategies

WHEN REGULATORY AGENCIES understand and accept the deficiencies of their traditional reactive strategies, they seldom progress immediately to a risk control strategy. Along the way, their strategic development passes through a number of distinct and recognizable stages.

First, there is the experimental, shaking loose stage, when executives begin a search for a broader range of compliance tools, experiment with different kinds of partnership, and begin to reject aggregate enforcement statistics as the principle indicator of agency performance. It does not take long to establish the value of some of the newer tools. For some types of problem, and for certain segments of the regulated community, they really do reach further and work better than traditional enforcement methods. The second stage involves learning through experience and then accepting, as a matter of agency policy, the value of a broader range of tools. At this stage, significant resources have been withdrawn from enforcement and reinvested in partnership programs, outreach, and facilitating voluntary compliance.

The third stage involves wrestling with the difficult strategic questions that then surface: Does the agency have an ideological preference for prevention over enforcement? Is deterrence still important? If so, how will it be defended under the rubric of customer service? Eventually, management recognizes and announces that the goal is to improve compliance and that all these tools usefully contribute toward that goal. At the end of this phase, agency executives embrace all the compliance tools, recognizing that a strategy aimed at improving compliance benefits from a broader and more comprehensive range of tactics.

This leaves executives facing the inevitable question: How much of each? Although it was clear to them during the shaking loose stage that resources had to be moved away from enforcement, now they begin to feel the pressure to specify a stable end state. They seek to *balance*, for the longer term, the agency's investments in different methods. They search for an optimal allocation that retains a credible deterrent, while garnering the public relations benefits and resource efficiencies of more cooperative methods. At the conclusion of this fourth stage, executives decide on the relative weights to be applied and specify resource allocation ratios across compliance tools. They have achieved what one might reasonably call a balanced compliance strategy.

When regulators reach this point they have accomplished much. They are well along the normal route that leads to development of an effective risk-control capacity. But they are not there yet. A balanced compliance strategy falls one step short of where we would like them to end up. Judging by the number of agencies that reach this point and yet fail to take the final step, this last remaining step—which would take them from a balanced strategy to an integrated strategy—represents a formidable challenge.

This chapter highlights the differences between a balanced compliance strategy and an integrated compliance strategy. My purpose is not to detract from the accomplishment of having come so far, nor to assume that agencies occupied with how much of each cannot see past that question or do not want to progress past it. My purpose, given the number of regulatory agencies that seem to have reached the balanced stage and stopped there, is to illuminate the remaining distance.

A Balanced Compliance Strategy

While a balanced compliance strategy specifies a mix of tools and resource allocations among them, it does not normally coordinate or integrate the work of the different tools, nor organize them around any specific risk. Once the overall activity levels have been specified—often within the context of budget preparation—each regulatory tool (function, or program) is then allowed to operate in isolation from the others and to find its own targets of opportunity. Thus the work remains organized around functional tools. Only the range of tools available and the resource allocations among them have changed.

Policymakers then search for the optimal mix. In some cases legislatures (having their own tool-based preferences) may endeavor to mandate a certain mix. For example, when the methods of the Occupational Health and Safety Administration were so much in the spotlight during 1995, Congress considered designating 50 percent of OSHA's annual appropriation for use in cooperative programs, which would have substantially cut into enforcement activities. Commentators, using OSHA as a case study to consider the relative merits of "punishment versus cooperation in regulatory enforcement," note that OSHA's experience "confirms the importance of both cooperation and appropriate punishment" and regretfully acknowledge that "the policy literature does not provide a basis for such a change [shifting 50 percent of resources into cooperative programs] because the optimal mix of cooperation and enforcement is unknown."[1] In other words, the relevant literature provides no satisfactory answer to the optimal mix question.

Does that mean that academia in general, and analysts of regulatory policy in particular, simply failed to give this question enough thought? Or is the question unanswerable? A number of scholars familiar with the challenges of regulation clearly think it can be answered. For example, an expert on fisheries compliance, in a report to the Australian Fisheries Management Authority, explicitly considers the "optimal mix of compliance services" and states that "the amounts and types of compliance services should be the mix which yields optimal compliance at least cost."[2] With resource efficiency factored in, the question takes on the form of a constrained optimization problem. The agency has a finite number of resources to distribute across a number of well-defined program areas, each one of which produces a certain marginal gain in compliance for each additional dollar spent. Resource allocation models based on this formulation would have to take into account interaction effects between programs (for example, partnership plans that work better because of a background level of enforcement). Nevertheless, the mathematical solutions to such problems are well understood.

Not only academics but also regulatory executives believe these optimization problems can and should be solved and that the models used to solve them should provide the basis for resource allocation across entire regulatory agencies. For example, the national director of compliance research at the Internal Revenue Service, in testimony to the (bipartisan) National Commission on Restructuring the IRS in January 1997, acknowledged that the "IRS is aware that it has not yet achieved an optimal allocation of its resources."[3] He also explained to the commission how the IRS hoped to calculate, and then implement, the standard mathematical solution to this constrained optimization problem. That solution involves allocating resources in such a way that marginal returns are equalized across all programs. Hence the IRS "should strive for equal marginal revenue-to-cost ratios in every activity at every location." He spelled out the practical details of how this would work for the IRS:

> This will involve dividing the universe of all potential work units into very narrowly-defined categories (including the type of activity, the size of the case, the district, etc.) such that each case in a given category has practically the same expected revenue-to-cost ratio, and each category can be worked independently of all others. The model will then allocate resources to these categories in descending revenue-to-cost order until all resources have been allocated.

But wait! What of all the IRS's recent experience in adopting and using a broader range of tools and inventing tailor-made solutions to specific noncompliance problems? How does all that innovation and learning get absorbed within such a technocratic model? Apparently, it gets sucked up quite easily—for the IRS's resource allocation model, like this:

> We established the NORA/DORA structure to look at groups of taxpayers and the causes of noncompliance in nontraditional ways, to help identify ways to foster improved compliance with less effort than through traditional enforcement mechanisms. Once such an "alternative strategy" is fully tested, we will incorporate it into the model to compete for resources on a marginal revenue-to-cost basis.

The fact that alternative strategies may have been designed for specific problem areas and may not work for others gets lost in this calculus. Once proven, a new tool simply gets added to the set of defined programs and then competes against all the others on the basis of marginal returns.

Once regulators frame the resource allocation issues in these terms, they can then use sophisticated technical methods to hone in on the "solution." The IRS recently enjoyed such help from an econometrician, who set out to provide "the first empirical basis for choosing the best combination of major IRS activities to improve voluntary filing and reporting compliance among individuals."[4] One can appreciate the complexity and sophistication of the requisite analysis. It requires up-front estimation of not only the *direct* marginal returns from each program activity but also the indirect marginal returns (when activities contribute to the agency's public image and affect broader compliance psychology). These indirect effects are notoriously hard to estimate. (Assessing the indirect compliance effects for the enforcement tool is the same problem as trying to measure the magnitude of the deterrent effect.)

After heroic technical effort, this analysis of IRS tools and programs turns up, among other things, the predictable finding that criminal investigation ranks at the bottom of the list in terms of its "marginal indirect revenue/cost ratio." The criminal conviction rate, according to the analysis, is less efficient by a factor of 3 than "audit starts" and less efficient by a factor exceeding 200 than the mailing of certain taxpayer deficiency investigation notices.[5] These findings accord with what one would expect: if regulators analyze choice of compliance methods on the basis of marginal returns, then they will end up chasing the easy targets and decimating the agency's capacity for the most serious (and costly) investigations.

Whatever the level of technical proficiency that attaches to such analyses, the overall approach seems intuitively flawed for a number of reasons. First, regulators should consider justice at least to some extent (even as they optimize effectiveness). Ignoring the harder targets just because pursuing them is more expensive does not seem fair. Second, many scholars of regulatory policy and compliance psychology point out the special significance of pursuing the toughest cases. If bad actors get away with their transgressions, trust in and respect for the system begins to collapse. Jon Sutinen, on fisheries:

> Even if the subgroup of chronic, flagrant violators is small and the amount of their illegal fishing is minor, they need to be controlled. Weak enforcement would allow chronic flagrant violators to flaunt violation of the law. Being seemingly immune to the regulations sends two signals to normally law-abiding fishermen. One is that regulatory procedures are unfair, having no effect on flagrant illegal fishing. The other is that the regulatory program is not

effectively managing the fishery (protecting the resource). Each of these signals weakens the moral obligation to comply and the moral basis on which social influence is exercised.[6]

These observations may poke some holes in the vogue technologies for optimal resource allocation. Greater technical wizardry, taking such observations and factors into account, might repair those holes. But I would prefer to demolish the entire framework, rather than just poke holes in it. And it is demolished, I think, by pointing out that none of the regulatory innovations described in chapter 6, nor any one of the delightfully effective and tailor-made solutions described elsewhere in these pages, would or could have resulted from the workings of an optimal resource allocation model. In virtually every case—the Customs Service's port-running problem, Operation Ceasefire, New York City's red light camera program, and so on—the solution that fixed the problem was not a mixture of things the agency did already. No amount of shuffling resources between well-defined program areas could ever have produced those results. What did produce those results? Focusing on the problems, not on the tools.

The IRS is by no means alone in having considered entrusting agency-wide resource allocation decisions to an econometric model. (I am pleased to say I am not aware of any major regulatory agency that actually operates under such a model.) During the early stages of OSHA's redesign program, one of the more technically minded of OSHA's senior executives proposed (and partially constructed) a computerized model that could calculate exactly how many enforcement actions, how many consultations, and how many of anything else each area office should perform. The model would be driven by accident and injury rates, broken down geographically and by industry sector. Regression analysis against historic agency activity rates would provide the parameters of the model, which would then prescribe activity mixes all across the country and across every industrial segment, optimizing the impact of OSHA resources upon injury and illness rates.

One might prefer efficient resource allocation to inefficient resource allocation. One might also welcome a greater technical sophistication among regulatory managers. Nevertheless, regulators should utterly reject these "big brain in the sky" models of regulatory management. They leave no room for human ingenuity and inventiveness. They create no obligation to solve specific problems. They render the life of field staff barren, failing to recognize any contribution staff might make other than playing the role of functional, productivity driven cogs in a vast model-driven machine. And they reduce the role of middle management to enforcing field-level compliance with the model's prescriptions.

Even the crudest notion of regulatory craftsmanship makes nonsense of such a picture. Consider what such analysis would look like if we applied it to a *craft*. Imagine that in the course of running a furniture maker's craft shop, we want to determine the optimal allocation of time among the following activities: drilling, sawing, planing, gluing, and using the lathe. We pick a sample of five leading craftspersons whose work is much in demand and who bring high prices. Five terrible ones, who produce junk, are also chosen. Data are collected for a year, recording how much time each of the ten furniture makers spends with each tool. The data are fed into a mathematical model that identifies the usage patterns that best account for the differences in performance. The most successful craftspeople use the lathe and the glue more, and the other tools less, than the unsuccessful ones. Subsequently, the craftshop management specifies levels for each activity to match the optimal balance, imagining that the products will fetch higher prices as a result. Time allocations and budgetary resources (in terms of supplies) are shifted away from drills, saws, and planes and toward lathes and glue.

Just as such analysis so obviously fails to capture the essence of the furniture makers' craftsmanship, so optimal resource allocation models will forever fail to produce regulatory craftsmanship. Which tools to use, as any craftsperson can attest, depends on what one is trying to do, on what one is working on, and on one's experience with similar tasks. Tool selection, within the context of a craft, is a field-level tactical decision, not a high-level strategic one. The right tool selection decisions arise from a combination of experience and a clear sense of what the carpenter is trying to accomplish. A clear focus on the task in hand makes perfectly plain those times when no suitable tool is available and a new one needs to be invented. (A task orientation produces relevant innovations.)

What is obvious in the context of craftsmanship also seems obvious to some of those who study a wide range of compliance problems. The wider the range of problems, the easier it is to recognize the foolishness of a generic optimal mix of regulatory instruments. Writing in 1997 about the vast range of new crime problems emerging in the field of computing and telecommunications, Peter Grabosky and Russell Smith

Table 14-1. Distinguishing Characteristics of Balanced and Integrated
Compliance Strategies

Characteristic	Balanced strategy	Integrated strategy
Strategy	—Identifies range of tools desirable —Decides overall resource allocation (balance) —Each functional tool finds its own targets	—Identifies important risks —Develops coordinated, multifunctional responses —Often invents new tools, techniques, solutions
Organization	—Work organized around tools	—Tools organized around work
Key phrases	—"Opportunities for use" —"Identify targets" —"Right mix of tools for the agency"	—"Identify problems" —"Invent solutions" —"Impact"/"effect" —"Mix of tools that work"
Organizational challenges	—Competing styles or orientations —On-site conflicts —Mixed signals to outside world	—Lateral coordination —Project-based approach —Dynamic resource allocation —Budgetary flexibility
Impacts or effects	—Functionally specific credit for direct effects of actions	—Shared credit for major accomplishments

considered which compliance instruments might be most important.
Their conclusion moves beyond the notion of finding an optimal mix, to
the appropriately differentiated response, It depends: "The varied nature
of telecommunications-related illegality defies a single policy solution.
Indeed, each of the basic forms of illegality . . . is sufficiently complex
that if a solution exists at all, it is likely to entail a combination of
instruments."[7] Table 14-1 lays out the core differences between a balanced approach (which many regulatory agencies have now achieved)
and the integrated approach necessary to support the types of risk control or problem-solving capacity upon which the last several chapters
have dwelt.

An integrated compliance strategy (problem-solving approach)
organizes the tools around the work, rather than vice versa. It identifies
important risks and then it develops coordinated, multifunctional

responses. Often it invents new tools, techniques, or solutions tailor made for the problem in hand. Almost every problem-solving success story reveals this: effective solutions to identified risks involve either artfully crafted, properly coordinated combinations of actions or the design of something new. Such solutions could never be created by moving resources between existing functions or programs and allowing them to operate in isolation.

My friend Mike Phillips, who has acted as point man for much of the Florida Department of Environmental Protection's strategic reform over the past four years, delivered a presentation on his agency's environmental problem-solving program at an international conference early in 1999. Surrounded by regulatory managers at the close of his presentation, he was asked by several of them what mix of compliance tools his agency had chosen and could he help them determine the right mix for their agencies. Describing his frustration to me later, he said, "Why, when I've been talking about problem solving for an hour, do people ask *that question*? Weren't they listening?"

Regulatory executives continue to ask that question for two reasons. First, if their human and other resources are insufficiently fungible, their budgetary planning processes may require them to make advance allocations of resources, even before they know what problems they will be working on. As a consequence of this, executives pursuing a greater problem-solving capacity need to pursue more fungible funding sources. They should also attempt as far as possible to attach funds and resources to risk areas rather than to functional areas. They might also explore the greater flexibilities that result from contracting out certain regulatory functions. Mostly, they need to use every device available to increase the versatility and internal mobility of existing resources.

Second, they ask *that question* because that is where they are—still trying to establish the right aggregate balance. Why the apparent reluctance or inability to contemplate the last step from there? I think, because it is a huge step. In fact this last step seems to be the most difficult of them all. Why? Because executives of any agency that had managed to build an integrated approach and had operated it would be able to provide an account of this work in the following terms: they could show their inventory of specific risks or problems identified as worthy of attention; they could describe the bases upon which the agency chose them from the list of possibilities; they could state unambiguously which problems have been selected and who was responsible for working on them; and, for each such project under way, they could provide a record of the work done so far.

In other words, regulators that choose to operate the integrated compliance strategy must first grapple with the subtle and complex art of problem solving (as laid out in chapters 9 and 10) and to construct the institutional apparatus necessary to support and direct it (as laid out in chapter 11). Well, that's a lot! Most agencies have not. Hence their best hope, for now, is to settle for some sense of overall balance.

The Continuing Search for Results that Count

Despite its limitations, the balanced compliance strategy is a substantial advance over traditional, enforcement-centered, reactive strategies. Many useful lessons have been learned along the way, many new tools embraced, and the balanced agency is now poised to understand and address the formidable challenges of institutionalizing a risk or problem orientation. The one factor most likely to reveal the shortcomings of the balanced approach and most likely to create the incentive for an agency to take the remaining step is the balanced agency's continuing inability to demonstrate effectiveness in the terms to which it aspires. For the distinction between balanced and integrated strategies has profound consequences for the kinds of performance account an agency can give.

The balanced approach, preserving a functional orientation, offers *functionally specific* credit for the direct impacts of *functionally specific* actions. It does not provide the opportunity for the agency to claim it addressed and successfully tackled major risks, because the work is neither conceived nor organized that way. By contrast, an integrated compliance or problem-solving strategy directly tackles identified risks and permits the agency to demonstrate elimination or mitigation of those risks as accomplishments. When an agency adopts a balanced approach but stops short of developing the coordinating mechanisms and organizational structures necessary to support an integrated approach, staff will likely remain frustrated—as will overseers and stakeholders. The agency's work will remain organized around individual functions or programs, with the functions and programs acting largely in isolation. Nobody inside nor outside the agency will be able to match these isolated functional activities to any important outcomes.

PART III

The Elusive Art of Risk Control

CHAPTER FIFTEEN

Centrality of the
Risk Control Challenge

IN SEPTEMBER 1998, at the Florida Department of Environmental Protection's annual Compliance Conference, I participated in a session to review and assess the status of the department's environmental problem-solving program. In the room for that discussion, among others, were the majority of the department's internal problem-solving consultants, a group of young, energetic, and analytically minded staff from across the agency who had taken on the responsibility for promoting and facilitating environmental problem solving within their respective divisions and districts. Most of them had volunteered for that role more than a year earlier and had been given some training in the relevant methods.

The session was somewhat depressing. After reviewing a small number of projects (most of them incomplete, and several having apparently ground to a halt) the subject quickly turned to, Why isn't it happening? After all, the agency's senior management were committed to problem solving; seminars on problem solving had been conducted throughout the agency to give every staff member the opportunity to understand what it was and how it fit into the agency's operations; middle management had been educated regarding their role with respect to problem-solving projects; and assistance with project management and facilitation of team meetings was available to anyone who asked. Nevertheless, promoting and sustaining problem solving, the consultants felt, was like "pushing a boulder uphill." Why was it not easier, and why was more of it not happening?

The Obstacles to Problem Solving

A list was compiled of the major organizational impediments that had surfaced during the first fifteen months or so after the official launch of environmental problem solving. It was an impressive list and surprisingly easy to generate—sufficiently impressive, in fact, that several participants suggested that problem solving was not just difficult, but outright impossible! Here are their top ten reasons (as I noted them down) why problem solving seems impossibly difficult within a major regulatory agency:

— It is viewed as extra. Everyone is already busy with more structured, manageable tasks, all of which have deadlines and therefore take precedence.

— The required analytic support (data analysis and help with statistical work) is not available.

— Problem solving has no formal budgetary support or legislative mandate. Everything else the department does has both.

— Real-world problems come in awkward shapes and sizes, which do not fit established groups or units. Dealing with them properly requires coordination and commitment across units and agencies. Establishing those commitments, the consultants claimed, is "like pulling teeth."

— Management fails to understand or support it. "We are left to push from down here. It should not be up to us."

— Problem solving brings an unfamiliar degree of discretion and uncertain degrees of authorization. Teams are not sure what they are allowed to propose and whether they can commit agency resources through their action plans. The persistent uncertainty brings projects to a standstill.

— Staff are not clear whether problem solving is really new. Many staff think it is not. Several managers declared that it is not. If it is not new, why should anyone worry about it? But if it is new and important, then it demands attention, recognition, and dedicated resources. But problem solving will never get the commitment it requires if the majority of staff are not sure whether it is *different* from what they already do.

— Project teams are generally incapable of sticking to the imposed rigor of the approach. They do not understand why each different stage is necessary. "That puts enormous pressure on us [the facilitators], if we are the only ones interested in doing it right."

— Engaging external parties (representatives of regulated industries and interest groups) without offering them a veto or vote over the action plan strikes participants as awkward. These terms of engagement are unfamiliar to all the participants.

— Problem-solving is regarded by many as an alternative to enforcement and is consequently written off as "one of the fashionable new soft options being pushed by senior management as they sell out to political pressures."

That was the day I decided to write this book, because that was the day the irony of the situation struck me. Why create environmental agencies? Presumably in the hope that they can identify significant environmental issues and act upon them in such a way as to make a difference. If they cannot do that, then we would not want them. And here was an attempt, in a major environmental agency (the largest state-level agency, with over 4,000 employees), to do precisely that—to identify important environmental problems and fix them—with a minimal semblance of order. After more than a year of pushing and pulling in every conceivable way, what did the agency have to show for it? Ten rather compelling reasons why problem solving could not work!

Anyone else who has tried to implement an operational risk control strategy, particularly in a large organization, has most likely developed the same deep respect for the nature of this challenge that I now have. Risk control is obviously central to much of what the public expects from government; yet despite its pervasive relevance, risk control presents a formidable collection of intellectual and practical challenges, which remain unresolved. The environmental problem-solving consultants in Florida's Department of Environmental Protection are by no means alone in experiencing problem solving as elusive and troublesome. A 1996 study of problem-oriented policing in England and Wales examined over two decades of experimentation with the concept, spanning many police forces. Police officers gave an overlapping, but not identical, list of reasons in accounting for the general failure of problem-oriented policing to "take off." [1]

— There is no time for it. Police in Britain are already overstretched.

— There is nothing new about it. Problem-oriented policing is just a fancy way of describing what is delivered routinely anyway.

— Problem-oriented policing is impossible. Real issues are so complex and deep rooted that piecemeal problem-solving efforts cannot succeed.

— The police's job is to respond to incidents. It is up to others to solve problems.

— Policing in Britain is about crime and detection. Addressing other problems is for other agencies.

— British police culture is so deep rooted and wrapped up in crime detection that there can be no serious prospect of implementing problem solving.

— Objectives are set nationally, which leaves little room for the concerns of individual communities.

— Management structures are not well adapted to the bottom-up approach that characterizes problem-oriented policing.

With these beliefs widespread throughout police ranks, it comes as no surprise that problem-oriented policing had not taken off. The same review notes that most problem-solving initiatives had so far been relatively small scale and had affected only a small number of dedicated officers.[2] The review also notes the absence of appropriate managerial systems for problem identification and project monitoring: "In particular, none of the past POP [problem-oriented policing] initiatives in England and Wales has adopted a formal and systematic model linking incident identification and analysis with the construction of responses and subsequent assessment of the actions taken."[3]

Herman Goldstein, commenting on the American police experience, also observes that highly localized responses have frequently been effective, yet police departments lack a higher-level vision or structure for implementing the strategy: "Too often, these commendable efforts [of individual police officers] are peripheral to everything else they do; sporadic; improvised; lacking in official support; and achieved *despite* the formal requirements of the bureaucracy."[4] In other words, a problem orientation seems to work fine in practice, provided it does not call for resources, management involvement, or a significant amount of staff time.

Constructing the proper supporting infrastructure would help overcome many of these obstacles: creating room, allocating personnel and resources, tracking progress, and specifying the nature and frequency of managerial attention. Yet the difficulties seem to run deeper than the absence of systems, to an absence of understanding. Surely, if executives knew what they needed to create to sustain an effective risk control operation, they would do it. Many of them seem committed enough to the underlying premise. Perhaps they do not truly grasp the concept. Perhaps the intellectual task of defining the art, and communicating it to practitioners, remains unfinished.

I am convinced now that the concept itself—not just the practice—remains elusive. In fact, so poorly is the concept generally understood that many do not even recognize it when they see it. When practitioners—and academics, and even awards committees—see artfully constructed and creative solutions that have been devised in response to specific, well-identified, problems, they celebrate them. And so they should. But too often they celebrate the wrong things. They celebrate the *solutions*, when the real value lies in the method used to reach the solution. After all, the particular solution may have no relevance beyond the specific problem. Yet the method used to reach it—provided we can distill the essence of it—may have relevance for a much broader class of issues.

Replication

Nowhere is the failure to grasp the concept more evident than in the way officials approach the business of replication. Consider the following examples.

Customs Service: Port-Running Project

By mid-1995 the Customs Service project on port running began to show signs of success. The indicators were all moving in the right direction. The number of port-running incidents had declined; the number of "returns to Mexico" had peaked and then fallen off; and the price being paid by the drug smuggling organizations to drivers to run a load had risen sharply. One senior customs executive familiar with the project suggested that the agency had enjoyed such success, in this case, with a biregional, multifunctional, and multiport team that the agency should create teams like that all around the country. I asked if he was aware of any other problems of that particular size and shape (biregional, multifunctional, and multiport, but smaller than national). He said he was not aware of them but was confident that the agency could find them if they looked for them.

Occupational Health and Safety Administration:
Maine 200 Program

On May 16, 1995, President Bill Clinton, accompanied by Vice President Al Gore and Secretary of Labor Robert Reich, publicly celebrated the Maine 200 program at an event in Washington, D.C. They each heralded the program as an example of commonsense regulation. President Clinton, in the course of his remarks, announced that the Maine 200 program would be replicated across the nation: in his words, "as goes Maine, so goes the nation."[5] Within two months a one-page memo (unsigned and undated) was issued from OSHA headquarters to all the regional and area offices throughout the country, detailing the method for "expanding the Maine concept." The memo specified the data to be used and the analysis to be performed on it. It laid out the choice that should be offered to employers identified through the analysis—exactly the same choice that had been offered in Maine—and laid out the procedure to be followed, depending on which path employers chose.[6]

Risk-Control as a Strategic Innovation

Both of these cases (and countless similar examples in other fields) show how readily officials fail to grasp the heart of this concept. In the customs example, the executive in question genuinely appreciated the way that collaborative work on the port-running project team had brought staff from different functions together, and he wanted to see more of that. That piece is perfectly reasonable. But he also wanted to reproduce, elsewhere, the peculiar size and composition of that project team. In other words, he was attracted to the *administrative* innovation and wanted to replicate that.

In the OSHA case, the memo directed faithful replication of the *programmatic* innovation used in Maine. In Maine, the efficiency of the program rested on the fact that a mere 200 companies accounted, among them, for more than half of the state's workdays lost to injury and illness. This particular form of analysis, applied to data for the state of Maine, found a specific, and very useful, *risk concentration*. Addressing this risk concentration through employers would be efficient precisely because OSHA could influence over half the days lost in Maine by working with only 200 of them. Unfortunately, the same analysis applied in states such as Texas and California yielded lists of several thousand companies—far too many to handle in the same kind of partnership arrangements as in Maine. In other words, the same risk concentration did not exist elsewhere, and so the same program would not work elsewhere. The complaints, "That wouldn't work here," heard from around the country, were in many regards justified.

When the memo was sent out, Assistant Secretary Joe Dear began receiving vociferous objections from his own redesign team and from the area office problem-solving teams. The newly formed problem-solving teams complained that replicating the Maine 200 program contravened the spirit of local problem solving and would consume all their time. Joe Dear withdrew the memo as soon as he heard about it (it had been issued without his knowledge, by someone just doing what the president said). Subsequently, the senior management team met with the redesign team to work out what the core elements of the Maine 200 program were and how they should be replicated. They all liked the fact that the program was data driven and results oriented, and that partnerships had been used to leverage scarce public resources. But almost any greater level of detail would potentially run afoul of local particularities. As OSHA considered the Maine 200 program, the question, What exactly is this thing? turned out to be difficult to answer. What was the innovation? What should they celebrate? And which pieces of it should they replicate?

In reforming regulatory practice, executives should focus if at all possible on a *strategic* innovation, that is, a whole new way of thinking about the work of regulatory agencies and the value those agencies can produce.[7] When the nature of the strategic innovation is not grasped, one is limited to celebrating the particular administrative or programmatic innovations that risk control produces. Once regulators grasp the strategic innovation, they concern themselves more with innovativeness than with particular innovations, and they will want to devise the organizational apparatus necessary to generate innovations, wherever they are needed, as a matter of routine operations.

Vocabulary

Part of the problem with grasping the core of the concept, and with communicating it, is finding the right language to describe it. Upon the advice of colleagues, I have avoided settling on any particular vocabulary and use a number of terms almost interchangeably to describe this strategic innovation: risk control, problem solving, and compliance management. Each of these terms has its drawbacks, and none of them adequately conveys the complexity of the business.

The term *compliance management* leaves room for the identification of patterns, selection of the important ones, and design of tailor-made strategies to increase compliance. But it suffers the obvious deficiency of limiting attention to patterns of behavior that are regulated, when many other kinds of behavior count too. *Problem solving* sounds commonplace. And, as Goldstein's writings make plain, it would be a mistake to confuse a problem solving procedure with a problem-oriented strategy.

The term *risk control* (at least until recently) has belonged more to the fields of finance and insurance than social regulation. *Risk management* may overcome the objections of anyone who finds *control* unnecessarily coercive, but *risk management* sounds even more particular to the domain of finance, where the business of portfolio management juggles risk and return. One expert on risk control (writing in the context of the overseas operations of American corporations), expresses his preference for the term *risk control* over the term *risk management* on the basis that "man *manages* only man," and so the word *management* should not be used for risks.[8] Besides, he says, director of risk control sounds a loftier and more weighty title than risk manager.

My colleague Bill Hogan (an expert on economic regulation) tells me that the word *problem* is much broader than the word *risk*—*risk,* within the realm of regulation, refers mostly to health and the environment. Others tell me that *risk* is broader, because *problem* sounds local and petty. If the word *risk* is used as the generic descriptor for those bad things that regulators seek to suppress, then the control process will involve risk analysis, which unfortunately smacks of technocracy rather than democracy and of research rather than operations.

Other fields have their own language for similar strategic concepts, such as *disease control* (public health), or *threat assessment* (military and intelligence). But none of these vocabularies translates particularly well into other domains, and many carry with them assumptions about the forms of analysis that should be done, the dimensions in which threats should be defined, or the range of tactics available.

The challenge in trying to describe the strategy is to hold fast to the core ingredients (identification, selection, definition, measurement, intervention, monitoring, and reporting); to orient the portfolio of projects around the core mission of the agency; to sweep away, and keep on sweeping away, assumptions about the right way to define or subdivide problems, the forms of analysis that count, the right times to intervene, or the methods that might work.

Given the awkwardness of these semantic choices, I often wonder whether anything of substance lies at the core. If it is so hard to describe, maybe it is a mere apparition. And then, occasionally, and in the most unusual places, I find comments that suggest that others too are seeking to capture and codify the same ideas. I am impressed, for example, by J. B. R. Matthews's study of risk management in the operation of dental clinics, in which he lays out a formal risk management cycle and then describes risk management as a professional skill, acquisition of which might take many years of study and experience.[9]

Another example is much closer to the issues of regulatory practice. The Office of Pipeline Safety in Washington, D.C., according to Associate Administrator Richard Felder, seeks to "transform the fundamental relationship between the regulator and the operating companies it regulates." From a tradition in which regulations state all the problems to be addressed and largely specify the solutions, the Office of Pipeline Safety intends to use risk management as an "alternative basis for operations and for relationships with the regulated community." The office has been exploring the idea under a demonstration program approved by Congress in 1996. According to Felder, "Simply put, we believe that risk management can provide us a structured way of being flexible."[10]

The notion of "a structured way of being flexible" resonates with the quandary in which many regulators find themselves, having explored a much broader range of tools over the last few years. They have learned how to be flexible; but what they have lacked to date was any structured way of being flexible. Felder's description of this risk management program shows clearly that the Office of Pipeline Safety has learned the limitations of purely technical analysis. It has also recognized the need to create supporting organizational infrastructure:

> Risk management is much more than the technical models used to calculate probabilities and consequences. To be useful as an alternative regulatory approach, risk management must be an integrated program of activities institutionalized into the way that the company conducts its business on a day-to-day basis.[11]

The U.S. Coast Guard also, within the context of a pilot project under the Government Performance and Results Act, has discovered the usefulness of risk management as an orienting framework. Commander

Rick Kowalewski (describing the early experience of the Coast Guard's Office of Marine Safety, Security and Environmental Protection under the pilot program) states bluntly, "Our business is risk management."[12] The Coast Guard's experience with a risk control orientation apparently mirrors the Office of Pipeline Safety's: risk management provides an alternative basis for operations and for relationships with the regulated community. With respect to operations, Kowalewski equates risk reductions with outcomes, and reports:

> Outcomes . . . commonly cut across organizational lines. A variety of programs will influence the outcomes in areas like safety and environmental protection . . . and this fact tends to blur traditional organizational boundaries. Maybe more significantly, the search for outcome-oriented goals is a process of examining the very basis for existence of your programs.[13]

Echoing Felder's point about the relationship with the regulated community, he says:

> We have several new partnerships with our stakeholders in the maritime industry. In our experience, conflicts commonly arise over activities, such as the scope and frequency of inspections, or specific corrective actions. Outcomes [risk reduction objectives], on the other hand, give us common ground in things we all care about, and it has been helpful in general to be able to agree first on the scope and magnitude of the problem before addressing solutions.[14]

Reductionism and the Battle of Ideas

Leaving aside these bright points, consider for a moment the myriad ways in which these subtle ideas more normally get reduced. They get reduced whenever practitioners focus on a solution rather than the orientation that generated it; or when replication focuses on tactical prescriptions invented elsewhere, in unlike circumstances; or when problem identification relies on only one data source; or when particular forms of analysis dominate and preclude others; or when problems are always defined in shapes and sizes that fit existing units or functions; or when traditional measures of success are thoughtlessly applied to nontraditional forms of work.

Many police officers are baffled by the crime reduction accomplishments of the New York City Police Department. They ask us (academics) whether Compstat (computer comparison statistics) is the same as problem solving? I say no, it is not. Compstat is particular in four ways: it focuses only on reported crime, not on other types of problems; the analysis slices the reported crime data geographically, specifically, by precinct; it uses the existing precinct structure (notably, precinct commanders) as the system for allocating responsibility; and it focuses heavily on the tactics of aggressive order maintenance as a method for establishing police control over streets and public places. None of that is intended as criticism. The point is, the Compstat system is *quite particular* in many ways in which a problem-solving strategy is *quite general.*

Particular, also, was the city of Minneapolis's Repeat Call Address Policing Unit (RECAP) program in focusing on repeat-call addresses. Particular, also, are the forms of analysis conducted by the Consumer Product Safety Commission (focusing on products) and the methods it uses to interact with manufacturers. Particular, also, are the risk assessment models used by the Pension Benefit Guaranty Corporation to rank order pension plans. In each case, the operation of these particular systems may well reflect a risk orientation, and the systems and methods implemented might be regarded as products or manifestations of a risk control strategy. But they are not the same thing as the strategy itself; the strategy itself is highly dynamic and avoids getting locked in to any such particularities.

Some might see this argument as unreasonable. What use is an idea without a practical implementation? And if we are to have practical implementations, then do not such particular choices have to be made? Just because somebody made those choices, does that make the underlying strategy any less valuable? For sure, such choices do have to be made. Perhaps the architects of Compstat or of RECAP considered a broader range of analytic, structural, or tactical systems; and perhaps they made these specific design choices consciously and pragmatically, to exploit existing structures, focus on feasible projects, and use readily available statistics and indicators. But when folk ask, as they so often do, whether this one particular system is the same thing as problem solving, or as a risk control strategy, I still have to answer no. And I will continue to answer that way, because I want regulators to keep their minds open to a much broader range of possibilities. They must also learn that any pragmatic choices they make, given the dynamic nature of the business, may not be relevant for long and may not be relevant for other important problems.

I have heard champions of ecosystem management confidently proclaim that ecosystem management *is* problem solving, presumably in an effort to subsume an emerging focus on problem solving within their established domain. No, these are not the same thing. Ecosystem management could certainly use the *procedures* of problem solving as it addresses ecosystem-shaped problems. Ecosystem management may share, as part of its philosophical underpinnings, the same results orientation and appreciation for cooperative action that problem solving also embraces. But if environmental practitioners imagine that the two are the same, they may make the mistake of assuming that the structures created to deal with ecosystem issues (committees formed around watershed areas) can properly deal with problems of all shapes and sizes. Trying to force, through the ecosystem management system, problems that do not coincide with specific watershed areas (for example, the problem of pesticide-induced arsenic concentrations on golf courses, or threats to manatees from speeding boats, or radon in homes, or asbestos in schools) will produce predictable inefficiencies and probable confusion. One of the basic lessons of a problem-oriented strategy is this: *organize the resources around the problem* and avoid the temptation to force the problem into machinery created for another purpose. When anyone says that the problems must be defined *this way*, they are usually trying to extend their own turf or elevate the status of systems they already operate. In so doing, they substantially diminish the strategy.

In the field of crime control, contention over the right way to accomplish crime reduction goals has been more visible and explicit than in many other areas of regulation. Many crime control choices, which a mature risk control approach would treat as tactical and risk specific, emerge instead as a priori ideological preferences. Politics gets involved. Liberals traditionally favor intervention through social controls early in the lives of potential offenders. Conservatives favor the "get tough on crime" rhetoric, which acts after the fact with "three strikes and you're out" and similar punitive measures. The operational reality is that most opportunities for effective crime control interventions lie between these extremes, somewhere in the infinitely textured domains where offenders, victims, and opportunities for crime come into close proximity.

Among practitioners and academics, alternative problem definitions are often presented as *beliefs*. For example, in considering the choice of goals for an organized crime strike force, one commentator writes:

> What is the Strike Force supposed to accomplish? Its goals are often taken to be entirely criminal-justice related: the conviction and incarceration of members of organized crime groups. However, this is a narrow interpretation of a Strike Force's mandate. A Strike Force's goal should be viewed more broadly as an effort to reduce the harm to the American public caused by organized crime. Note that reference is not made to reducing crime, but to reducing the harm caused by crime.[15]

That's a perfectly plausible way to define the goal. But so is "reducing crime," or "controlling corruption," or "shutting down the operations of more than half the organized crime groups within ten years," or "taking the profits out of organized crime." Each conception of the goal suggests different forms of analysis, different intervention opportunities, and different tactics. Of course such choices must be made, but they should be managerial and operational choices, rather than matters of doctrine.

Baltimore County Police's Citizen-Oriented Policing Enforcement (COPE) unit shifted its emphasis from a solitary focus on crime toward a focus on "fear of crime" and the debilitating effects of that fear on community life. The instruction to focus on fear, given by Chief Neil Behan, sprang not from his personal beliefs or preferences but from his continuing observation that fear of crime, even when detached from crime itself, brought its own serious consequences. Behan's decision, in establishing COPE and focusing it (at first) on fear, was an operational and managerial one. He simply spotted, and carefully defined, an important problem that traditional police methods had failed to address.

In the broader literature of criminology, crime prevention, and crime control (all of which are different), Goldstein's "problem-oriented policing" philosophy has had to compete with other ideas. Proponents of situational crime prevention, for example, claim that they already have all of this problem-solving business covered. For example, consider the definition of situational crime prevention given by one of its leading proponents, Ron Clarke:

> Situational crime prevention . . . refers to a pre-emptive approach that relies, not on improving society or its institutions, but simply

on reducing the opportunities for crime. . . . Situational crime prevention comprises opportunity-reducing measures that are (1) directed at highly specific forms of crime, (2) that involve the management, design or manipulation of the immediate environment in as specific and permanent a way as possible (3) so as to increase the effort and risks of crime and reduce the rewards as perceived by a wide range of offenders.[16]

This seems reasonably broad, although the definition hints strongly at a preference for intervention through environmental design. (The American equivalent has been called "crime prevention through environmental design.")

Clarke has produced sixteen specific techniques of situational prevention. Which idea is bigger: problem-oriented policing or situational crime prevention? Does it matter? I think it does matter, because if the theorists cannot sort these things out, then practitioners are even less likely to listen to anything the theorists have to say. According to Clarke, situational crime prevention is bigger:

Goldstein recognized the need for evaluation, and his formulation of problem-oriented policing appears to reflect the same action research paradigm underpinning situational prevention. Nevertheless, some important differences exist between the concepts. In particular, problem-oriented policing is a management approach designed to make the most efficient use of police resources, while situational prevention is a crime control approach open not just to the police but to any organizational or management structure.[17]

By characterizing problem-oriented policing as a management approach peculiar to policing (which it clearly is not, as the problem orientation often pulls police into cooperative ventures with other agencies and communities), Clarke claims his approach is broader because it naturally brings in other professions, notably architects, city planners, and security consultants.

Conversely, Goldstein welcomes situational prevention but points to its limitations:

Clarke identified sixteen techniques of situational prevention. Problem-oriented policing would embrace all of these—but, in its concern for the range of community problems that the police must handle beyond crime, embrace many additional strategies as well.[18]

If I had to arbitrate the question, I would go with Goldstein. Situational crime prevention does seem explicitly focused on crime (important as that is) and heavily focused (although not exclusively) on interventions relying on the redesign of places and spaces. Such approaches work well for crime problems in which places and spaces present a useful mode of analysis and a useful way of concentrating risk (such as crimes within a transit system or in densely populated urban neighborhoods). But for many other types of crime problem (date rape, domestic violence, or corruption), place- and space-based analysis is not the right way—at least, not an efficient way—to approach the problem. Focusing on any particular set of interventions (even sixteen categories of them) represents a loss, as it may prevent staff from spotting some other, quite different, avenue of attack.

As Peter Senge states,

Small changes can produce big results—but the areas of highest leverage are often the least obvious. . . .

Tackling a difficult problem is often a matter of seeing where the high leverage lies, a change which—with a minimum of effort—would lead to lasting, significant improvement. The only problem is that high-leverage changes are usually *nonobvious* to most participants in the system. . . . This is what makes life interesting.[19]

In the early 1990s the Australian Tax Office established a matrix structure by which to assess and address risk. First, they divided taxpayers into industry segments (as do most tax agencies), and then they divided each segment according to seven predefined risk areas:
— Failure to enter the system.
— Dropping out of the system.
— Deliberate underpayment of tax.
— Inadvertent under- or overpayment of tax.
— Use of tax planning arrangements.
— Failure to pay tax.
— Failure to withhold tax.
Senior management carried the responsibility for determining the level of risk in each risk area and for each industry segment. Compliance and enforcement resources were then focused on those areas classified as medium to high risk. For each of these selected risk areas, the agency quantifies the risk, manages the risk, and evaluates the impact of agency action over time.[20]

The risk matrix was formulated from executives' joint understanding of noncompliance issues. This, they felt, was an appropriate way to slice and dice the world of taxpayer noncompliance. The matrix—at the time they created it—did not sit well with existing organizational structures, for the tax office had previously been organized along functional lines. They eventually overcame that hurdle. Later, having worked with this particular risk matrix for some time, Commissioner Trevor Boucher observed that some newly emerging problems did not seem to fit even that (comparatively sophisticated) structure. The nature of the emerging problems suggested a rearrangement along the lines of large and international business, domestic business, and individuals. Does that mean the tax office got it wrong first time? Did they miss some better matrix? Of course not. As Boucher points out, "Market segmentation and risk analysis is an iterative, dynamic and organic process. It does not have a defined finishing line that we can cross."[21]

The dynamic nature of the risk control business can provide a recipe for perpetual reorganization if an agency tries to match each new problem with a new piece of permanent or semipermanent apparatus. There is nothing like perpetual reorganization for driving people crazy and destroying morale. Huge, long-term problems may require permanent or semipermanent apparatus. Any predefined risk matrix (of two or more dimensions) may support systematic identification and prioritization of certain types of problems and miss others. And executives might choose specific structures, from time to time, to give staff a home, to create a semblance of order, or to facilitate the agency's response to one particularly pressing set of issues. But reliance on any permanent structure likely detracts from a risk control strategy—dynamic and fluid business that it is—more than it adds to it.

The most formidable *organizational* challenge associated with a risk control strategy is to maintain the maximum possible flexibility over the mechanisms through which problems might be identified, the dimensions in which they can be defined, the ways in which they might be subdivided, the forms of analysis that count, the times for intervention, the tools to use, and the configurations of personnel and resources best suited to address each one. The most formidable *executive* challenge associated with a risk control strategy is to keep an open mind on all of these structural questions and to counteract all the powerful inclinations of personnel and administrative systems to snap back into familiar forms. While executives struggle to keep an open mind on all the major structural and tactical questions, they should also insist on a reasonably high level of methodological rigor whenever and wherever their agency tackles specific risks.

Now there's a tricky combination: *tight on methodology, and loose on operational methods and structures*. Most of the regulatory and enforcement world has it the other way around.

CHAPTER SIXTEEN

Finding Resources, Making Space

"LOOSE ON STRUCTURES" brings with it a certain vulnerability. Risk control operations must compete against other forms of work for resources and attention. Those other forms of work (many of them functionally or process based) enjoy the security of fixed units, dedicated budgets, and established patterns of operation. Some of them might be less important than they once were or even obsolete. Nevertheless they survive and continue to consume vital resources, precisely because of these organizational comforts, which—coupled with lack of rigor over measurement—make long-standing programs difficult to dislodge.

To make room for risk control work, executives face a choice. Either they create dedicated units, giving problem solving the same organizational roots that other programs enjoy (but introducing the danger that the particular configuration and staffing of the unit will limit the kinds of problem that it can address). Or they avoid creating a fixed or additional unit, in which case they must devise other methods for preserving commitment and focus in the face of competing pressures. This chapter considers these very practical questions: how to find resources; whether or not to create separate units; where problem solving fits within the organization; and how it might (or might not) show up on an organizational chart.

Finding Resources

In the long-term steady state, a problem-solving or risk control strategy ought not to be highly consumptive of resources. Indeed, such strategies, if well managed and monitored, should be considerably more resource efficient than alternatives. Here are some reasons why:

— *Improved targeting of resources and attention* ("only important stuff"). An explicit emphasis on problem selection, before projects are launched, should enable the agency to target its time and attention on the most important areas and to explicitly deemphasize unimportant ones.

— *Analysis revealing the nub of the issue* ("more thought, less muscle"). The analytic process of picking a problem apart—understanding its components and precursors, its causes and consequences—reveals opportunities for intervention that would not have been apparent without such analysis. Extra investment in analysis up front produces more surgical interventions, making it possible to achieve ambitious risk reduction goals by using existing resources more incisively.

— *Insistence upon resource-efficient solutions* ("managing efficiency in"). The action-planning phase of the problem-solving procedure (stage 4) requires that project teams consider only resource-efficient solutions and that they include in their intervention design a long-term plan for withdrawing resources from the solution, without the problem reappearing. Management oversight reviews should examine the issue of resource efficiency, rejecting (or sending back for amendment) any intervention plan that appears overly consumptive of resources or that threatens to tie up resources in perpetuity.

— *Quicker recognition of ineffective plans* ("ditching what doesn't work"). The results orientation, with a set of performance indicators specific to the project, allows unsuccessful plans to be recognized as such and abandoned relatively quickly.

— *Decreased process loads* ("relief elsewhere"). Successful interventions should eventually decrease the load on reactive processes, breaking the cycle of harm and reducing the associated resource demands.

— *Organizational learning, producing efficient solutions and efficiencies in identifying them* ("learning what really works"). Over time, an agency will accumulate a repository of ideas from prior projects—intervention strategies that turned out to be both efficient and effective. Access to such a knowledge base enables project teams to identify approaches that worked elsewhere, in similar circumstances, and speeds the process of intervention design by bringing a broader range of ideas to the planning table early on.

For all of these reasons, the benefits of a well-managed risk control operation ought to outweigh its costs. Nevertheless, practitioners consistently place "lack of time" high on their lists of factors that make problem solving difficult or impossible. Part of the explanation, no doubt, lies in the general absence of systems for allocating time or for granting relief from other duties.

Four Approaches

Another part of the explanation may lie in the particular difficulties of starting up—when the value of such work has not been well established, when positive results seem few, and when the organization has not yet experienced relief in its process loads. We should pay particular attention, therefore, to the various ways in which organizations have managed to *begin* their problem-solving work. Four quite different approaches to the introduction of problem-solving follow.

Baltimore County Police Department: COPE Unit

Even though Baltimore's Citizen-Oriented Policing Enforcement (COPE) units ended up as general purpose problem-solving teams, they did not begin that way. In 1982 Chief Neil Behan was granted funding for forty-five additional officers in response to specific local concerns centering upon fear of crime. He used that funding to create three new units of fifteen officers, which he staffed with experienced volunteers, freed up by the increase in the department's strength.[1] The COPE units initially focused on the specific problem of fear and its debilitating effects on community life, particularly among the elderly.

Along their way, and partly because the problem of fear was not susceptible to traditional enforcement approaches, the COPE units discovered the relevance of problem-solving techniques and eventually received instruction from Herman Goldstein (on the invitation of Chief Behan).[2] Subsequently the role of the COPE teams broadened as they took on other community problems, and they adopted the problem-solving approach as their core method of operation. Chief Behan had not set out to create problem-solving units. Rather, he set up the units to solve a specific problem. In due course, however, he was able to capitalize on their newly acquired problem-solving skills by broadening the terms of their deployment to cover a wider range of issues.

Customs Service: Strategic Problem-Solving Program

The Customs Service kicked off its Strategic Problem-Solving program with a $2 million auction, held in El Paso on July 9, 1996. Management had already laid the groundwork, providing extensive training throughout the organization, and creating an Office of Strategic Problem Solving at Headquarters to coordinate the new program. The agency had also launched the port-running project, and some others, on a pilot basis. By July 1996 senior executives decided it was time to get serious about problem solving.

The deputy commissioner issued an invitation to the field office staff to prepare and present problem-solving proposals at the El Paso conference, at which each proposal would compete on its merits for selection and funding. The invitation stated that more than $2 million was available from the commissioner's discretionary funding; that not all projects would be funded; that proposals must be multidisciplinary; and that proposals that were "creative, innovative, and cognizant of limited resources" would be well received.[3] Each local office was allowed to propose up to three projects and was given twenty minutes to present them all. Participants then voted among themselves (each being prohibited from voting for their own) to select the most attractive projects. Based on the votes tallied, funds were allocated and projects were launched. Despite the substantial injection of funds, the only personnel dedicated to problem solving on a full-time basis were the four senior managers (plus clerical staff) who made up the coordination unit at headquarters.

Occupational Health and Safety Administration: Redesign of Area Offices

OSHA's reinvention effort, which began in 1994 and focused primarily on the redesign of the agency's sixty-six area offices, coupled the *efficiencies of process improvement* with the *effectiveness of problem solving*. Implementation of the plan began in the spring of 1995, with two area offices "rolled out" at a time. For five weeks before roll out, area office staff underwent intensive training in newly reengineered complaint response procedures, and they were also introduced to the techniques of problem solving. Neighboring area offices covered for them while they underwent training.

After the training period, the following Monday morning brought instant transformation to that area office. The reengineered complaint responses were implemented, which, being more resource efficient, freed up between one-third and one-half of the area office staff. Those resources were immediately reinvested in an intervention team, whose job it was to identify patterns and trends in workplace injuries and illnesses and to implement tailor-made solutions ("the problem-solving approach to hazard mitigation in the workplace"). OSHA used the efficiencies of process improvement to produce the resources for problem solving and tied them together in one redesign plan.

Florida Department of Environmental Protection

The FDEP has led the way among state-level agencies in formally implementing environmental problem solving. However, the agency has never had any special appropriation for problem solving, nor has it internally designated any funding for it. District and division directors have to make room, within existing resources, for projects they choose to run. Each district and division has internal problem-solving consultants, trained as facilitators and guides (although these are part-time responsibilities). A small headquarters-based unit—the Office for Strategic Projects and Planning—handles the central tracking and coordination role for environmental problem solving but does so among many other duties. Despite the lack of dedicated resources, as of the summer of 1999, the department had more than fifty significant projects approved and running, including some jointly coordinated with the Environmental Protection Agency's Region IV under a negotiated "performance partnership agreement."

The Strengths and Weaknesses of the Four Approaches

Each of these arrangements has its strengths and weaknesses. Separate, dedicated units—like Chief Behan's COPE units—provide an incubator for fledgling problem-solving skills. But setting the problem-solving work aside from mainstream operations can serve to insulate the rest of the department from the need to learn, or even think about, this type of work. Chief Behan realized that, to transform policing, he and other chiefs would have to spread problem solving throughout their departments, making the problem-solving orientation and skills central to normal operations.

Some police chiefs, hoping to capitalize on the early successes of dedicated units, have subsequently abolished them and spread the personnel
around their departments, hoping to leaven the whole. More often than
not, this kills problem solving rather than diffusing it, because the organizational crutch of having a dedicated unit has been removed and no
other kind of organizational support has been provided in its place. The
pressures of other work then drive out problem solving, and problem
solving is swiftly reduced to a question of personal style for those few
officers who remain committed to it.

The Customs Service's $2 million launch—separate money but no
separate units—reflects an extraordinary degree of early commitment
and confidence on the part of agency executives. But even this has its
dangers. By requiring problem-solving proposals with a price tag, the
agency was asking for problem nominations with a solution already
worked out. This short circuits the early analytic stages of problem solving and predisposes project teams toward solutions that use a lot of
technical equipment, which can be priced. Worse still, field staff may be
tempted (when they see significant sums of money on the table) to dress
up ordinary equipment requests as problem-solving projects, when in
fact they are nothing of the kind. Other side effects include the possibility that teams not awarded special funds might assume they were
excused from any obligation to attempt problem solving. Teams locked
into equipment purchases might not feel sufficiently free to adjust their
interventions when their first idea fails. And the problem-solving program might be less likely to spread into other areas of the organization,
where no special funding is available. What customs bought itself with
the El Paso auction was a very quick and energetic start; the price it paid
was the need for some methodological repair work later.

OSHA's redesign roll-out, area office by area office, usefully combined process improvement (with its emphasis on efficiency, timeliness,
and customer satisfaction) with investments in problem solving (with its
emphasis on effectiveness and risk reduction). Either one without the
other would not have worked as well. OSHA could not have found the
resources for problem solving without the process improvements, as
Congress was squeezing its budget mercilessly at the time. And process
improvements alone could not have produced the kind of results OSHA
wanted—demonstrable risk reductions. Besides, if OSHA had freed up
half its area office resources without a plan for their useful redeploy-
ment, it would surely have lost them.

The OSHA approach also had its downside. In terms of reaching throughout the organization, the roll out was excruciatingly slow. In the first year, the redesign project rolled-out only seventeen of the sixty-six area offices. It took three years to finish the job and to begin work on the regional and national offices. By focusing so heavily on the field level at the outset, redesign scored quick local successes, but it left those offices vulnerable, lacking support or understanding from their regional and national managers. Because middle and upper management had been left out at the beginning, problem solving within the area offices smacked, to them, of organizational subversion. Regional managers who tried to exercise oversight of problem-solving projects were told by subordinates that they should not interfere, because they had not been trained in problem solving and so they could not possibly understand it! It was a recipe for organizational chaos, even as the local teams began to chalk up successes. OSHA's regional and national managers were brought into the problem-solving picture in due course, but at a relatively late stage.

Of all these examples, the Florida Department of Environmental Protection's approach provides the slowest start of all. Senior management did a lot of urging and encouraging but provided no designated funding for problem solving, nor any special organizational home for it. They just told their middle managers that they should start using environmental problem-solving methods. Headquarters tracked the flow of problem nominations and project launches and could see clearly which parts of the organization had adopted it and which continued to resist it. Senior executives resisted the temptation to set quotas for problem-solving projects, as they did not want to invent just a new kind of bean-count. Nor did they want other work to be dressed up as environmental problem solving. For almost two years, therefore, implementation was patchy and was regarded by many as experimental. When district or division directors did not see the need for it, or did not recognize it as different from what they already did, no projects were launched.

On the upside, when environmental problem-solving did happen, it happened within the existing fabric of the organization, and mid-level managers had to figure out how to administer it, monitor it, and make space for it within existing budgetary and personnel allocations. Despite the slow start, this approach at least established the sense that risk control operations were integral to the mission of regulators and not somehow peripheral or extra.

Forms and Structures for the Long Term

Until a range of regulatory agencies have run mature risk control operations over a period of years, it will be tough to say what organizational forms and structures provide the best support for it. Even then, it might be foolish to assume that a set of organizational arrangements that suited one agency would necessarily be optimal for another. Rather than specifying one set of arrangements, let me present a few broader observations about the nature of the risk control task—from what we have seen already—each with implications for organizational forms, structures, and relationships. How agencies choose to accommodate these observations will vary a great deal and will inevitably depend on their existing structures, the location of relevant skills within their organization, and the nature of their regulatory tasks.

The Need to Maintain Other Forms of Work

Not all work will be conceived or organized this way. Functional expertise needs to be maintained. High-volume core operational processes need to be operated efficiently and managed professionally. A problem-solving or risk orientation does not displace these other organizational competencies; it augments and supplements them and changes the context for them. An effective risk control operation will probably affect the process workload, and many problem solutions will involve adjustments to processes. But even the most effective risk reduction operation will not completely eradicate traffic accidents, environmental spills, industrial accidents, mechanical failures, or human error. All these will still require expert regulatory response, and many of the resulting incidents will not fit into a particular pattern, trend, or risk concentration. Departmentwide adoption of a risk control strategy, therefore, will never mean that all regulatory work fits the mold of problem solving. At this stage, I cannot predict what proportion of a regulatory agency's work might eventually be conceived and organized this way. Perhaps 30 percent, or 50 percent at most. All I know for now is that most agencies do precious little, and I hope they will find a way to do much more. Executives would do well to give some advance consideration to where the balance, in the end, may lie. They would also do well to give staff some indication of the pace at which they want to shift resources into that kind of operation.

The Scarcity of Problem-Solving Skills

Problem-solving skills are rare, valuable, and slow to develop. One major advantage of using separate, dedicated units is that they provide an incubator for fledgling problem-solving skills and a protective shield from competing demands. Such units also serve as training grounds, through which staff might be rotated. In the absence of such a training ground, executives should bear in mind that most newcomers to the business of problem solving usually flounder, baffled by the range of choices they face. They need a lot of support, encouragement, and expert guidance. Inexperienced project teams need experienced facilitators to help run their meetings. Even senior managers, new to the business of selecting or overseeing projects, may need technical and methodological guidance. It takes a long time, and sustained investment, for staff to grasp the conceptual underpinnings of problem solving and to come to terms with its analytic and methodological demands.

Problem Solving as an Operational Method

Problem solving should not be isolated from operations. Problem solving is an operational method, not a research task. The argument for adopting it is predicated on the hypothesis that a significant proportion of day-to-day accidents, incidents, violations and crimes fall into patterns that can be discerned and that regulatory effectiveness is enhanced by treating the patterns intelligently, rather than processing the incidents one by one. If problem-solving operations become isolated and insulated from the rest of operations, they lose their relevance. The problem-solving operation must be constantly informed about shifting operational demands; in a position to identify emerging patterns within routine process loads; and able to influence operational responses. Given the highly analytic nature of problem solving, any hint that a problem-solving unit is insulated from operations will lead the rest of the agency to assume it is yet another research unit, producing reports for consumption mostly by outsiders, irrelevant to operations, enjoying a comfortable and cerebral existence, detached from the grinding pressure of daily business. No. Problem solving is an analytical approach to operations.

The Fluid Nature of Problem Solving

The only permanent apparatus is for coordination and support. Problem areas and risk concentrations come and (one hopes) go. Given the dynamic nature of the risk control business, one would expect the majority of the operational work associated with it to be conducted by temporary project teams. Of course, *temporary* is a relative term, and some teams formed around specific risks may remain in place for long periods and may involve team members on a full-time basis. Even though project teams may be long term or full time, or both, they should still not be regarded as permanent. If the problem turns out to be intractable, or diminishes in importance when stacked against other emerging priorities, the team should be abolished and resources redeployed elsewhere. If the team succeeds, the team should similarly be abolished or wound down as the project moves into long-term maintenance mode. The responsibility for stopping project teams from becoming permanent fixtures in the organization lies with the managerial infrastructure. In particular, the rigorous focus on results, coupled with mandatory periodic reviews, obliges managers to question whether projects should continue, whether resources allocated to them need adjustment, and whether project teams have accomplished their goals.

However, the support and coordination infrastructure (described in chapter 11) should be permanent and should be embedded in existing management structures. This infrastructure might include—as in the case of the Customs Service and the Florida Department of Environmental Protection—a permanent (but small) coordinating and tracking unit at headquarters and a trained group of internal consultants or facilitators. But this apparatus does not conduct problem-solving operations; rather, it coordinates, manages, and supports them.

Problem Solving and Staff Versatility

In response to a broad range of problems, regulatory agencies must be able to produce a broad range of tailor-made interventions. They must maintain their competence across a broad range of methods and tactics and even be able to respond with different regulatory styles. Hence the need (as presented in chapter 2) for regulatory agencies to have more than one act. But agency versatility is not the same thing as agent versatility. Agency versatility is a managerial product, not a personal one. Response design can specify *who* to send.

There are natural limits to the degree of versatility one can expect from individual agents. Research on regulatory styles indicates higher levels of stress for inspectors when they are required to move between legalistic and conciliatory styles. Consistently playing one role is less stressful.[4] Maintaining separate units for different skills does not necessarily damage a risk control strategy, provided such resources are all available to the risk control operation and provided the work of multiple units can be coordinated in the context of integrated intervention plans.

Moreover, not all regulatory staff will adapt readily to the intellectual and analytic demands of problem solving; and not all of them need to. Some regulatory tasks require thoughtful, creative individuals. But others (such as riot control and emergency response) require high degrees of central coordination, efficiency and obedience to orders.[5] Some staff can comfortably play multiple roles. Others do not have such chameleonlike versatility and are much better at one thing than another. Part of the management task, within the context of problem solving, is to diversify the skills and interests of staff. But management, through its human resource management policies, must weigh agent versatility against preservation of expertise, and produce agency versatility without stretching individual staff members beyond reasonable limits.

The Interface between Intervention and Process

The problem-solving apparatus and the core operational processes interact with each other in many ways. Understanding the myriad ways in which they relate, without jumping to the erroneous conclusion that the processes therefore take care of risk control, is fundamental to successful implementation of a risk control operation. Here are six specific ways in which interventions and processes may be intertwined:[6]

— Intervention plans, oriented around a specific problem, may involve adjustments to processes (the use of Jersey barriers behind the border inspection operation to control the Customs Service's port-running problem).

— Analysis of a problem may require data drawn from processes. The process may be adjusted or augmented to collect additional data, either to support initial analysis of a problem or to help monitor the effects of an intervention.

— Studying the impact of experimental strategies might require the administration of controlled or randomized experiments, which may be conducted through the administration of processes.

— Problems may be identified through analysis of process workloads. (repeat-call address analysis in the Minneapolis RECAP program).

— Interventions may alter process workloads. If an intervention successfully eliminates or mitigates a problem or risk, the parts of the process load associated with that risk should decline. Conversely, if the problem is one of nonreporting, improved compliance rates may increase administrative loads. If a problem is underreported or underrepresented in process loads, the initial phases of an intervention plan might deliberately increase the visibility of the problem by stimulating reporting, in which case process loads would increase during this phase of the intervention.

— Processes and interventions might involve the same staff (membership of a problem-solving project team might be a part-time responsibility).

Despite all these interactions between process management and problem solving, the two forms of work remain quite different. They have different goals and require different patterns of thought. Each needs its own management system, and the two forms of work need carefully delineated responsibility. Otherwise one form of competence will suffer at the hands of the other.

A New Perspective on the Enforcement Function

A risk control operation, and the kind of regulatory craftsmanship it demands, treats enforcement as one of the tools in the compliance tool kit. But the tool kit idea does not reveal the full extent of the contribution that investigative and enforcement personnel can make. It tells us only that this tool may or may not be deployed with respect to any one compliance problem. A control strategy places quite a different emphasis on enforcement and investigation and considers those functions valuable in a number of other ways. First, each investigation produces valuable knowledge and insights about the failures of control or prevention. Information about the failure—how and why it happened, what the violators knew or did not know, what factors or incentives produced this behavior—is vital information for improved control and, if fed back into the control operation, may be significantly more valuable than the immediate disposition of the case itself.

Second, prosecutions (and even investigations that do not result in prosecutions) become devices for influencing behavior. A control strategy will exploit cases for publicity and leverage and will design and time media releases for optimal effect. (Think how artfully Operation Ceasefire in Boston used a few cases to maximum effect.) A control strategy may even produce requests for an enforcement unit to seek out particular kinds of cases at particular times, so that prosecutions or convictions can be publicized as part of a communication strategy.

Third, intelligence-gathering techniques and investigative field craft can be used *outside* the context of a case to uncover invisible risks, determine the scope and nature of emerging problems, identify the components or vulnerabilities of a particular noncompliance trend, and to suggest remedies. This is a form of strategic intelligence analysis, relying heavily on investigative skills, thoroughly operational, and yet not case specific. (See chapter 18 for a more detailed discussion of the role of strategic intelligence analysis in supporting risk control operations.)

Fourth, control operations may need to deploy field investigative techniques in a preventive, or early-detection, mode (before a serious offense has been committed). Background checks in the context of screening or qualification of contractors, for example, may require investigation of undisclosed ownership arrangements. Previously excluded or ineligible parties (for example, medical providers barred from the Medicare program, or building contractors prohibited from a school construction program) often reappear under different guises, and investigative skills may be needed to track them and trace their relationships.

An enforcement operation that sits passively on the end of a referral pipeline and that lacks formal mechanisms for passing information and intelligence back to the rest of the organization misses all of these important opportunities. To make the fullest possible use of enforcement and investigation, a control operation demands a much higher level of communication and coordination between the enforcement operation and the rest of the agency.

When Resource Constraints Present an Insurmountable Obstacle

This chapter opened with a list of reasons why, over the long term, a risk control strategy should be not only effective but also resource efficient. Nevertheless, shortage of resources persistently tops the list of reasons why problem solving "can't be done," even though the pressures of the Government Performance and Results Act and other performance-based budgeting systems in theory favor projects with clearly identified, outcome-oriented goals.

For executives whose agencies still cannot find the time or resources to operate risk-control operations the way they would like, I have only one remaining suggestion. I invite them to consider whether they really understand and embrace the choices that such a strategy requires. A strategy that requires them to *pick important problems* will founder if they cannot face the prospect of *turning down unimportant problems*. Focusing on important risks—and doing so within constrained budgets—obliges executives to state with some clarity what will *not* be done, what programs will be discontinued, and why one initiative is dropped in favor of another.

The business of risk control not only obliges regulators to make such choices but to defend them and sometimes to reconsider them in public. Regulators will have to explain and defend their right to choose and the criteria and systems they use for choosing. Explaining new projects is always comparatively easy—much harder to explain what regulators have chosen not to do, or to admit which laws are not being enforced, or to explain to problem nominators outside the agency why their problems were not selected.

The traditional myth of regulatory practice is that regulators enforce all of the laws all of the time, uniformly, across the board. The risk control story is very different. It requires regulators to understand and to embrace various forms of discretion, including the right to choose what to work on and how to work on it. Without that piece of the story, regulators will never find the room or resources to maneuver.

CHAPTER SEVENTEEN

Managing Discretion

SOME SAY THE ANSWER to regulatory unreasonableness is to give regulators more discretion. Others say the regulators themselves are the problem and that the solution is to take away their discretion by exerting tighter legislative control. The dilemma is familiar and ages old. Too little discretion produces legalistic, nitpicky behavior and denies regulators the means to tailor their responses to local or particular circumstances. Too much discretion creates opportunities for corruption and discrimination and opens a regulatory agency to capture by the regulated community.

In its most general form, the dilemma is between centralization (which increases uniformity and control) and decentralization (which allows frontline workers to respond effectively to local or particular circumstances in ways that remote lawmakers could not have considered).[1] This basic dilemma appears at multiple levels. At the highest level it concerns the relationship between branches of government, with Hamiltonians favoring a strong executive, and Madisonians favoring tighter congressional controls. But it also appears *within* regulatory agencies, wherein discretion may be pushed down to the field level for the sake of local responsiveness or held tightly at the center for the sake of uniformity and control.

The majority of the voices now clamoring for regulatory reform press for greater use of discretion by regulators as an antidote to what they perceive to be a legalistic, adversarial style. They want commonsense regulation rather than rule-bound regulation. The kinds of regulatory commonsense that now find favor nearly always involve a shift away from straightforward enforcement of the rules through adoption of some regulatory alternative.

The idea of regulators simply enforcing the rules, without exercising their discretion, has its appeal. Alan Altshuler points out how the "bureaucratic paradigm" is based upon the principles of scientific management methods, imported from manufacturing industry, and that such methods appeared in their own time as the antidote to patronage and ad hoc political meddling:

Execution of laws should be organized as a ministerial activity. The laws should be crystal clear; their execution should be thoroughly routine. The aims of managerial reform, quite simply, should be honesty, efficiency, and a day's work for a day's pay. The demons to be slain are corruption, arbitrariness, and sloth. There is no room within this paradigm for bureaucratic intelligence or creativity, because these imply discretion, an invitation to the above mentioned demons.[2]

But as far as regulatory practice is concerned, the idea of regulators devoid of discretion is just that: an idea. In reality, they have always exercised their discretion, and they always will. They do so partly out of necessity, because there are far too many regulations and far too many instances of noncompliance and insufficient resources to tackle more than a small fraction. They do so partly because society has always expected it of them, knowing that life would be intolerable if they did not. As Eugene Bardach and Robert Kagan put it in 1982:

In sum, the criminal law on the books may be relatively clear and legally specific, but as a society, we willingly enable legal decision-makers to suspend the rules (in the direction of leniency), to rely upon warnings and informal adjustments, to distinguish between serious and non-serious violations, to consider extenuating circumstances, to use the rehabilitative potential of giving a second chance, and to strike a more discerning balance between social control and liberty than lawmakers, far removed from a particular case and a local culture, could envisage in advance.[3]

So why does the idea of discretion-free regulation persist? Why is this idea still available for critics to attack, when the practical reality is so obviously different? Mostly, I believe, because regulators like this idea, because it makes their position easy to defend. They can say, "We have no choice in the matter, we are simply enforcing the law." They do not have to explain their use of discretion if people imagine they do not exercise it. In fact, regulatory practice is not as rule bound as reformers suggest. It is not that regulators do not use their discretion; they just do not admit it. If they admitted it, they would inevitably get drawn into discussions over the criteria and methods they used to make enforcement decisions (none of which would be specified in law), and such discussions could be embarrassing if they revealed a lack of a defensible rationale for the choices made. Worse, regulators fear that admitting their use of discretion might be interpreted as a sign of laziness, dereliction of duty, favoritism, or corruption. Regulators also fear that failure to enforce a particular law might render them liable for subsequent harm if continuing noncompliance resulted in an accident. "Adhering to rules, on the other hand, provides regulatory officials a relatively safe harbor from such storms of criticism."[4]

James Q. Wilson observed the inevitability of discretion for police patrol officers and the tendency of police administrators to deny it:

> The patrolman necessarily exercises wide discretion, but the police administrator is obliged publicly to deny that there is much discretion in police work and may have to act out that denial by deciding complaints about police behavior as if no discretion existed. . . . The patrolman is not a professional, and thus the opinion of a professional colleague cannot be sought to justify his actions (the way doctors may justify each other's actions as in accord with "approved medical practice").[5]

If regulatory practice was regarded as a profession, then the use of discretion might be more readily defended as the exercise of professional judgment. As it is, regulators experience considerable difficulty in *not* enforcing the law almost any time they have to declare it—and especially when they have to write it down.

Part of the Environmental Protection Agency's difficulty with its flagship reinvention project, Project XL, has been that site-specific agreements (which trade regulatory flexibility for superior environmental performance) had to specify which rules the facility was permitted to break.

Hence the in-house motto, "If it ain't illegal, it ain't XL." As the program developed, the EPA shifted the emphasis away from waiving enforcement of a specific regulation and instead took to issuing site-specific rules under the authority of existing federal statutes.[6] In other words, it was easier for them to *change* a rule than to record and defend an agency decision not to enforce it. Generating highly detailed regulations (differentiated, in the case of Project XL, right down to the level of individual sites) apparently sits more easily with the traditions and myths of regulatory practice than accomplishing the same ends through the use of discretion.

To advance regulatory practice, the option of simply granting more, or less, discretion fails to provide an adequate foundation. The fact is, regulatory practitioners already have plenty of discretion, and they use it constantly. The important questions for now are, On what basis should regulators use their discretion; and Can regulators learn to engage in substantive, open discussions about their exercise of discretion? For both of these questions, the business of risk-control has profound implications.

The usual arguments over enforcement discretion are really quite narrow. They focus on the dichotomous nature of an inspector's choice once a violation has been observed or reported. Discretion means choosing whether to initiate enforcement action or not. Inspectors can make errors of omission or commission—either failing to enforce in circumstances that seem to demand it or taking enforcement action in circumstances that make such action appear harsh or unfair.

Recent expansion of the regulatory repertoire has made this a little more complicated. Inspectors, faced with a violation and deciding not to initiate enforcement actions now have a broader range of alternatives from which to choose. They can offer education, guidance, or technical assistance; or set a schedule for violators' return to compliance; or issue warnings; or negotiate other resolutions, perhaps involving compensatory good deeds. Rather than simply choosing whether to enforce or not, inspectors now have a more graduated list of options available. All they have to do is select an appropriate disposition for each violation that comes along.

This model of enforcement decisionmaking (which I call *enforcement discretion*), even if no longer a dichotomy, still feels like a *process*. The units of work that enter the work stream are violations observed or reported. After examination and verification, the violations arrive at branch points within the process, from which they can be routed along different paths, toward different dispositions. These routing decisions are made by field agents and are sometimes reviewed or approved by superiors. How much discretion field-level agents or inspectors exercise depends only on how much they are permitted to use their own judgment in making these branch-point determinations, as opposed to using detailed criteria prespecified in policy or procedure. Whether the discretion is centralized (encapsulated in policy) or decentralized (allowing use of field-level judgment), the question is the same: Which way should this one go?

This conception of discretion cannot adequately support a risk control strategy. It fails to capture the significantly richer forms of discretion that allow regulators to pick important problems, define and formulate them, and devise creative tailor-made solutions for them. Nor does the *enforcement discretion* model envisage a meeting of agency managers at which the participants decide whether to allow a project team to continue its action plan for another month, or decide it is time to try something else, or terminate the project and shift the resources elsewhere. Compared with these choices, the enforcement choice model seems one dimensional—a process model in disguise—with violations passing through a sequence of decision points and routed according to preset criteria, one by one.

Mitchell Adams, when he was commissioner of the Massachusetts Department of Revenue, once a year would call in his enforcement staff and say to them, "It's time. Go find me a yacht." It had come time, within the context of the department's compliance strategy for child support payments, to find a deadbeat dad whose yacht could be seized in front of television camera crews and paraded on the evening news. What Adams wanted had nothing to do with appropriate processing of a violation already known to the department. Rather, he wanted to carry out a symbolic enforcement act, designed for public consumption, as one element of a broader compliance plan. His enforcement staff then had to go and search for a suitable enforcement target, with a yacht, to fill the slot. Not all such deadbeat dads; just one.

The enforcement discretion model could never contemplate such an action and would probably reject it as inequitable. Nor would it contemplate the kind of structured discretion employed by Operation Ceasefire in Boston, in which enforcement decisions against one gang member became dependent on the behavior of other gang members. Nor would it provide any basis for determining whether the Australian Securities and Investments Commission acted reasonably when its staff constructed a bogus Internet investment site, as a method of identifying and then educating gullible investors, and convinced 233 people to part with $4 million over the Internet.[7]

Madisonians might view such regulatory creativity, particularly when it involves enforcement actions, as evidence that regulators cannot be trusted with discretion and that their actions ought to be much more tightly prescribed. Indeed, many public administration scholars have had exactly this kind of reaction to the reinventing government movement, perceiving it as "a dangerous aberration from increasing and rightful congressional control of the executive branch."[8] Others have observed how sharply the idea of government as customer driven, service oriented, and locally responsive conflicts with the bureaucratic or legalistic paradigm.[9]

The good news here is that a risk control orientation ought to be much less dangerous (from the point of view of those worried about regulatory accountability) than other reform ideas, particularly those centered around customer service. If one really wants to launch a regulatory agency toward capture, stressing the satisfaction of the regulated community above all else would probably be the way to go.

Risk control presents much less of a threat than this. It sticks closely to the regulatory mission. It does not imagine that keeping people happy takes precedence. It is highly analytical in the choices it makes, outcome oriented in the goals it sets, and rigorous about measurement and monitoring. It provides systematic forms of accountability. Choices are explained publicly and can be reviewed and appealed. Risk management provides a rational, defensible, and structured way of being flexible; not a careless, arbitrary, or corrupt one.

Four Types of Discretion

Chapter 1 examined the pressures for regulatory reform and sought to infer what those pressures might mean for regulatory practice, with or without changes to the framework of regulatory law. That chapter closed by suggesting a mandate for regulatory practice, derived from demands for regulatory reasonableness, greater effectiveness, and resource efficiency. That mandate contemplates many forms of discretion that a risk control orientation would have to recognize. Here it is again:

Acknowledge the constant need to make choices. Make them rationally, analytically, democratically. Take responsibility for the choices you make. Correct, by using your judgment, deficiencies of law. Organize yourselves to deliver important results. Choose specific goals of public value, and focus on them. Devise methods that are economical with respect to the use of state authority, the resources of the regulated community, and the resources of the agency. And as you carefully pick and choose what to do and how to do it, reconcile your pursuit of effectiveness with the values of justice and equity.

Enforcement decisions still have to made, and violations—reported or observed—still have to be dealt with. But enforcement discretion (choosing how to dispose of particular violations) is superseded by three other forms of discretion, each of which involves larger and weightier decisions. The exercise of these three will substantially alter the framework for enforcement decisions. The three superseding forms of discretion are the right to set the mission, the right to choose *what* to work on (to pick important problems within the scope of the mission), and the right to choose *how* to work on it (freedom to design solutions, drawing from a wide range of available methods). Enforcement discretion then appears as the fourth of four types of discretion. Regulators need to understand how the types relate to one another under an operational risk control model.

The Right to Set the Mission

When regulations are rendered obsolete by advances in technology or by the waxing and waning of risks, regulatory agencies should "correct, by using their judgment, deficiencies of law." The mission of public agencies is not adequately defined by statutes, nor is it static over time. Issues come and go, and law seldom keeps pace. Moreover, law typically specifies only a part of the role that society expects regulatory and enforcement agencies to play. The police do much more than deal with crime. Occupational safety and health agencies do much more than enforce existing standards. And the EPA deals with many environmental issues not covered by its authorizing (and mostly media-specific) statutes.

Regulatory executives constantly engage in drawing and redrawing the boundaries of their mission and in choosing which aspects of it to emphasize. The EPA engages with congressional overseers over the question of how far into the realm of public health an environmental agency should go. OSHA executives have to decide what to do, if anything, about ergonomic injuries in the absence of any ergonomic standard. Police chiefs have to decide whether their departments should continue to deal with damage-only road accidents or whether they should pull out of that.

The Kennedy School of Government teaches a model of public management (developed by Mark Moore and others) that embraces this particular form of discretion, even though it clashes with traditional doctrines of public administration. Rather than viewing public managers as implementors or executors of programs devised by legislatures, this model sees them as navigators over a terrain of possible strategic choices. Mark Moore describes public managers as "explorers commissioned by society to search for public value. In undertaking the search, managers are expected to use their initiative and imagination. But they are also expected to be responsive to more or less constant political guidance and feedback."[10] Madisonians might object, viewing this model of public management as undermining the Constitution and subverting the normal mechanisms that legislatures use to hold the executive accountable. If regulatory executives are mere implementors, then their accountability rides squarely on the question, "Did they do what they were authorized and required to do?" But when they take on the regulatory craft, and begin to exercise these forms of discretion openly, overseers will have to examine their exercise of professional judgment.

The safeguards against subversion of the constitution, according to Moore, lie in how such exploration is conducted.

> [Public managers'] most important ethical responsibility is to undertake the search for public value conscientiously. "Conscientiously" in this context means something quite simple: they have to be willing to openly state their views about what is valuable, and to subject those views both to political commentary and to operational tests of effectiveness. They should not hide their views or frustrate efforts to test the value of their operational or administrative theories. They must report honestly on what their organizations are seeking, doing, and accomplishing.

Moore argues that this conception of strategy is not an undoing of accountability but an enhancement of it. As public managers search out important new forms of work, they are duty bound to check that their plans fit with the political aspirations of overseers, and appeal to citizens and taxpayers as important work for government to be doing.[11] Other scholars have from time to time urged regulatory agencies to accept more responsibility in setting and shaping their own agenda and to be bolder in seizing the initiative.[12] Of course, they must do all this openly, ready to engage in debate, even deliberately provoking debate on important issues; always democratically responsive.

Legislatures, for their part, need to allow room for executive agencies to exercise their professional judgment—as National Academy of Public Administration's 1995 report on the EPA stresses: "At present, EPA is hobbled by overly prescriptive statutes that pull the agency in too many directions and permit managers too little discretion to make wise decisions. Congress should stop micromanaging EPA."[13] The same report presses hard for a coherent integrated governing statute but says that even in the absence of such a statute, the "EPA should promulgate a mission statement on its own." The report even suggests that setting the mission might lead to the statute, rather than the other way around, and that the agency itself might propose the statute.

Regulatory practice cannot wait for regulatory law to catch up. Legislatures will never fill all the gaps, or resolve all the conflicts, or provide adequate guidance on what takes priority, or pass laws that anticipate next year's problems. The risk business is too dynamic for regulatory practitioners to wait; they have to step out.

The Right to Choose _What_ to Work On

The second type of discretion involves _picking the important problems_, within the scope of the mission. As the discussion of the problem-solving infrastructure showed (chapter 11), agencies need a system for making explicit decisions about what to address and what not to address. All the more so (given constrained resources) if executives first extend the boundaries of their agency mission to cover risks not yet recognized in law.

NAPA points out the lack of a formal mechanism for making such choices. Even though they refer specifically to the EPA, their comment applies equally well across the entire regulatory spectrum: "There is no statutory definition of a general mission for the agency and no established criteria that the agency might use to set priorities that cut across statutory lines. EPA lacks formal mechanisms to enable it to choose among different statutory requirements."[14]

Again, some might object: these are statutory requirements after all, so what business does the executive have in choosing among them? Answer: given the resources available, and limited public tolerance for the use of state authority, such choices are inevitable. No one in their right mind would want agencies to enforce all the laws all the time. Regulators are going to make these choices one way or another. A risk orientation offers an orderly and rational system for making them.

Experienced regulatory executives recognize the need to pick and choose. To varying degrees, they do it already. Observers of the EPA point out that some managers have been able to set priorities and reallocate resources according to their own judgment about where the richest opportunities for risk reduction lie and have even been able to cut back activities in some program areas to make room for new initiatives. But apparently it helps to be out of sight, and it gets easier the further you are from Washington.[15] Also, it helps if these choices are neither announced nor formally recorded. In other words, the exercise of this form of discretion remains sporadic, subterranean, and deniable. A risk control strategy exposes and promotes this form of discretion and constructs formal systems within which it can be exercised.

The next question is who, within a regulatory agency, gets to make these choices? Senior executives? Field staff? All of them? As agencies begin to develop their risk control capabilities and recognize their need to pick and choose what to work on, at some stage they will discover the tension between centralized and decentralized exercise of this discretion. Within an agency, who gets to do the picking? Headquarters? Perhaps the unit that coordinates and tracks problem-solving activity? Or is it better to leave this to local, field-level teams that can respond to local priorities and pressures?

For OSHA, this tension arose shortly after President Clinton announced, "As goes Maine, so goes the nation." National office managers tried to replicate the Maine 200 program across the country. Meanwhile, OSHA's redesign program was encouraging each area office to engage in problem solving, which meant identifying and focusing on local priorities. Area office problem-solving teams complained that national initiatives (even national problem-solving initiatives) would swallow up all available local resources and squeeze out local problem solving. They worried particularly that problem solving at the national level, if conducted without due regard for methodological rigor, might produce action plans highly consumptive of resources (resource inefficient) and lacking adequate means for assessing their effectiveness (guaranteeing their longevity). Proponents of the centralized version—who based their case in part on the importance of national consistency—responded, in effect, "Why can't we (the national office) do problem solving too? What makes you (the area offices) think you have a monopoly on this?"[16]

Eventually, as agencies' problem-solving capabilities mature, one would expect them to be able to handle problems large and small and of every conceivable shape. The way that most agencies choose to begin is much narrower, focusing either on problems of a particular size (for example, local) or of a particular shape (for example, specific to industry segments, or to ecosystems, or to police beats). The mature version would bring a versatility that distributes the right to choose what to work on across all levels of the agency. Agencywide projects would be conceived and organized at the headquarters level, and they would have to coexist with local initiatives. Inevitably, such coexistence would require negotiation and understanding as to who can claim access to field-level resources—where the rubber meets the road regardless of the size and shape of the vehicle. Some field office time would be reserved for local projects, some for national or regional initiatives, some for interagency initiatives. Thus distributing the right to choose what to work on between levels of the agency represents another awkward balance, which the problem-solving infrastructure has to recognize and manage.

Herman Goldstein, commenting in 1996 on the surprising immaturity of most police departments' problem-solving capabilities, notes that "as much as ninety percent of all of the efforts to address problems has been at the beat or neighborhood level." He too expects to see a better balance eventually:

> Ultimately, I would hope that a pattern will emerge whereby we can efficiently blend efforts to address problems at different levels; that beat level officers can be expected to identify and often address problems on their own, but also to identify problems that can benefit from analysis at higher levels by their supervisors and by management (because they have broader jurisdiction and perhaps access to more resources); and that some problems of national significance can be appropriately addressed at the national level.[17]

With the benefit of chapter 11's examination of the organizational infrastructure necessary to support problem solving, it is rather easy to guess why police departments have been slow to extend their problem-solving capabilities up the hierarchical chain and to move beyond the implementation of problem solving as a question of personal style for beat officers. Problem solving at higher levels depends on a supporting organizational infrastructure in a way that beat-level operations do not. Selecting and commissioning larger projects also requires that the right to choose what to work on be embraced and defended at the executive level, rather than being relegated to the street.

The Right to Choose *How* to Work on It

Once the mission is set and important issues selected, the opportunity comes to exercise the regulatory craft. All the tools should be available. Those responsible for solving the problem should have the latitude to experiment, to try different methods and different combinations. When no suitable tools exist, they should be encouraged (or required) to invent new ones.

Enforcement staff and investigators join in the problem-solving process. They sit down with educators, negotiators, rule writers, and process managers, all of them drawn together around a problem (not a case) and sharing responsibility for solving it. Solutions may involve enforcement actions, often coordinated with other "offers" or outreach campaigns. Action plans might deploy investigative field-craft in a preventive (for example, screening) mode; or intelligence operations in a proactive capacity, to help uncover the true nature of the problem or to identify opportunities for intervention. Some solutions might involve more complex structuring of enforcement-discretion, making enforcement decisions dependent upon *other behaviors* (as in Maine 200), or even upon the *behavior of others* (as in Operation Ceasefire). And all such solutions—before they are implemented—have to pass the test of legality, feasibility, and economy with respect to public and private resources.

Enforcement Discretion

What happens to enforcement discretion in this more complex scheme? Enforcement decisions still have to be made. Violations, reported or observed, still have to be disposed of one way or another. In the early days of the Compliance 2000 philosophy at the Internal Revenue Service, criminal investigators were trying to figure out what it all meant for them. They sought reassurance from their boss, Inar Morics, head of the Criminal Investigation Branch at the time. According to Morics:

> I tell them it's not going to change the way you do business. You are still going to go out and interview people and gather evidence and try to put people in jail if they deserve to be there. What it should change is *who you do it to*. You should now be doing it not to targets of opportunity that come along . . . but because in this district we have a major problem with this particular type of tax-payer.[18]

As regulatory agencies shift more and more of their energy and attention into risk control operations, we should expect case disposition decisions to be derived, increasingly, from decisions already made about which problems to work on and how to work on them. Investigations conducted and cases made will be justified less often on their own merits and more often for the contribution they make to integrated compliance strategies. Enforcement attention will be carefully aimed at patterns of violations closely related to specific problems upon which the agency has chosen to concentrate. So this (fourth) form of discretion should become increasingly dependent upon, or derived from, the first three.

But what of the serious violations that surface, not a part of any particular pattern or trend? Clearly regulators should still pursue serious offenses, lest the credibility of the agency and respect for the law be undermined. Risk control should not displace a concern for justice, nor permit bad actors to walk away. Rather, the requirements of risk control have to balanced with the requirements of justice and equity, and the setting of this balance (like so many others) will occur as agency executives make their resource allocation decisions. Given the high cost of enforcement actions and the constrained capacity of the justice system, executives may have to raise the bar a little for the one-off cases that have no broader context, to free up sufficient investigative and enforcement resources to serve risk reduction operations.

There is no reason why well-articulated and well-coordinated control strategies should not engage a substantial proportion of an agency's enforcement effort. In fact, the proportion of enforcement cases that derive from explicit risk reduction strategies, rather than arising from routine process loads, may act as a useful indicator of how far problem-solving has penetrated the organization.

Responsiveness versus Consistency

And as you carefully pick and choose what to do and how to do it, reconcile your pursuit of effectiveness with the values of justice and equity.

Risk control effectiveness may conflict with the values of equity and consistency. The Massachusetts commissioner of revenue's "go find me a yacht" seems unfair from the point of view of the hapless victim. Yes the deadbeat dad had been delinquent, and the agency acted within its rights with respect to that delinquency. But many others dads, equally delinquent, were not selected. Perhaps more significantly, those others did not have their delinquency broadcast on the evening news. Regulatory fairness would seem to call for uniformity and consistency. Regulatory effectiveness seems to call for focusing, targeting, artful selection, symbolic actions, and unusually harsh treatment in select cases (remember Freddy Cardoza, the Boston gang member who went to jail for nineteen years for possession of a single bullet).

Reconciling or balancing these different values is challenging. Fairness normally requires equal treatment and handling of like offenders, plus a sliding scale of punishment appropriately aligned with the degree of severity of the offense. The justice system normally judges severity of an offense only by reference to the culpability of the offender (including their past history) and the degree of actual or potential harm. Severity of an offense has little or nothing do with an agency's current priorities or project plans. In the context of a risk control strategy, however, an overriding concern for fairness can take away any room to maneuver. It is not possible to prosecute one offender without prosecuting them all. There is no place for symbolic actions or for picking a few for the sake of making an example. There is no place for randomness or experimental treatments. Certainly there is no place for enforcement decisions based upon other behaviors or the behavior of others.

Regulators need to understand the other values with which equity competes and the reasons that equity might not always win. It is appropriate for regulators to stress equity (and create systems and policies to guarantee it) as a way of driving out irrational inconsistency—and the accompanying demons of arbitrariness, capriciousness, sloth, and corruption. But it is also appropriate to allow the value of equity to be superseded by *rational inconsistencies*, which arise as a result of special projects, targeting schemes, symbolic actions, leveraging of scarce resources, and optimization of behavioral impacts (for example, when tax agencies go after celebrities for the sake of the attendant publicity). But if regulators are permitted to be inconsistent, how will the regulated community, the legislature, and the public distinguish between rational and irrational exercise of such discretion? Answer: by calling the agency management to account, and having them explain the basis for their choices.

Some of their answers, perfectly reasonable within the context of a risk control operation, might surprise stakeholders and onlookers. If they ask why A was prosecuted, whereas B (who behaved similarly) was not, they might hear explanations they do not normally hear from regulators: "A's local area office was running a special project on this type of noncompliance, whereas B's was not; and we have given the area offices the freedom to make these choices." Or "We only needed one for our compliance plan, and the timing was good in A's case." Or "We chose A because of the density of his network connections and the effect we expected our action against him to have among his associates." Or "An important element of this particular compliance plan is that we not reveal the basis for target selection. We've explained this to the oversight committee; you can take your concerns there." Or "We prosecuted A for A's violations because he failed to control C's behavior, whereas B succeeded." Or "A fell into the experimental group, whereas B fell into the control group."

The risk control business introduces a rich variety of rational inconsistencies. All of them are perfectly defensible and regulators will grow accustomed to describing and defending them as they learn to exercise more deliberately these several forms of discretion.

A Challenge to Programmed Discretion

However much we may applaud regulatory interventions involving structured use of enforcement discretion, we should not assume that all segments of the regulated community will take readily to the idea. OSHA's experience with its cooperative compliance program suggests there may be some legal obstacles yet to be overcome.

The cooperative compliance program (CCP) evolved out of OSHA's earlier efforts to replicate the Maine 200 program. The CCP was designed to encourage employers with relatively dangerous workplaces to enter into a partnership with OSHA—under the threat of a comprehensive inspection if they did not—and to construct comprehensive safety and health programs. The dangerous workplaces were identified through analysis of national statistics on workplace injuries and illnesses; roughly 12,500 workplaces were identified as having particularly high rates. The analysis was performed, and the program conceived, centrally.

The way the program would have operated (if it had ever been implemented) was as follows: OSHA would place all 12,500 high-risk workplaces on its primary inspection list and then approach the employers with the same choice offered under the Maine 200 program. The employers in the target group could reduce the probability of an inspection by 70 to 90 percent (but not eliminate it entirely) if they participated in the cooperative compliance program. An agreement with OSHA under the program obliged them to identify and correct hazards and to work toward a significant reduction in injuries and illnesses. Particularly troubling for industry, participants in the program were also required to establish a comprehensive safety and health program that moved beyond existing OSHA standards. An adequate safety and health program was required, for example, to address specific substantive problems associated with ergonomics: "An effective [program] looks beyond specific requirements of law to address all hazards. It will seek to prevent injuries and illnesses, whether or not compliance is at issue."[19]

In March 1998, the Federal Appeals Court for the District of Columbia issued a stay against OSHA's cooperative compliance program, based on objections presented by the U.S. Chamber of Commerce. The chamber and other critics attacked the compliance program on two fronts. First, they said that when an agency "fetters its own discretion"—in this case, by removing discretion from field-level inspectors and mandating what OSHA should do when rates of injury at a site exceed a certain threshold—it has made, in effect, a new rule; and the making of rules is permitted only when accompanied by adequate public notice and opportunity for comment. OSHA, they claimed, had failed to follow the notice and comment procedure.[20]

Second, critics saw the compliance program as OSHA's attempt to regulate ergonomic injuries through the back door, knowing that Congress was unlikely to support promulgation of an ergonomics standard. Baruch Fellner, lead counsel for the Chamber of Commerce, said "OSHA has to deal with these issues straight up" and that they were engaging in "mischief." OSHA's approach was, he said, "far too clever by half."

Over a year later, in April 1999, the Court issued its final verdict. The structuring of discretion had, in the Court's view, the practical effect of a rule, and therefore OSHA should have provided a public notice and comment period. OSHA had argued that its compliance program represented little more than a formalized inspection plan and that such rules of agency procedure were exempt from the notice and comment requirement. OSHA also argued that participation in the compliance program was voluntary, so nothing in the program design or content carried the force of law. The Court rejected these arguments, vacating the rule, but leaving open the path for OSHA to repromulgate it with an appropriate notice and comment provision. In the meantime, for OSHA to proceed with the program would have constituted contempt of court. Within a week of the Court's decision, OSHA announced that it had no plans for reviving the cooperative compliance program through formal rule making, but would instead target 2,200 dangerous workplaces (identified through the same analysis) for formal inspections by the end of the year.[21] If the regulated community did not appreciate novel programs based on structured discretion, OSHA figured, they could have it the old way.

In the grander scheme of things, the demise of OSHA's cooperative compliance program probably represents only a temporary setback. As risk orientation takes firmer hold, regulators will continue to devise rational, sensible, and artful ways of structuring their discretion; and they will continue to influence behaviors beyond the strict limits of existing law. Of course, the design of such structures should be open to challenge and review. But eventually such practices will come to be accepted as a normal component of the regulatory craft. (The alternatives are hardly appealing; they are just more familiar.)

Meanwhile, OSHA's experience with the program serves as a reminder that such practices are not yet considered normal and that regulatory agencies are more likely to face legal challenge when they declare the basis for their exercise of discretion—however rational—than when they exercise their discretion in an arbitrary manner without declaring it.

CHAPTER EIGHTEEN

Intelligence
and Analysis

Never to be undertaken thoughtlessly or recklessly, war was to be preceded by measures designed to make it easy to win. The master conqueror frustrated his enemy's plans and broke up his alliances. He created cleavages between sovereign and minister, superiors and inferiors, commanders and subordinates. His spies and agents were active everywhere, gathering information, sowing dissension, and nurturing subversion. The enemy was isolated and demoralized; his will to resist broken. Thus without battle his army was conquered, his cities taken and his state overthrown.

SUN TZU, *The Art of War*

THE ART OF WAR, according to Chinese military strategist Sun Tzu— writing roughly 2,400 years ago—is more about thought, analysis, and outwitting one's opponent than about military force. Tzu downplays the importance of destroying the enemy, treating that as an option of last resort, a sign of failure. The better the planning, the less force that is necessary. Note how little emphasis he places on military might, and how much on functions that are essentially analytical: "Now the elements of the art of war are first, measurement of space; second, estimation of quantities; third, calculations; fourth, comparisons; and fifth, chances of victory."[1]

War is waged against conscious opponents, as are some parts of regulatory and enforcement strategy. Drug smugglers, terrorists, and fraud perpetrators, for example, pit their wits against the authorities, searching for ways to thwart control strategies. When regulators face conscious and deliberate human opposition, their control strategies must take the possibility of displacement into account, as opponents constantly seek out alternative avenues for their illicit enterprise. Other regulatory risks—those concerning health, safety, and the environment— generally do not have a mind of their own and do not adapt or mutate to thwart authorities' interventions. There are interesting exceptions to this that have consequences for control strategies. For example, pollution problems may move if humans shift pollutants from one medium to another, which is particularly likely when environmental enforcement is not coordinated across different media programs; and certain diseases, through natural processes, have produced mutations resistant to commonly used antibiotics. But generally, suppression of one type of workplace injury, or one cause of airplane crashes, or one kind of disease does not increase the likelihood of any other kind of harm.

The wisdom of Sun Tzu can be applied across the regulatory spectrum, whether the risk involves conscious opponents (bringing the possibility of counterintelligence and adaptation) or not. The better one understands a risk and the more insightfully one picks it apart, the less brute force will be needed to contain or suppress it.

This chapter explores the role that intelligence and analysis play in supporting regulatory risk-control operations. First, let us consider a series of effective interventions, and ask what role analysis played in the design and implementation of the solution.

Effective Interventions

Regulators usually associate analysis with *science,* emphasizing formal knowledge and known methods of enquiry. By contrast, Sun Tzu associates analysis and intelligence with the *art* of war, which shifts the emphasis toward insight, perception, and creativity. In the following examples, there is something almost playful about the analyses that underpin the various intervention plans.

The French Connection. Strategic analysis played a crucial role in destroying the heroin supply operations of the Alberto Larrain Maestre system during the early 1970s. The smuggling operation was dubbed the French Connection because drugs were routed to the United States from source countries via Paris. Analysts identified one crucial *role* in the smuggling operation—that of smuggling organizer—which represented a vulnerability of the criminal enterprise. Smuggling organizers recruited couriers among the traveling public, a specialized task requiring considerable insight into human nature as well as an understanding of the behavioral and demographic profiling techniques used by law enforcement. Concentrating enforcement attention on this one specific role produced a shortage that eventually incapacitated the entire organization.[2]

Street Drug Dealing in Tampa. During the late 1980s, drug dealing and drug-related crime dominated the streets of Tampa, Florida. Tampa police, working with the Federal Bureau of Investigation and the Drug Enforcement Administration, used traditional methods to target mid- to upper-level traffickers (the familiar kingpin strategy). It did not work. Rather it produced a healthy promotion system within the drug organizations. Later, a newly formed police squad attacked street dealers, making more than 12,000 arrests in a three-year period. That made no dent in the problem either; apparently there was no shortage of street dealers. Finally, Tampa police recognized that convenient *spaces* for street dealing were in short supply, so much so that rival gangs were fighting over control of them.

Police made an inventory of these "dope holes," identifying sixty-one of them. They assigned these locations to police teams, who were tasked with making drug dealing awkward at each one by whatever means they could dream up. Officers used a variety of methods, from parking a police car at the spot, to sitting on the sidewalk in a lounge chair, to enlisting spotters in nearby apartment complexes to tell them where the dealers hid their drugs when the police came by. Within six months from inception of this program (in 1989) drug dealing had declined substantially. By March 1990 only nine of the original sixty-one sites remained active. By 1991 street drug dealing was virtually eliminated, and the level of complaints about drug dealing had dropped to zero.[3]

Operation Ceasefire. The Boston gun project set out to control juvenile homicide and violence by uncovering, and then interrupting, the means by which juveniles obtained guns. As the project developed, the analytic base broadened and other opportunities for intervention were identified. The population at risk turned out to be active gang members: highly concentrated, tightly networked, and mostly well known to the criminal justice system. Most homicides were results of intergang conflicts, which were enumerated and mapped by debriefing street-level workers with knowledge of them. An intervention strategy, which came to be known as Operation Ceasefire, was then crafted to exploit the tight concentration of homicide offenders and victims within the gang network and to turn gang loyalties and peer pressure to the authorities' advantage by threatening action against the whole gang for the actions of any one member. Youth gang violence decreased dramatically.

Maine 200 Program. Staff at OSHA's area office in Maine purchased from the state government a database of Maine's compensation claims for workdays lost to injury and illness and set to work sorting the data in various ways. They found that a significant concentration of risk lay with just 200 employers (205 employers originally, but the list was later pared down). These represented only 1 percent of Maine's employers but employed 30 percent of the state's work force and accounted for 44 percent of the state's compensable claims. The new partnership program, Maine 200, was then designed to act upon and through these 200 employers.

The analysis focused upon *numbers* of days lost rather than *rates* of injury and illness per worker. In other words, there was no adjustment for company size. The 200 employers therefore did not represent the most dangerous places to work. Rather, this relatively small set of employers provided OSHA an access point, or intervention opportunity, allowing them to reach a high proportion of workers at risk in a resource-efficient manner.

Eradicating Sweatshops in the Garment Industry. The Department of Labor's Wage and Hour Division, with only 800 investigators and inspectors, knew that noncompliance with labor laws was rampant among the 22,000 contractors that supplied the $45 billion garment industry. The division's investigative resources were spread too thin to make any significant impact, but analysis showed the garment industry to be structured like a pyramid, with relatively few retailers at the top buying finished goods from manufacturers, who in turn contract the work out to the contractors. To gain leverage over the whole industry, the Wage and Hour Division focused its scarce resources at the top of the pyramid by enforcing prohibitions against interstate shipment of goods made in violation of labor laws. The division threatened to mobilize media and public opinion against violators, thus pushing retailers into monitoring compliance among their own suppliers and contractors.

Marine Safety in Commercial Shipping. The U.S. Coastguard's Office of Marine Safety, Security, and Environmental Protection disaggregated statistical data relating to worker fatalities in commercial shipping.[4] Although the raw numbers were not high, fatality rates were particularly high for commercial towing operations. The office shared this data with the towing industry, leading to a collaborative study to identify the major causes of fatalities. It turned out that a significant proportion of the casualties were deckhands, most of whose deaths resulted from falling overboard. The standard form of towboat inspections did not address that particular problem. The Office of Marine Safety subsequently formed a partnership with the towing industry to find targeted solutions (mostly nonregulatory in nature) for this problem. Fatality rates dropped from 77 per 100,000 workers in 1992 to 27 per 100,000 in 1995.

Orange County (Florida) Sewage Spills. One of Florida Department of Environmental Protection's earliest problem-solving projects, run by the Orlando district office, tackled the problem of sewage overflows and spills in Orange County (the Orlando metropolitan area). In the base year (fiscal year 1996–97) the 181 spills amounted to 900,000 gallons of raw sewage, 70 percent of it ending up in Orange County surface waters. The project team, named Team SOS (sewage overflows and spills), collected data on historical spills, mapped their locations using geographic information systems, and broke the data down in as many other ways as they could think of.

Everyone assumed at the outset that spills would show significant seasonal variation, but the data showed no such trend. So Team SOS categorized spills by cause, then by location, by repeat offenders (different municipalities or sewage treatment contractors), by surface water destination, by season, by size. They found that the greatest number of spills were the result of blocked sewage lines (with restaurant grease high on the list of causes) and that the largest spills in gallons were the result of electrical power failures at pumping stations. Team SOS shared these findings with Orange County Utilities and worked with the utility companies to address the major causes. As a result, Orange County installed cell phone autodialers on lift stations to report imminent spills before they happened; enlisted the help of citizens living nearby by mailing out refrigerator magnets explaining what to if they saw an overflow; diverted hydrogen sulfide away from switch boxes at the lift stations to reduce the corrosion that leads to malfunctions; and (with the Department of Environmental Protection) educated restaurant owners on how to trap kitchen grease. By the year's end, raw sewage spills had been cut by 30 percent (270,000 gallons) and the amount spilled to surface waters by 65 percent.

The analysis—and the risk-control orientation—has enabled Orange County to focus its capital improvements. Orange County Utilities and the Department of Environmental Protection published a paper on the lessons learned from Team SOS's experience for use by other Florida utilities. The project continues.[5]

Strategic and Operational Analysis

What do these stories have in common? Certainly not that they used the same kind of analysis or similar sources of data. In six of the seven examples, the analysis required data not normally kept by the agency. In all seven examples, the specific form of analysis that provided the insight had never been done before. And the specific form of analysis was, for each of the seven, different. Yet the contribution of analysis in all cases—despite the different settings, data sources, and analytic methods—is exactly the same: analysis revealed a concentration of the risk, or a previously undiscovered view of the problem, that indicated an opportunity for resource-efficient intervention. In one case, analysis revealed a role vulnerability (courier recruiters); in another, a concentration of the risk (deckhands falling overboard); in others, an opportunity to leverage scarce resources by acting through a relatively small subset of the regulated community (garment retailers; the 200 employers in Maine). In every case, new insights opened up new possibilities for intervention. This analytic focus is intensely practical. The objective is not to produce research (although research may appear along the way) or to establish causality definitively; the object is to produce *insight with a view to action.*

The law enforcement, military, and intelligence professions normally draw a distinction between *strategic* and *tactical* analysis, although many other regulatory professions do not use that language. In the context of criminal intelligence analysis, tactical analysis—also called *operational* or *investigative* analysis—is defined as "the analysis of data collected as part of an investigation of a criminal violation." Strategic analysis, by contrast, focuses upon larger objects: "the analysis of a crime group, overall criminal activity, or situation which results in the production of a report on that group, activity, or situation and includes recommendations for future action."[6] In the military context, strategic analysis is associated with figuring out what long-term capabilities are needed and *which* battles to fight, whereas tactical analysis is about *how* to fight them.

Advocates for better use of strategic analysis by law enforcement complain than the prevailing emphasis on tactical intelligence produces a certain myopia:

> In [the] investigative process a crime occurs, it is reported to the police, and an investigation is initiated. In essence, investigation is usually a reaction to an external stimulus. Seldom do we find intel-

ligence units undertaking detailed assessments of criminal markets or organizations and transmitting these assessments to operational units for investigative action. Rather, the intelligence process is subservient to the investigative process. In effect, the "tail is wagging the dog"; investigations guide the intelligence process. For sound policy to emerge, it is essential that the intelligence process be used as a mechanism to develop well-reasoned assessments, which are ultimately transformed into investigative plans implemented by operational units.[7]

Now, back to the seven examples. Is the analysis in those instances strategic or tactical? The question is confusing, given the advent of the new, intermediate-level unit of work, variously called *problems, patterns,* or *risk concentrations.* As objects of study, these are each smaller than a strategic focus yet larger than a case. If the work of an enforcement agency consists of choosing cases and then making them, the distinction between strategic and tactical analysis would remain fairly clear. Strategy is about choosing them; tactics are about making them. But when a regulatory or enforcement agency turns to risk control, this binary or polarized distinction between strategic analysis (at the highest levels of the organization) and tactical analysis (in the context of specific investigations) is replaced by a more complex continuum.

At the highest levels of the organization, executives engaged in strategic planning set long-range goals for the agency and manage portfolios of projects contributing to the attainment of these goals. Permeating every level of the risk control organization is assessment, comparison, and evaluation; and a new hunger for analytic insights that reveal better ways of defining problems, carving them up into actionable pieces, tackling them, and measuring progress. Just as the supporting organizational infrastructure stretches from high-level strategic planning down to individual projects with their action plans (and connects them), so analysis supports that fabric at every level: breaking down mission and strategic focus areas into risk areas; identifying risk concentrations and subcomponents and subcomponents of subcomponents; assessing, prioritizing, and breaking them down into actionable projects; and finally supporting each one through the stages of the problem-solving procedure. The whole operational structure is intensely analytical.

We might anticipate, given this heavy dependence on analysis, that an agency embracing risk management as an organizing philosophy could not proceed far without fathoming the nature of the underlying analytic support. Witness the experience of the U.S. Coast Guard in the context of a Government Performance and Results Act pilot program. Commander Rick Kowalewski served as chief of the Strategic Planning and Analysis Branch (for the Office of Marine Safety, Security, and Environmental Protection) from 1992 to 1995, a period during which the branch explored what it meant to get into the risk management business. Kowalewski reports:

> Data analysis presented a surprisingly contentious issue. For several months, agreement could not be reached on whether the data analysis function ought to be distributed or centralized in the organization, or, if centralized, what part of the organization should be responsible for it. There were basic differences about what analyses needed to be done, and what needed to be done first. . . .
>
> A focused, short-term effort to *demonstrate* the development of performance measures was proposed to break the logjam. We created an ad-hoc Program Evaluation Group of "experts"—with academic backgrounds and experience in economics, operations research, and policy analysis—from throughout the organization. This group substantially advanced the sophistication of our baseline measures, began to disaggregate the data to identify important risk factors for targeting, outlined a range of external factors potentially affecting achievement of our goals, and identified several possible unintended effects of our programs for further study.[8]

With respect to the issue of marine safety, the approach was to start with high-level data on fatalities and injuries and begin breaking them down. Disaggregation of the data (the same term Herman Goldstein uses) provided the basic analytical fabric that connected high-level strategic focus areas with low-level, actionable, projects. This disaggregation became *strategic* in the sense that it changed the Coast Guard's priorities and resource allocation decisions:

> By disaggregating high-level measures like worker fatalities and passenger vessel casualties, we have begun using trend and risk information to redirect activities and resources toward achieving our goals. We found several surprises, including some risks we had underestimated, and some program successes we didn't realize we could claim.[9]

But this analysis is also *tactical* (at a finer-grained level) in that it provides insight into the causes and components underlying specific risk concentrations (for example, deckhands in the commercial towing industry falling overboard), insights that, in turn, suggest possibilities for resource-efficient interventions.

The traditional culture of law enforcement has not always appreciated analytic insights. Civilian law enforcement agencies lag behind their counterparts in other disciplines—notably the professions of defense, intelligence, and medicine—in appreciating the wisdom of basing operations on analysis and assessment. Some enforcement agents display a hostility toward intelligence functions, a hostility that arises in part from the traditional focus on tactical analysis. It is not always clear to investigators what distinguishes the role of analyst from the role of investigator, and the investigator may feel threatened by the possibility of an analyst discovering something that the investigator did not know.[10]

Why do law enforcement agencies fail to appreciate the value of strategic analyses (above the level of case support)? To the degree that these agencies are locked in a reactive, case-making, and process-oriented mode, it should come as no surprise. If their organizational and operational practices revolve around cases and processes, and if there is no practice of organizing around patterns, problems, trends, or risk concentrations, then nothing in the daily routine results in the commissioning of such analysis. Nobody asks for it, because no one's job requires it. No resource allocation decision or intervention plan depends on it. Moreover, even if strategic intelligence is offered by an analyst or an intelligence officer (a potentially threatening moment for any middle manager, as intelligence might reveal their energies to be misdirected or their methods ineffective), as often as not there is no managerial mechanism capable of absorbing and using it. The rigidity of operational forms and methods precludes such adjustments, and so managers are obliged to reject or ignore new insights and certainly never ask for them.

In the civilian law enforcement community, the discipline of intelligence analysis is relatively young and weakly established, but it is growing. The International Association of Law Enforcement Intelligence Analysts was created in 1980 with the purpose of professionalizing the field of law enforcement analysis, and in 1990 the Society of Certified Criminal Analysts, with formal testing and certification requirements, was created in the United States. The Federal Bureau of Investigation's training academy at Quantico, Virginia, instituted crime analyst training only in 1993.[11]

Within this still relatively young criminal intelligence field, a new concept has popped up in the last several years that seems to be exactly what the risk control model needs: *intelligence-led policing*. Although the concept has so far been only weakly connected with the literature on problem-oriented policing, intelligence-led policing has been called "a model of policing in which intelligence serves as a guide to operations, rather than the reverse. . . . Police managers must be prepared to stand away from traditional police philosophies and methodologies; to believe that operations can and should be driven by intelligence; to act rather than react."[12] This concept embraces the notion of disaggregating data at multiple levels of granularity. "The intelligence-led policing environment requires the analyst to be capable of viewing multiple data and finding both small and large patterns to guide police efforts."[13]

One proponent of intelligence-led policing (Russ Porter, special agent in charge of the Intelligence Bureau for Iowa's Department of Public Safety) recognizes the role that analysis should play in identifying and assessing problems and monitoring the impact of interventions: "Should we plan and carry out law enforcement operations in ignorance? Of course not. We need accurate and timely information that will identify and prioritize our most important problems. We can then use that information to develop effective responses, and tell us if our actions made a difference."[14] A British observer, describing a review and revamping of Kent County constabulary's intelligence function undertaken between 1993 and 1995, points out the weaknesses of traditional intelligence functions: "The review described the force's intelligence capability as passive, poorly resourced, lacking management attention and producing little in terms of usable products for either uniform patrols or detectives. . . . The review team envisioned an intelligence function at the very heart of the decision making process."[15]

The idea of an intelligence or analysis function at the very heart of the decisionmaking process contrasts sharply with the traditions of law enforcement agencies' research and planning departments or policy units attached loosely to headquarters, producing reports read mostly by outsiders and isolated from daily operations. As John Eck points out, for police "applied research is a management tool."[16] In a risk control setting, analysis cannot be separated from operations. If analysis and operations do remain (or become) separate, then each loses its effectiveness. Analytic units will be unable to commission a field investigation of newly identified or emerging issues (having no operational arm), and their findings will be largely written off by operational units as research. Operational units will focus on traditional areas, using traditional means; they will remain oblivious to emerging or evolving risks, missing the benefits of analytic insight and new perceptions that would offer opportunities for intervention.

In the context of risk control, operations and analysis go hand in hand. Analysis is operational, and operations are analytical. Separate them, and the whole strategy falls apart.

The Roles of Analysis in Risk Control

Certain aspects of a risk control operation impose special demands on information management. Special attention is required to perform each of the following functions

Scanning for emerging or evolving threats, as well as periodically reassessing the extent and nature of more familiar threats. When agencies have responsibility for risks that do not reveal themselves, or that are not properly represented in the work that arrives in the in basket, they may have to invest in the construction and operation of systems designed to *make the invisible visible*—to show them what they otherwise would not have known.

Defining risks, risk concentrations, or problems in the clearest, most natural ways, and helping operational officers avoid the temptation to define risks in terms or dimensions that mirror existing agency boundaries, internal divisions, existing capabilities, or traditional responses.

Exploring and assessing risks (after they have been nominated for attention but before they are presented for selection). Management may need to commission further data gathering and analysis before making their selection decisions. Initial data gathering and assessment, coupled with collection of external perspectives on the problem, may result in a restatement or redefinition of the problem and a reappraisal of its core components. These early assessments should establish (a) an understanding of the nature and sources of a problem and (b) an assessment of its relative significance compared with others that compete for attention and resources.

Prioritizing risks. Managers, not analysts, ultimately have to make the selection decisions. They often wish they had more complete or more definitive information on which to base those decisions. To support managers in their role, analysts must provide the best available information about the nature of the harm or hazard, the degree of exposure, the nature of the population at risk, and information regarding public and political attitudes toward the risk. Where managers have to choose between unlike risks, they may need some creative analytic help in converting the hazards or harms, as far as reasonable, into comparable units. (For an example of some creative work in this area, note the Environmental Defense Fund, which established an Internet site in 1998, taking existing Toxic Release Inventory data on emissions from 17,000 industrial facilities, and calculated for each chemical release a *toxic equivalency potential* to help the public understand the relative risks posed.[17] For carcinogens they used *benzene equivalents*. Other methods of ranking dissimilar carcinogenic hazards include use of the HERP index, which relates human exposure to carcinogenic potency in rodents.[18])

Disaggregating risks. It is also the analyst's job to dive into the data, slicing and dicing in every conceivable way, in search of insights with a view to action. These insights help provide artful ways and the right choice of dimensions in which to subdivide big, broad risks into discrete subcomponents, each of which comprises an actionable project with a substantial core. Risks are addressed most efficiently and effectively when problems are defined, and then subdivided, in terms natural to the problem rather than natural to the agency. Herman Goldstein emphasizes the multidimensional nature of the analytic task in the context of policing, urging analysis of the actors (victims, offenders, and third parties) and the nature of the incidents (sequences of events, immediate effects, long-term effects) and careful examination of existing responses from the agency, the community, and other institutions.[19]

Most regulatory agencies have their own preferred methods of dividing regulated risks. These methods may derive from their authorizing statutes or their internal structures, from the kinds of problem they have faced in the past, or from their analytic capabilities. The Consumer Product Safety Commission, for example, by virtue of its mission, thinks in terms of products or classes of products, analyzes injury and illness data that way, and fashions its interventions around specific products or manufacturers. Such analysis produces fascinating, and sometimes surprising, data. For example, extrapolating from the caseloads of a sample of hospital emergency rooms, the CPSC found that in 1997 an estimated

411,689 Americans were injured by their beds, mattresses, or pillows seriously enough to warrant emergency room admission, a figure that dwarfs the numbers hurt by skateboards (48,186), trampolines (82,722), and razors, shavers, or razor blades (40,773).[20] And apparently more people were hurt by sound-recording equipment (38,956) than by chain saws (29,684). Often such findings, perhaps products of quirky or unrepresentative data or data collection techniques, are counterintuitive. Perhaps the data for bedding-related injuries includes folk who simply became sick during the night. Perhaps being injured by sound-recording equipment includes being hit by a car while wearing a Walkman. In any case, the extraordinary figures for bedding-related injuries prompted one commentator on the American way of life to question whether Americans were "more inept than the rest of the world" when "it comes to lying down for the night."[21]

The Occupational Safety and Health Administration, like the CPCS, might classify injuries according to the nature of product being used at the time of an accident, but that is only one of many conceivable lines of inquiry. They might also want to know the demographic characteristics of victims, in order to identify populations at risk. They might slice the data by industry segment in order to target their routine inspection programs. They would want to discover geographic concentrations and to understand the effects of climate and season. They might also identify particularly dangerous tasks being attempted, in order to influence industrial practices. They would probably want to discern what items of safety equipment were either in use or not in use; compare different times of day, or week; and consider the effects of shift work. The ways of examining these issues are endless. The task of analysts is to find *useful* ways: ways that suggest courses of action.

Where risk management experts have examined specific risks in other fields, one sees this playful and experimental slicing and dicing all the time. Consider, for example, the problem of sudden death among competitive athletes (just one of the risks that sports program administrators are advised to consider). One assessment of this particular problem examines, first, the medical causes of death. The principle causes, based on a study of 134 sudden deaths, turn out to be hypertrophic cardiomyopathy (37 percent) and coronary anomalies (19 percent). Second, by sport being played: basketball (35 percent) and football (33 percent). Then, considering possible interventions (and screening programs in particular), the analysis explores the extent to which early warning signs were displayed or could have been uncovered; and then, deeper into the costs and benefits of intervention strategies, how to focus screening programs on the population segments most at risk.[22]

An investigation into the causes of tractor overturns, conducted by the National Institute for Occupational Safety and Health (NIOSH), shows the same kind of analytic versatility and open-mindedness. NIOSH studied the problem in the first place because tractor overturns account for 50 to 60 percent of tractor-related fatalities. In other words, tractor overturns represent a significant risk concentration in a specific subset of injuries (tractor-related fatalities) in a specific industrial segment (agriculture). In disaggregating this data even further, NIOSH considers front, rear, or side overturns; then, the effects of topography (roadsides, roads, fields, ditches); the nature of loads carried; the tractor's age; effects of engine horsepower; effects of tractor design; then, the effects of compliance with roll bar and seat belt requirements; then, determination of criteria affecting roll bar protection; then, special problems regarding the carrying of passengers; and so on.[23]

The public health field finds it useful to divide opportunities for intervention by the chronology of an illness. So they have primary prevention (for example, vaccination), secondary prevention (for example, screening for early symptoms), and tertiary prevention (response and treatment) as one method of classifying intervention opportunities. The emerging injury field employs its own chronological distinctions, dividing opportunities for intervention among the pre-event phase, the event phase, and the postevent phase. The injury field also considers a broader range of other cross-cutting factors, including individual behaviors, the agent (object or mechanism) of injury, the physical environment, and the socioeconomic environment.[24]

By comparison, civilian law enforcement and regulatory agencies display a distressing lack of analytical imagination, even as they move away from reactive, incident-based processing. Some focus on repeat offenders as the relevant objects for study and containment. Others focus almost exclusively on criminal organizations, aiming to incapacitate them one by one (even in situations in which there are far more criminal organizations than enforcement agencies could ever hope to close down). Some focus on spatial (hot spot) analysis to the virtual exclusion of all other methods. Some do industry segmentation, equating that with risk analysis or problem solving. These agencies need to spread their analytic wings and produce much greater analytic versatility, lest their risk control capacities remain one-dimensional. (Several times, I have been asked, "What is wrong with taking a one-dimensional approach?" Only that it means an agency will be good at dealing with one kind of risk and bad at dealing with every other kind.)

Action planning. In the problem-solving methodology, action planning comes relatively late, but effective intervention plans—as the examples above suggest—rests on analytic insights gleaned during the problem definition, assessment, and disaggregation stages. Sometimes the most valuable insights relate not simply to the nature of things (incidents, crimes, accidents) but to their relationships to one another, their sequences, structures, and cycles. Several regulatory Innovations in American Government finalists claim to have *broken the cycle*—of prostitution in San Francisco, of hiring illegal aliens in Texas, of gang-related violence in Boston. Analysts have the opportunity, therefore, to study dynamic objects as well as static collections of data and to identify critical links in those structures or cycles that regulators can then uncouple.

Monitoring impacts and outcomes. Analysis obviously plays a critical role in monitoring the effectiveness of control strategies. Project teams need help designing portfolios of measures relevant to their problem, making sure the indicators are outcome oriented, collecting and filtering the data necessary to benchmark those indicators at the outset, establishing mechanisms for collection of data as the project proceeds, and (occasionally) reconsidering the appropriateness of performance indicators as a team's understanding of a problem changes over time.

The Information Craft Shop

So much for the analytic *demands* of the risk business. What about the analytic *supply*? Obviously most agencies will be short on analysts, analytic skills, and analytic versatility. They may cobble together a new analytic unit, as did the U.S. Coast Guard. They may identify particular parts of the organization rich in analytic skills and figure how to make them more broadly available throughout the organization. They might choose analytically minded and technically competent personnel as their problem-solving consultants and facilitators. They might commission their statistics office or their research and planning units to appoint staff members to support the operational work of project teams.

Whether the provision of analytic support turns out to be centralized or decentralized, executives and managers need to be clear how it will differ from the kinds of analytic support traditionally provided for functional and process-based work. First, analytic support for risk control will have nothing routine or predictable about it; almost every analytic request will be different. Second, information about what the agency does or has done—of paramount importance in supporting and describing functional and process work—is less central to risk control than information about the risks themselves, their components, their precursors, their sources, and their dynamics; the objects of analysis are external rather than internal. Third, the analytic support required for risk control is a service, not a system: it is intensely human as well as technical.

Chapter 4 of my earlier work, *Imposing Duties,* explored the characteristics of information support for problem solving, pointing out a number of key ways in which it differed from predominant modes of analysis. Routine and reactive processes are normally supported by a data warehousing operation, characterized by the fact that what goes in ultimately comes out in exactly the same form, upon request. I used the term *data warehouse* then, in 1994, to mean the routine warehousing of operational data; that was before the term acquired its distinctive technical meaning as a product description.[25]

Risk control, however, requires a support system more akin to an information craft shop than to a data warehouse. (Ironically, the technical products called *data warehouses* can provide the underlying data access, which then has to be overlaid with a broad suite of flexible analytic tools.) The information craft shop, whether centralized or decentralized, would be staffed by analysts skilled in a range of analytical disciplines, adept at drawing raw materials (data) from a range of sources, skilled at selecting the right analytic techniques for the job, and capable of producing made-to-order information products that support decisionmakers. The nature about information support, derived from an understanding of the nature of problem solving, is summarized here.

— The dominant form of analysis will no longer be regional and national aggregation of production data. Risk identification and control places a premium on *disaggregation*, exploiting the multiple dimensionality of problems, to scan for patterns or concentrations.

— Analytic support should be provided for problem-solving initiatives at every level of the organization, from street level to nationwide programs. The cost and sophistication of the supporting analysis should be commensurate with the size and importance of the project. A practical rule of thumb, based on nothing other than my own practical observation of risk control operations, is that managers should expect to spend around 20 percent of the cost of a project on analytic support, more during the earlier stages of the procedure and less during the action phase once problem definition and measurement frames have been set in place.

— As agencies adopt a broader range of tools and techniques, so the intelligence function (accustomed to supporting enforcement and investigations) must broaden its outlook and become accessible to a wider range of functions.

— The ad hoc, unpredictable nature of analytic requirements puts a premium on improvisation, creativity, and versatility. Many problems tackled will be unfamiliar, even unique; they bring, therefore, no standard or predetermined analytical approaches.

— A risk orientation draws upon a much richer variety of data sources, many of them outside the agency. These sources will include relevant literature, agency files, and department archives (history of earlier attempts to control similar problems); rank-and-file officers, victims, and those who appear to be causing the problem; the community, other agencies, and other communities (what has been learned about this problem elsewhere).[26] The most valuable database will be the database of databases, which will grow as analysts accumulate knowledge from a variety of sources, learning their content, their strengths and weaknesses, and how to access them. Like a woodworking craft shop, standard items of raw material (data) might be kept in-house, but many others require a "special order" once a job order is received. Analysts may place less emphasis on perfecting data infrastructures and maintaining complete, accurate, and timely databases (the normal preoccupation of bureaucrats) and greater emphasis on knowing what is available and where, how to get it in a hurry, and how to integrate data from multiple sources to provide valuable intelligence products.

— Many intervention plans involve active public dissemination. These information products and analyses will therefore be shared with outsiders in the context of collaborative problem-solving projects. Information products must be designed, therefore, with the technical limitations of the audience, and the public nature of the forum, in mind.

— The "learning organization" needs searchable knowledge databases, providing access to historical and current problems, projects, solutions, and points of reference.

— Risk control operations increase the need for interagency data sharing and cross-matching, when problems fail to fit organizational boundaries neatly and when an agency's own data sources (built from its process load) do not properly reflect important problems.

— Finally, a risk orientation elevates the importance of analysis and the status of analysts and probably stretches the analytic and technical resources of most regulatory and enforcement agencies beyond their existing capacity. An investment plan is needed, therefore, to keep pace with the development of risk management operations.

Particular Classes of Risk

Three classes of risk place special burdens on analytic support and are therefore worth considering briefly.

Invisible Risks

The first class involves invisible risks, or non-self-revealing problems—issues that either by conscious design (as in the case of white-collar crime) or by a quirk of their nature are not adequately represented in the organization's process workloads. These problems do not present themselves; if an agency wants to control them, they must first deliberately uncover them.

An Australian study puts telecommunications crimes in this category, pointing out that risks might be invisible to the authorities and to the public even after they are visible to the victim. "Some of the most deftly perpetrated offenses with or against telecommunications systems are never detected, not even by their victims; of those that are, some are concealed from authorities because disclosure could prove embarrassing or commercially inconvenient to victims."[27]

Other risks that do not reveal themselves or that have extremely low reporting rates include extortion, gambling, prostitution, drug dealing, date rape, fraud, white-collar crime, and crimes within the family such as incest and sexual or physical abuse. Some harms (other than crimes) may also go unreported because of an associated stigma or because the population at risk is indisposed to complain to authorities (for example, illegal immigrants failing to report abusive work conditions) or because the harm manifests only years after the exposure.

In dealing with such issues, regulators cannot rely on the content of their incoming workload to reveal a problem's true scope and magnitude. The Consumer Product Safety Commission (CPSC), for example, cannot rely on reports from industry regarding defective products, as they have good reason to expect biased or inadequate reporting patterns. Instead, CPSC's own Compliance Special Investigative Unit integrates data from sources outside the commission, a proactive analysis that identifies many more problems than industry reports.[28]

The special challenge for intelligence and analysis, with respect to such risks, is to make the invisible visible; to scan the horizon for emerging problems, so they can be tackled before they become serious or systemic; to quantify risks so that adequate resources can be devoted to controlling them; to reveal the true nature and components of the risk, so that interventions are not structured only around the visible (unrepresentative) parts; and to sustain the quantification process over time to prevent the agency taking its eye off the (otherwise invisible) ball.[29]

To maintain this broader view, agencies need mechanisms for searching out issues that might not otherwise come to light or that might not come to light soon enough. That puts a premium on proactive intelligence gathering, undercover operations, information sharing with other agencies, creative and exploratory data mining (using both internal and external data sources and cross-matches), focus groups, questionnaires, victimization surveys, even the use of tiger teams to identify institutional or programmatic vulnerabilities. The possible existence of invisible risks elevates the importance of incorporating a random component into inspection and audit programs to show regulators what they did not know. Random inspections or audits need to be quite rigorous to serve this purpose—otherwise the manner in which the inspections are conducted may focus only on known or expected forms of noncompliance, which would defeat their purpose.[30]

The heart of the analytic challenge for invisible risks is to help regulatory, enforcement, and intelligence agencies avoid the circularity trap, in which they fish in the same parts of the river day after day because that is where they caught fish before. They focus on what they believe are the central problems, and because they focus on them, they learn more about them, and those problems become even more central in their thinking. As time passes, they work on problems they know about, and they know about problems they work on. Meanwhile, trouble may be brewing elsewhere, quietly, and out of sight. Strategic intelligence analysis reveals the broader picture, allows an agency to understand its traditional emphases against a more fully revealed landscape, and holds up newly discovered and unfamiliar issues long enough, and in a convincing enough manner, for the agency to adjust its sights.

Risks Involving Opponents

When a risk involves conscious opponents—drug smugglers, fraud perpetrators, thieves—authorities must appreciate the dynamic nature of the risk-control game. They must anticipate that problems will adapt and mutate. And they must think especially carefully about what it means to succeed.

Part of the analytic challenge is to make sure that actionable risk concentrations, or problems, are defined at a sufficiently high level that suppression of them would constitute a significant accomplishment. If the Customs Service port-running project, for example, had been defined too locally, the elimination of port running at a few border-crossing points might have presented little inconvenience to the smuggling organizations. They could have moved their operation, at almost no cost to themselves, a few miles along the border. But the discovery of a method of suppressing port running that could be implemented at all relevant ports imposed substantial costs and inconvenience on the smuggling organizations, as they had to find alternative smuggling methods.

When dealing with conscious opponents, most interventions will produce some displacement. Skeptical observers of customs' strategic problem-solving program, both inside and outside the agency, might conclude that the possibility and probability of displacement nullifies any problem-solving accomplishments against smuggling organizations. Extending this argument, some might conclude that the only success that counts in such an environment is taking out entire criminal organizations (that is, taking out the conscious opponents themselves) so they can no longer do anything.

Experience, however, suggests that defining problems in terms of criminal organizations is not always the best way to go. If there are many criminal organizations in an area of criminal enterprise, it may not even be useful. Sometimes it is better to eliminate methods (port running), or behaviors (violence in Boston's gangs), or places (dope holes in Tampa), or roles (courier recruiters), or whatever other vulnerabilites or potential scarcities analysis can reveal. For many crime problems, there is no shortage of relevant organizations, and so picking them off one by one is not a particularly hopeful strategy.

The idea that displacement renders specific problem-solving accomplishments meaningless should also be rejected. When the opposition consists of a less-than-determined criminal enterprise, evidence suggests displacement is partial, is seldom a serious threat, and that there is frequently a diffusion of benefits as crime reduction spreads beyond the confines of a specific project.[31] Even when the opposition is determined, forcing criminal enterprises to develop alternative methods, routes, and partnerships not only imposes substantial costs on their operations but also makes them vulnerable. Their adaptations produce flurries of new intelligence information (especially when agencies are deliberately watching for indications of adaptation) and may provide law enforcement special opportunities to introduce undercover agents as new partners. For criminal enterprises, setting up systems is much more dangerous than operating them. The more often they are forced to adapt, and the more substantial the adaptations they are forced to make, the more costly and dangerous their enterprise becomes. When law enforcement agencies focus on specific subcomponents of major crime problems, they must ensure that problem definitions are ambitious enough (that is, that the selected subcomponents are large enough) to do substantial damage to a criminal enterprise if the project succeeds.

For many risks involving conscious opponents, the kind of success authorities ultimately pursue—by spotting new patterns, jumping on them quickly, and suppressing them using the most efficient means available—is to harass the opposition out of the business. In games involving intelligence and counterintelligence (like narcotics interdiction, like fraud control, like chess), he who wins is he who monitors the opponent's moves most closely, understands the opponent's strategy best, and undermines it most effectively.

A failure to invest adequately in proactive intelligence gathering and strategic analysis can have serious consequences. Without systematic efforts to uncover emerging risks, to measure their significance, to understand their nature and their key components, agencies fly blind. They remain oblivious of the magnitude of what they face. Resources are allocated without any clear sense of relative priorities, resulting in underinvestment with respect to non-self-revealing categories of risk. Without early warning when opponents change tactics, control strategies remain static, and operational methods fixed. One might as well try to play chess blindfold, and with one's chess pieces bolted to the table. Effective risk control, given the peculiar properties of this category of risk, depends utterly upon an organization's ability to commission strategic intelligence gathering and analysis and to structure its operations around the intelligence these yield.

Risks for Which Prevention Is Paramount

The kind of risk for which prevention is paramount presents extraordinary challenges for intelligence and analysis. Considering these risks carefully is instructive because they make nonsense of many familiar approaches to regulatory analysis.

Consider, for example, the prospect of nuclear or biological terrorism, in which a single successful attack could kill millions of people and irreparably damage a nation's economy and infrastructure. Not only is prevention of paramount importance, but the possibility of reaction after the fact (which would fall in the domain of emergency planning, civil defense, and disease containment) is curiously disconnected from the means of prevention (which falls to intelligence and enforcement agencies).

Immediately one realizes the futility of imagining that we could study patterns of such terrorist incidents, grouping them in artful ways and identifying major causes after the fact. A *pattern* of such incidents is unthinkable. Just *one* would be a major disaster. Nor is it particularly useful to think about enforcement after the fact, because any consequences that might be visited on perpetrators could never come close to matching the harm done. Deterrence does not count for much either, as many terrorists are prepared to die. So the normal machinery of detection, arrest, and prosecution loses its normal preventive potency. A reactive posture—wait and see what happens—is out of the question.

Given the risk of catastrophic terrorism (which, according to my colleagues at the Kennedy School who know about such things, is severely underestimated), one would expect government to spend a lot of money and effort in controlling or reducing it. But the more resources government invests in control, the more it would have to think about how to subdivide the task—and subdivide it further and further. The special analytic problem here is determining how to break down (disaggregate) the control task into specific, actionable projects so that each could be assigned and have a clear purpose and progression. The reason why this disaggregation turns out to be particularly difficult is because it has to be done way back in the chronology of a terrorist incident—long before an "event" takes place, long before an event is even imminent or proximate, way back in the realm of precursors, and precursors to precursors, and subcomponents of precursors to precursors. Interventions must be designed, and their effectiveness measured, early in a chain of events that, if uninterrupted, might lead to a catastrophe.

Many of the obvious ways to divide such a task rely on proximity to the event. It is understood how to separate domestic law enforcement issues from foreign or overseas intelligence operations and which agencies normally carry responsibility for each. If it is known that a bomb is going to be detonated on American soil, that it is of a certain type (chemical, biological, nuclear), then one can determine which agency has jurisdiction and thus responsibility for prevention. But can a nation afford to wait until it is clear where the attack might happen and what kind of weapon might be used before the work of prevention begins? Of course not; that would bring us uncomfortably close to the event itself. Besides, major terrorist groups have both domestic and foreign operations and may engage in development work, straddling national borders, long before they decide where to attack or what kind of weapon to use.

Working so far back in the chronological development of a threat renders virtually all the ways we normally divide tasks—between domestic and foreign, between intelligence and enforcement, between functional competencies—largely irrelevant. If broad strategic objectives are set but not picked apart explicitly, agencies will most likely interpret the broad strategic objectives in accordance with their own existing capabilities and preferred methods of operation. They will each want a piece of the financial pie and will use it to do more of what they do already, which may or may not be relevant. The efforts will certainly be uncoordinated; the sum of the contributions will not amount to an effective control plan.

For control to be effective, all contributing agencies must gather around these central analytic tasks, just as multifunctional teams gather around a problem-solving project. Collectively, they must formulate the analytic structure that breaks down the lofty goal of preventing catastrophic terrorism into meaningful, actionable, and specific projects, before they jump into operations.

Here the importance of analytic creativity and exploration of the multiple dimensions of the problem emerges. The problem can be sliced in many ways, and each cut (or view) could spawn a whole new set of actionable projects. Some projects might focus on potential or likely targets; others on terrorist groups; others on critical weapon components and technologies and ways of controlling or restricting their availability; others on specific chemicals and agents; others on delivery mechanisms and technologies that might be regulated or controlled (for example, the nozzle spray technology necessary to deliver anthrax spores). Other projects might focus on constructing profiles of potential terrorists and then figuring out where such people might be found. The possibilities are almost endless, and hours and hours should be spent poring over them, seeing where each leads and what each might uncover.

In a recent discussion of these issues, I stressed the importance of placing a strategic intelligence unit at the heart of the operation—creating a central "brain"—and making it responsible for chopping up the problem and parsing it out (not just once, but continuously). Another participant asked me why I was so keen on chopping up the risks. The answer is that if those responsible for controlling such risks lack the analytic fabric to disaggregate the overall problem into actionable projects, then they cannot work on them intelligently; nobody will know what to do tomorrow—except to do the same things they did yesterday.

With risks where prevention is paramount, intelligence and operations are virtually the same thing. The most important component of the control operation will be the analytic operation at its core. Strategic analysis lies at the very heart of such operations.

PART IV

Demonstrating Results

CHAPTER NINETEEN

Measuring a Risk Control Performance

CHAPTER 8 RECOUNTED the experience of regulators searching for performance measures that count and the frustrations many of them have felt as they struggle to escape reporting traditions that focus heavily upon enforcement outputs. In that discussion, we saw how regulators were turning toward more balanced portfolios of measures, augmenting their focus on *business results* with indicators of customer and employee satisfaction.

As they did so, the most significant unsolved puzzle was how they would report the business results in some way other than through enforcement statistics. If the central business of regulatory agencies really is risk control, then *business results* would mean *risks controlled*. Regulators and overseers have all recognized the need to focus on outcomes—risks mitigated, hazards eliminated, patterns of noncompliance addressed—but few to date have had much success in producing satisfactory performance accounts of that type.

At the end of chapter 8, I suspended that discussion, promising to return to it later, trusting that a better understanding of the risk-control business would make the nature of the corresponding business results seem a little less opaque.

Ten chapters later—and with most of the intervening chapters spent teasing out the practical nature of a risk control operation—I suspect that the nature of the corresponding business results will now seem rather transparent. Once one understands the nature of the risk-control performance, figuring the kind of performance *story* that goes with it becomes surprisingly straightforward.

The first step in understanding the risk control, or problem-solving, competency is to distinguish it from the competencies built around functions and processes (the work of chapter 9). The first step in performance measurement is therefore a consideration of the performance account that goes with each type of performance. Much of the frustration surrounding performance measurement stems from the fact that functional- and process-centered performance stories do not naturally include an account of risks mitigated, hazards eliminated, or patterns of noncompliance addressed. The performance account that accompanies a problem-solving or risk control operation consists almost entirely of such.

A Performance Focus

The three forms of organizational competency—functional, process, and problem solving—have different performance characteristics. The purpose of the matrix in table 19-1 is to answer the question, Where does the performance focus lie for each of these three types of competency? A simple graphic device—the allocation of eight asterisks per row across the four major categories of performance measures described in chapter 8 (see table 8-1, p. 119)—represents a crude consensus of practitioners' opinions on the question of where the emphases, in practice, rest.

As the first row of the table suggests, when performance of a specific *function* is considered in isolation, issues of productivity and efficiency dominate, because they are the easiest measures to isolate to a specific functional working group. Measures of quality, where they exist, are functionally specific and generally not extensible to other functions. (For example, the way the quality of an investigation might be assessed has little relevance to other functional activities, such as information campaigns or partnership programs.) Perhaps the most important point about function-specific performance is that credit for outcomes can be claimed only when the outcome results unambiguously and directly from the actions of one function alone—which is rare. Claiming credit for broader accomplishments is difficult and involves an assessment of the contribution to larger-scale outcomes made by specific functions.

Table 19-1. Performance Focus of Three Types of Regulatory Competency

Type of competency	Tier 4 Resource efficiency	Tier 3 Agency activities, outputs	Tier 2 Behavioral outcomes	Tier 1 Effects, impacts, outcomes
1. Functional expertise	***	***	*a	*a
2. Process improvement management	****	**	**b	
3. Compliance management/ problem solving			****c	****c

a. Limited to evaluating direct consequences of specific activities.
b. Focus on facilitation, education, outreach. Emphasis on "Voluntary Compliance."
c. But consider residual difficulties. (Inescapable Truths).

Parsing credit for major accomplishments among functions, apart from being difficult, may also not make sense. In medicine, a prescription combining several drugs may work beautifully, although any one of the component drugs used in isolation would fail. Once this combination is found, ascribing credit to certain component drugs would be meaningless. Similarly, regulatory prescriptions often involve a combination of tools (for example, carefully targeted enforcement activity coupled with an information campaign or partnership offer).

Enforcement programs, often culturally isolated within regulatory agencies, feel most acutely the limitations on outcomes they can claim as their own. Pressed to describe their performance in terms of outcomes rather than outputs, they are obliged to focus on the deterrent effects of their enforcement actions. But deterrence is notoriously difficult to isolate and measure, so the enforcement function, in describing enforcement-specific outcomes, is limited to the microlevel and local behavioral changes that result directly from individual enforcement actions.

The Environmental Protection Agency's Office of Enforcement and Compliance Assurance (OECA), reporting its fiscal year 1996 results, for the first time supplemented their enforcement numbers with information regarding direct microlevel outcomes resulting from their enforcement actions.[1] These outcomes were expressed in terms of tonnage of pollutants reduced by industrial facilities subject to enforcement actions, aggregated across enforcement targets.[2] Some of these reductions were reported in the press, although no connection was made, either by the

EPA or by the press, between pollutant reduction and associated environmental or health risks.[3] The OECA, happy to have constructed outcome measures associated with its enforcement actions, was nevertheless disappointed that these measures (not least by failing to capture deterrent effects) provided a minimal and misleading account of the enforcement function's contribution to broader environmental goals.[4]

The process management model (row 2 of the matrix) places its primary emphasis on improving productivity, efficiency, timeliness, and service in the context of the agency's core operational processes. Thus the obvious performance focus for process improvements lies within tiers 3 and 4. However, regulators (particularly the reform minded among them) believe that process improvement can increase voluntary compliance by facilitating it: make it easier for customers to comply, the argument goes, and they will. Investments in process improvement may improve levels of compliance, but these effects will likely be limited to segments of the regulated community willing to comply and to types of noncompliance caused by difficulties and frustrations associated with defects in those processes.

Apart from that particular subset of compliance problems, process improvement is seldom directly associated with the elimination or mitigation of specific risks or problems. Process improvement, after all, is organized around processes, not problems. Process improvement projects may well affect a range of problems, but they are not conceived or organized in terms of tackling risks and thus cannot usually be reported that way.

In contrast to the functional and process-centered models of professionalism, the problem-solving approach (row 3 of the matrix) aims squarely at identified risks. Thus the performance focus lies quite naturally within tiers 1 and 2.

Table 19-1 reveals one reason why regulatory agencies have had difficulty in establishing performance accounts concentrating on outcomes and compliance levels: a functional orientation supports the claiming of credit only for direct, microlevel results of specific functional actions. A process orientation may contribute to higher compliance levels, but only when facilitation and customer assistance leads to higher levels of voluntary compliance. The best hope for delivering and describing important outcomes clearly lies with the problem-solving orientation, the least mature and least well understood of regulatory competencies. Many regulators fail to produce that performance account because they are

not set up to deliver *that performance.* They struggle to squeeze a problem-solving performance account out of functional and process-based
performance.

Balanced versus Integrated Strategies

The distinction between balanced and integrated strategies laid out in
chapter 14 also has profound consequences for performance measurement. A balanced compliance strategy does not coordinate or integrate
the work of the different tools or organize them around specific risks.
Rather it sets a balance among tools. Once activity levels have been
specified—often within the context of budget preparation—each tool
(function or program) is allowed to operate in isolation from the others
and to find its own targets of opportunity. The work thus is organized
around functional tools. By contrast, an integrated compliance strategy
organizes the tools around the work, identifying important risks and
developing coordinated, multifunctional responses. Often it invents new
tools, techniques, or solutions, tailor-made for the problem at hand,
tools that would not have been created by shuffling resources among
existing functions or programs.

What kind of performance account can these strategies produce? The
balanced approach, preserving a functional orientation, offers functionally specific credit for the direct impacts of functionally specific actions.
It does not provide the opportunity for the agency to claim that it
addressed and successfully tackled major risks, because the work is neither conceived nor organized that way. By contrast, an integrated strategy directly tackles identified risks, permitting the agency to claim the
elimination or mitigation of those risks as major accomplishments.
Therefore, agencies that adopt a balanced approach but stop short of
developing the coordinating mechanisms and organizational structures
necessary to support an integrated approach will likely remain frustrated by their inability to match activities to outcomes. Their work is
still organized around functions, not problems.

Five Inescapable Truths

When agencies do eventually develop their problem-solving capabilities,
they will still face certain predictable difficulties in describing their risk
control accomplishments. Agencies and their audiences need to

acknowledge these inescapable difficulties and adjust their expectations accordingly.

Aggregating Outcome Measures

Outcome measures are usually problem specific and are therefore difficult to aggregate. The Customs Service team assigned the task of eliminating port running settled on a combination of three indicators that would show when they succeeded in reducing this form of drug smuggling: the number of port-running incidents observed (expected to decline), the number of "returns to Mexico" (expected to rise and then decline), and the price smuggling organizations paid port-running drivers (expected to rise). It is hard to imagine any other problem, even in the context of drug interdiction, in which this precise combination of measures would be relevant. The measures selected were unique to the problem addressed and of little value for broader measurement purposes. In general, measures of success in the context of the problem-solving strategy are specific to the problem at hand and thus do not lend themselves to broader aggregation.

Environmental agencies (whose landscape of possible outcomes is unusually complex and multidimensional) might point to a variety of accomplishments: restoration of endangered species' populations, protection of endangered aquifers, restoration of lakes or river to "swimmable" or "fishable" designations, reduction of rate of wetlands loss, higher compliance levels within particular industry segments, higher rates of adoption of environmentally friendly technologies by industry. Such accomplishments, described in many different terms, cannot be aggregated in a straightforward way.

Tax agencies may have some advantage here. As they tackle specific patterns of noncompliance, each pattern will have a revenue (dollar) impact, and those revenue impacts can be aggregated across unlike projects. Nevertheless, to give a compelling account of their compliance management accomplishments, even tax agencies will want to disaggregate such results and tell the particular stories of how they recognized, tackled, and eliminated different noncompliance problems. Otherwise such accomplishments will most likely be buried beneath the effects of broader economic trends.

Ultimately, the risk control model of operations is unlikely to produce a neat, simple aggregate statistical table of outcomes, representing overall agency performance. That failure may frustrate those who continue to search for a simple numerical summary to replace the old enforcement numbers (which did produce simple and unambiguous statistical summaries). Legislators and overseers, expecting outcome measures to appear in that same form, will need to adjust their expectations.

Rather than aggregate statistics, the problem-solving approach produces a performance account consisting of a collection of short stories. Each story describes a specific problem or risk, the evidence of its existence and seriousness, an account of solutions designed and implemented, and evidence of the results achieved. Each story relies on a different set of measures, tailored to the problem.

Observers should resist the temptation to dismiss these stories as anecdotes—they are neither anecdotes nor anecdotal; an anecdote is a data point suggestive of a broader reality but statistically inadequate for establishing or proving that reality. Problem-solving success stories describe significant accomplishments but are not anecdotes because they make no broader claims. When the Customs Service tells how it contained port running, it does not claim broad success against drug smuggling. Likewise, the account of the Boston gun project relates solely to juvenile and gang-related homicide—and solely to Boston. A project to control aggressive red light running in New York City makes no claim about red light running elsewhere or about other bad driving habits in New York.

The aggregate achievements of a problem-solving approach are simply the sum of individual problem-solving stories, not an extrapolation from, or generalization of, them. However, because accomplishments come in a variety of types, the sum of them cannot usually be presented in aggregate statistical form.

Proving Causality

Causality is usually impossible to prove. Seldom will a regulatory agency be able to prove causality—at least not convincingly enough to satisfy the customary standards of proof expected by academia or by scholarly social science or medical journals. Academics may be tempted to dismiss the problem-solving model because agencies are generally not able to prove that their problem-solving interventions *caused* particular outcomes.

I believe that academia has much to offer regulatory agencies—a risk control orientation demands substantial analytic sophistication, and problem-solving methods require attention to measurement and methodological rigor rare in government. As a model for regulatory practice, however, problem solving has to be an operational method, not a research method; and it has to work in an operational environment. Few agencies have the opportunity to conduct randomized, controlled experiments. Conceivably, the Internal Revenue Service, once it has the requisite information systems infrastructure, might be able to conduct massive, randomized, and controlled experiments to test taxpayer treatments, using differences in revenue raised to determine comparative effectiveness; but such opportunities are unusual. If and when manatees in the waters around Florida stop being injured by boats, the Florida Department of Environmental Protection—without the luxury of a control population of manatees—will be hard pressed to prove beyond doubt that their interventions produced this result. Critics might even claim that the situation would have improved sooner had the department left well enough alone; such claims may not be refutable.

Regulatory agencies should not feel obligated to prove causality. They should be content to demonstrate publicly their ability to focus on specific risks, to design and implement creative solutions, and to determine when the risk has abated sufficiently to permit them to move on to other priorities. A substantial collection of problem-solving success stories, accumulated over time, none of them claiming causality, constitute a compelling public account of intelligent resource allocation and agency effectiveness. I hope that academics will play the role of coach in raising the level of analytic sophistication in regulatory agencies, but they need to acknowledge the constraints imposed by an operational environment and avoid setting the analytic bar so high that practitioners turn away discouraged.

Assigning Credit

Credit cannot be assigned to an individual function, since effective solutions are seldom functionally specific. Given that many real-world problems do not neatly fit within defined programmatic or agency boundaries, successful interventions often involve many contributing parties. With increased emphasis on voluntary programs and partnerships with segments of the regulated community, some credit for regulatory accomplishments may even lie outside government.

For all these reasons, specific functions are unlikely to be able to say exactly how much credit they should claim for outcomes. Systems for parsing credit among contributors—constructed to satisfy the demands of performance-based budgeting—are likely to be arbitrary and artificial. All parties need to get used to sharing credit for major accomplishments, and performance-based budgeting systems need to acknowledge and accommodate the difficulties of parsing credit among contributors.

Measuring Prevention

Prevention is not measurable and is difficult to support over the long term. Once a regulatory agency has tackled a specific risk and brought it under control, keeping it under control may demand some long-term resource commitment. Budgetary systems are notoriously incapable of sustaining preventive operations in the long run, as long-term preventive successes are difficult to gauge. Few taxpayers are willing to keep paying for suppression of a problem that they never see.

Regulators are unlikely to be able to claim credit, or justify their budget, on the basis of problems that do not exist, even when the regulatory presence may largely account for the nonexistence of those problems. The Occupational Safety and Health Administration, for instance, cannot claim credit for all the accidents that did not happen. Nor can the Environmental Protection Agency expect to get credit for the fact that certain environmental problems do not exist within the United States.

Even as they operate successful preventive programs, in justifying their budgets and giving an account of results achieved, regulators will have to focus on *changes* in risk levels rather than on the risk levels themselves. By focusing on identified concentrations or subcomponents, and by reducing them one by one, regulators can take higher-level goals (for example, to reduce road accident fatality and injury rates, or enhance worker safety in the commercial shipping industry) and represent their success as a series of specific accomplishments, each directed at specific subcomponents of the higher-level goal.

Other Difficulties

Measuring and reporting compliance rates in a meaningful way also presents substantial challenges. Compliance, as determined by a facility inspection, might only signify compliance during the short period that an inspector is on the site. Many facilities are inspected infrequently, or never. Some forms of noncompliance are more observable than others. Some inspectors are more likely to find violations than others. And self-reported compliance rates are inevitably biased, with the extent of the bias dependent on the level of investment in verification.

Nor is compliance a simple binary affair. Some forms of noncompliance are more significant than others. In seeking to categorize the seriousness of instances of noncompliance, regulators often refer to the degree of willfulness associated with the violation, the history of the offender, and the degree of harm caused or likely to be caused by the violation. Despite attempts to define *significant* noncompliance or *egregious* violations more precisely, such categories will always remain to some degree subjective and, consequently, may appear to outsiders to be untrustworthy once incorporated into a performance measurement system.

Another difficulty relates to the fact that most readily available compliance data come from focused or biased inspection programs, which either deliberately target high-risk facilities or respond to incoming reports or complaints. Such focused or biased inspection programs help deal with specific risks that are already identified, but they cannot provide statistically valid estimates of general compliance behavior or reveal emergent risks. These purposes require representative sampling (either random or comprehensive) and require diversion of inspection or audit resources away from focused or complaint-oriented programs.

Random inspections or audits are usually as unpopular within the regulatory agency as they are among the regulated community. Employees often regard them as a waste of time, saying they could raise a lot more revenue and find more violations if they were allowed to focus on known problem areas (which is true). But that argument misses the point. The principal value of random audits by the IRS, or random searches by the Customs Service, or random audits of health care claims by Medicare is that they provide information about types of noncompliance that existing targeting strategies miss. They provide the opportunity, over the long term, to redirect resources, to make invisible problems visible, to adjust audit selection or targeting systems, to target resources, and to select enforcement actions with the greatest impact on significant areas of noncompliance. Cost-benefit analyses of such programs have to weigh the importance of the *information* they produce, which is the basis for long-term planning and resource allocation (that is, strategic intelligence), rather than focusing on immediate, case-specific returns.

Project-Specific Compliance Rates

Many problem-solving projects focus on particular patterns or forms of noncompliance (for example, failing to provide construction workers with full protection when working on scaffolding, or discharging heavy metals into slow-recharge lake systems). For focused projects of this type, selective compliance rates—measuring the rates of relevant forms of noncompliance—may appear as project-specific measures. Suppose, for example, that an environmental agency announces a special focus on gas stations' compliance with emission controls for volatile organic compounds. Measuring and reporting that specific form of compliance, in that specific industry segment, makes sense for the project, and it would make sense to the public once they understood the project.

The more an agency's compliance efforts are organized around specific patterns of noncompliance, the more often such project-specific compliance measures will be used. Unfortunately, however, these selective measures cannot normally be aggregated into meaningful macro-level measures of compliance—just as abatement of the associated risks themselves (which come in different forms and sizes) constitutes discrete accomplishments, not readily aggregated. The usefulness of such project-specific compliance measurements comes from the way they attach to the projects, not from their contribution to higher-level (aggregate) compliance measurements.

Problems Solved: So What?

Regulators have begun to explore the nature of the risk control business and the practical aspects of the problem-solving challenge. They are discovering the need to disaggregate risks into actionable projects and explore the stages through which such projects pass. Some have also developed a reasonable understanding of what a performance account associated with risk control operations would look like: a collection of stories, each one spelling out the nature of the problem, the method of its abatement, and the empirical evidence to show that the problem went away.

Critics might ask, So what? Suppose creativity flourishes, innovations proliferate. Somehow, through some motivational miracle, a thousand little flowers bloom, some involving three people, some involving fifteen, a few involving fifty. What of the national injury rate? What of the ozone layer? What of big, important risk control objectives, such as finding a cure for cancer? If one has to break important risks down so much in order to work on them, are the resulting accomplishments not simultaneously rendered insignificant? Does problem solving merely create a frontline, feel good experience with little or no relevance for agen-cywide goals?

That depends. It depends on whether the innovations are *the right ones*. It depends on whether creative energies are appropriately focused. It depends on whether the actionable projects, taken together, take meaningful bites out of meaningful risks. It depends on whether the messy, fluid proliferation of projects is a *miscellany*, or a *construct*.

CHAPTER TWENTY

Connecting
the Fabric

MANY REGULATORY INNOVATIONS are described as "bottom up." They arise from the field level, where thoughtful, motivated staff confront apparently intractable problems and figure out for themselves sensible solutions. Celebrations of such innovations emphasize the disconnection between them and the macrolevel functioning of the organization; innovators are said to be "good people locked in bad systems," who dared to "stick their necks out," who "bucked the culture." Meanwhile, at the highest levels of regulatory agencies, strategic planning—with its carefully formulated mission statements, value statements, and goals—sets lofty objectives but often fails to conceive of any apparatus or system for achieving them. When such apparatus *is* conceived, it usually consists of massive national programs that are highly consumptive of resources and that threaten to suffocate local or lower-level initiatives. Consequently, observers of large regulatory bureaucracies might easily get the impression that strategic planning and problem solving have absolutely nothing to do with one another or, worse, that they are at odds.

The failure to make the connection between lower-level activities and higher-level goals is never more apparent than in the context of performance measurement. Whatever it is that a regulatory agency counts, and however good the agency is at counting it, the question of significance remains. So you opened 1,400 cases. Were they the right ones? So you indicted 1,400 individuals. Did it make a difference? So, you solved 1,400 problems. Does that amount to anything?

Earlier chapters discuss a number of ways in which the nature of a performance account rests on the nature of the performance. In the same way, one cannot *stitch up the performance account* (that is, connect numerous lower-level achievements with important strategic goals) without *stitching up the performance* (which means constructing the apparatus to orient lower-level activities around higher-level objectives). Even before the units of work changed to *problems* or *risks*, the performance measurement issue stumbled over the question of connection.

One expert on the control of organized crime notes how organized crime strike forces relied heavily on counting cases, without questioning their significance:

> Using [case initiation reports] as the *primary* measures of Strike Force effectiveness is counterproductive. First, it is tantamount to determining how well they are doing in their battles with no indication of whether the war is being won. Second, since all [case initiation reports] are given the same weight, there is little indication whether the battles being fought are significant. Third, because no estimate of overall organized crime activity exists, it is unclear whether a Strike Force that is 'successful' has achieved its success by taking on only easy cases.[1]

James Q. Wilson, commenting on performance measurement challenges faced by police departments, suggests that police departments may ultimately be limited to describing their lower-level successes and that it may not be possible to connect these accomplishments to macrolevel trends.

> There are no "real" measures of overall success; what is measurable about the level of public order, safety, and amenity in a given large city can only partially, if at all, be affected by police behavior. . . . Proxy measures almost always turn out to be process measures—response times, arrest rates, or clearance rates—that may or may not have any relationship to crime rates or levels of public order.
>
> In my view, the search for better measures of police performance is doomed to failure so long as it focuses on city-wide or even precinct-wide statistics. Most police chiefs will agree on this point,

I think. No matter how we improve the Uniform Crime Reports (UCR) or the National Crime Victimization Survey (NCVS), they will not tell us very much (and certainly not very much in a timely fashion) about what difference the police make in the lives of the citizens. . . .

These considerations lead me to suggest that the better approach to defining police goals and performance measures involves thinking small and from the bottom up.[2]

Wilson goes on to say that police should make the production of safer, more orderly neighborhoods one of their goals, putting in place "micro-level measures of success" relevant to specific problems in specific neighborhoods. In other words, he encourages police to rely on the type of performance account that problem solving produces—a collection of problem-specific stories—without trying to build anything grander from them. "These micro-measures are likely to be among the few valid measures of police performance. They may well lead to conclusions quite at variance with city-wide, aggregate data."[3]

I, for one, am not prepared to give up hope of connecting lower-level projects to higher-level objectives. Nor are many of the regulatory executives whom I see grappling with these issues. To give up the connections would guarantee the marginalization of problem solving. If risk control operations cannot contribute substantially to strategic goals, or if they cannot be *shown* to contribute substantially to them, then performance-based budgeting and legislative pressures for results will drive problem solving out, rather than driving regulators to it.

The reason that lower-level problem-solving projects and higher-level strategic objectives appear disconnected is that the *connecting fabric* is too often missing. The middle is missing, the heart of the risk control operation. And now we know something of that connecting fabric. Chapter 11, describing the organizational infrastructure, explored the essential involvement of middle management in selecting and managing projects and managing portfolios of projects and portfolios of portfolios. And chapter 18 described the parallel analytic structure, which lies behind and supports the managerial structure, disaggregating high–level strategic objectives into risk areas, then risk concentrations, all the way down into actionable projects.

A few regulatory organizations have now begun the task of connecting the risk control fabric so that the insights and solutions of problem solving contribute directly to the core objectives of the organization. When these connections are made, executives stop regarding problem solving as an experimental or peripheral activity and come to rely on the systems and machinery of problem solving to identify and accomplish their core objectives.

U.S. Coast Guard: Office of Marine Safety, Security, and Environmental Protection

This office, selected as a pilot project under the Government Performance and Results Act of 1993, uses what it calls a planning framework, wherein everything flows from the mission (in order): strategic goals, performance goals, business focus, major initiatives, and detailed actions. Analysis, in particular the disaggregation of data, guides each successive decomposition. One of the strategic goals covers marine safety; another, environmental protection. The high-level performance goals for maritime safety, for example, include

— Reducing accidental deaths and injuries from maritime casualties by 20 percent over five years (using worker fatality rates per 100,000 workers as the relevant indicator)

— Reducing the risk of passenger vessel casualty with major loss of life by 20 percent over five years (using vessel accidents per thousand passenger vessels as the indicator)

— Reducing fatality rates aboard uninspected fishing and towing vessels halfway toward the average of the U.S. inspected fleet (using fatality rates per 100,000 workers, filtered by segment of the regulated industry).[4]

To track performance in a credible fashion, the office made substantial investment in data collection, cleansing, and analysis. The staff graphed historical data for the prior ten years, refined the definitions of the relevant measures, normalized the data for historical changes in exposure, identified and corrected significant data errors, smoothed random fluctuations by using moving averages, and then projected the trend lines over five years to ensure that the performance goals were a real "stretch." That was just setting the goals and putting the measures in place.

The next step was how to achieve those goals. Further data analysis, with the emphasis on disaggregation, helped identify risk concentrations and identify specific problems. This analysis fundamentally affected operations: "By disaggregating the data, we began identifying high-risk areas for targeting, and this provided the basis for the most important use of our performance measures—making real changes in safety and environmental protection."[5]

The disaggregation revealed some surprises, including the high rate of fatalities in the commercial towing industry. The identification of towing as a high-risk area led to further analysis of the accident data in that sector and revealed the problem of deckhands falling overboard as a significant risk concentration. From that, they launched a project focused on reducing these accidents. Other analyses showed different issues, and operations were reoriented to address each one that showed up.

> The group began to feel discomfort associated with the cross-organizational nature of outcomes. Many expected to see strategic goals in each of our traditional program areas, like maritime licensing or port security. Very likely, many wanted goals they could own and manage individually as program managers. The outcome focus upset the equilibrium.[6]

Notice how the analytic operation took over from the traditional program structure as the vehicle through which work was defined, subdivided, and allocated—hence the not-so-surprising degree of staff disorientation at the outset.

Occupational Safety and Health Administration

OSHA's arduous and painful reinvention journey reveals the tension within an organization when major national initiatives compete with local problem-solving initiatives. They compete, principally, for resources at the field level. After the abortive attempts to replicate the Maine 200 program nationwide, and the subsequent suspension of the cooperative compliance program, OSHA executives are eager to pursue their core performance objectives in a way that does not stifle local initiative and creativity. Redesigned area offices, with their newly formed strategic intervention (problem-solving) teams, have more than seventy significant projects up and running, each focused on issues of particular local concern. In the context of strategic planning, OSHA's national office does not want to quash that work; rather, it wants to provide a framework within which such work can be fashioned and reformulated.

The way OSHA has chosen to make the connection is to specify its outcome goals in a manner that directs the agency to high-risk areas, and to various methods of specifying high-risk areas, but leaves significant room within that framework for local offices to define their own projects and focus them on local issues. Thus OSHA hopes to optimize the contribution that local problem-solving projects make to the agency's higher-level objectives. The language of the higher-level objectives—written into OSHA's five-year strategic plans—might seem opaque if one did not know what the agency was trying to do. The language is deliberately crafted to encourage identification of substantial risk concentrations in a number of dimensions. At the same time, some higher-level targeting decisions have already been taken—for example, the focus on four categories of hazard in the construction industry. Here is the language used in OSHA's strategic plan for fiscal years 1997–2002:

OSHA Outcome Goal 1.1: Reduce the number of worker injuries, illnesses, and fatalities by focusing nationwide attention and agency resources on the most prevalent types of workplace injuries and illnesses, the most hazardous industries, and the most hazardous workplaces.

1.1A. Reduce three of the most prevalent types of workplace injuries and causes of illnesses by 15% in selected industries and occupations.

1.1B. Reduce injuries and illnesses by 15% in five industries characterized by high-hazard workplaces.

1.1C. Decrease fatalities in the construction industry by 15%, by focusing on the four leading causes of fatalities (falls, struck-by, crushed-by, and electrocutions and electrical injuries). . . .

1.1F. Reduce the total case rates for most Federal agencies by 12%.[7]

Notice how the specification of these objectives does not presume the outcome of analysis. Rather, it specifies that such analysis (identification of high-hazard workplaces and prevalent types of injury) will be done as part of the performance and that attention nationwide will subsequently be focused wherever that analysis leads. Notice also how the range of different slices—one by type of injury, one by high-hazard workplaces, one focused on construction, one focused on federal workplaces—leaves local problem-solving teams a great deal of latitude as to how best to define their contributing projects.

Florida Department of Environmental Protection

The Florida Department of Environmental Protection has appeared on the list of finalists for the Innovations in American Government award three times, most recently in 1998 for the introduction of the *Secretary's Quarterly Performance Report (SQPR)*.

Published quarterly since December 1997, the *SQPR* provides an umbrella framework for the identification of trends, patterns, and focus areas, and it publicly displays the agency's progress in addressing those concerns (or lack of it) via the Internet. The report separates out environmental impacts from compliance levels and agency activities. The first twenty-five pages or so of the report is devoted to environmental indicators and public health outcomes, followed by another twenty-five pages of information relating to compliance levels and other behavioral trends; then forty pages of information on departmental outputs and activities; and a final section on efficiency, budget, and financial management.

The senior management of the department has the opportunity to review the data before publication and to designate focus areas (most serious) and watch areas (less serious), where the data reveal worrying trends, environmental degradation, or anomalies in performance. As the foreword to the September 1998 edition points out, this reporting system "identifies status and trends, successes and failures, problems and opportunities. It enables need-based priorities to be set, cost-effective methods to be chosen. It drives the agenda, by focusing on greatest needs and best means. It enables internal programs, divisions, and offices to improve by comparing past and peer performance."[8] In the same period that the performance report was under development (1996–98), the department created its environmental problem-solving program, modeled on problem-solving techniques pioneered by the police profession. During Secretary Virginia Wetherell's last eighteen months in office, the department began to enjoy its first significant problem-solving successes, one of which was the reduction in sewage overflows and spills in Orange County, pursuant to the efforts of the Orlando district's Team SOS.

Just before she left the department in November 1998 (shortly after the death of Governor Lawton Chiles and the subsequent election of Republican Governor Jeb Bush), Wetherell announced that it was time for full-scale implementation of environmental problem solving—that it should no longer be regarded as experimental. Up to that time, no formal connection had been made between problem-solving projects (mostly ground-up) and the *SQPR* (which focused mostly on data aggregated to the district and division level). Some consideration had been given to attaching executive summaries of the projects to the *SQPR*, but even that did not seem to connect environmental problem solving with overall agency performance.

Incoming secretary David Struhs, appointed by Governor Bush, took up where Secretary Wetherell left off. He continued to use the *SQPR* to designate focus and watch areas, which clearly represented problem identifications of a kind, even if not problem definitions. Subsequent analysis of focus areas, however, often did reveal specific problems. For example, the petroleum storage tank program was designated as a watch area for its low compliance rate of 87 percent. Analysis of the sources and causes of noncompliance revealed that more than 70 percent of the significant violations related specifically to leak detection requirements. In this subset, violations fell into three main categories: those caused by financial inability to comply, those resulting from rule vagueness, and those involving blatant disregard for requirements. Plans were then devised to tackle each of these three categories.

The formal connection between the *Secretary's Quarterly Performance Report* and the environmental problem-solving program was made in March 1999, three months into the new administration. In a memo dated March 26, 1999, Deputy Secretary Kirby Green notified senior managers that environmental problem solving would become the method of choice for dealing with focus and watch areas:

> The exemplary response of the Petroleum Storage Tank program to a Watch area last year, and that of the Shellfish Sanitation program this past quarter, further underscore the benefits of using a structured approach. Both of these programs used the Environmental Problem Solving template to great effect in framing a response to [the senior management team's] designations. Therefore, we are directing that the EPS template be used on all future Watch and Focus designations.[9]

The administrative mechanisms put in place to connect the *SQPR* with environmental problem solving worked like this: Designation of a focus or watch area would be treated (from the point of the problem-solving infrastructure) as a problem nomination from Secretary Struhs. The executive team recognized the need for subsequent analysis and evaluation, to pick issue areas apart carefully, to identify potential projects in a risk area, and to compare these with other priorities. In other words, conversion of a focus or watch designation into a problem-solving project was not automatic, and the relationship would not necessarily be one to one.

For a watch area designation the nomination would go to the relevant division or district and would be handled in the context of the division or district's own environmental problem-solving review board, which would address the nomination as it would any other, decide whether it would be accepted, and report back to the Office of the Secretary, just as it would to any other problem nominator. For a focus area designation (the more serious of the two), once again, the designation would also act as a problem-solving nomination, but the appropriate division or district director would be required to report at significant milestones to an *Executive Focus Area Review Board,* consisting of the secretary and both deputy secretaries. In other words, for these more serious issues, the senior executive team took over the role of periodic managerial review.

The first Executive Focus Area Review Board meeting, held under the new rules, convened in Tallahassee on May 7, 1999. Three new focus areas were on the agenda, identified by the senior management team from data contained in the latest edition of the *SQPR*. The first related to air quality exceedancies and potential nonattainment in Escambia and Santa Rosa counties. The board decided this problem was not suitable for an agency problem-solving project because the problem went beyond these two counties, and federally prescribed efforts to address it were about to begin.

The second focus area involved failures by transient noncommunity drinking water systems to report quarterly monitoring results. It was submitted as a problem nomination by the secretary, to be acted upon by the Division of Water Facilities, on the grounds that it appeared to be a statewide reporting problem. An action plan outlining an approach to this problem was required from the division, for review by the executive team in June 1999, when the plan was approved and launched.

The third focus area concerned increased numbers and rates of manatee deaths due to watercraft. During the last six months of 1998 manatee deaths due to watercraft rose by 33 percent, with twenty times more deaths recorded in 1998 than in any year since 1989. Manatees are an endangered species whose recovery is the responsibility of the Florida

Environmental Protection Agency. This area was accepted as an environmental problem-solving project and assigned to the Division of Marine Resources and the Division of Law Enforcement, jointly, as the problem straddles their areas of responsibility. Again, an action plan was required for executive review.

When the connection was made between the high-level performance reporting system (*SQPR*) and (hitherto low-level) problem-solving projects, the effect—according to the department's internal problem-solving consultants—was stunning. Dave Herbster, from the Orlando District, had learned the environmental problem-solving business when he helped guide Team SOS in Orlando. He had been selected as one of the first internal problem-solving consultants and had earned respect throughout the department as a facilitator and adviser for environmental problem solving. Secretary Wetherell had created a position for him at headquarters, giving him the task of orchestrating and coordinating full-scale implementation of environmental problem solving. She told him before she left office that this was his chance to make a real difference, and he set about it with missionary zeal—cajoling, training, traveling to support the other consultants, and advising senior managers as they met to evaluate problem nominations or review projects under way.

Dave Herbster was on leave when he heard about the adoption of environmental problem solving as the preferred method for dealing with focus and watch areas. Before that change, he had likened the job of promoting environmental problem solving, without a system of support from the management structure, to pushing a boulder uphill and observed that, toward the end of 1998 problem-solving efforts "weren't getting much play. . . . This may have translated into an apparent lack of interest from management. And, in my estimation, with that lack of interest, problem solving dies a quiet death—the death of fast starts and no follow through."[10] But with the final push by the outgoing secretary, support from the incoming one, and the connection finally being made to high-level agency priorities, Herbster felt as if local administrators no longer had to provide all the energy or go begging for resources from disinterested management. This is how he described the changing environment:

> There are amazing things happening at DEP right now. I hope your book not only reflects the frustration of last September but also the opportunity this May [1999]. Right now, I would guess

there are fifty projects under way, almost half begun since we met in November. Directors are asking their team leaders about what they're measuring. They're making the distinction between problem-solving, pollution prevention, TQL and compliance assistance. Bimonthly reviews are held at every district and division. Staff know their problem [nominations] are sought and they know they'll get a fair hearing. People are being trained to support the projects, because shepherding is clearly vital. [The deputy secretary] has chosen problem solving as the operational methodology for any focus area that fits the selection criteria. Everyone around DEP is using the selection criteria. Former skeptics are fighting to keep their projects in the problem-solving loop. . . .

May we have a string of environmental indicators moving in the right direction by September [1999]. May your panel of judges [for an environmental problem-solving awards program] be torn over the best projects, because everybody's got one. Finally, Lord help us to seize this chance. There may never be a better one.

Connecting the fabric apparently makes all the difference. Because these connections are still relatively new, only time will tell exactly how much difference.

The Aggregate Risk-Control Performance Account

When the risk control performance finally gets connected, so does the risk control performance account. Once the managerial and analytic infrastructures are in place, then so is the explanation that connects the contributing activities with the outcomes. It is a project-based explanation. Figure 20-1 suggests the nature of that performance account. The top layer (termed the *outcome surface*) represents the underlying condition that regulators seek to improve. It might be the quality of drinking water, the injury rate in the construction industry, or the number of road accident fatalities in a state. Whatever the nature of the risk, at time t_0 the level is set, and at time t_1 it has moved (in the figure, for the better).

As observers constantly point out, aggregate risk levels are affected by many factors not under government control, so regulators have been understandably reluctant to hitch their horses to this particular cart (aggregate risk levels), in case it pulls backward—or even forward—in ways they cannot control. However, given the persistent pressure to

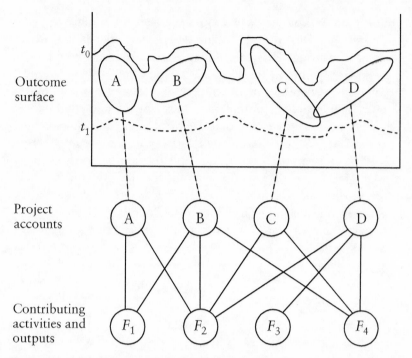

Outcome surface

Project accounts

Contributing activities and outputs

Figure 20-1. The Nature of the Risk Control Performance Account

demonstrate results, regulatory executives are forced back to these macrolevel risk measures time and time again. And each time they recoil, understandably reluctant to make themselves responsible for things they cannot control. But they are not permitted by legislatures and oversight agencies to give up on the task of establishing connections between their programs and changes in aggregate risk levels. In pursuit of such connections, they try to isolate the impacts of their programs from the impacts of external factors (such as the weather).[11] In other words, to use changes in risk levels as performance indicators, regulators feel they have to be able to tell exactly how much *they* changed them and how much other factors changed them.

Parse the Risk, Not the Credit

The risk control or problem-solving approach provides a way out of this analytic impasse by using a different kind of disaggregation: parsing the risk itself into its subcomponents or concentrations, rather than trying to separate the different causal factors for macrolevel movements. As figure 20-1 shows, aggregate risk level does not consist of a unitary, indivisible reality. It has *parts* (which is why it is presented as a surface, rather than a single level). Almost any risk typically has the nature of a lumpy surface, with high points and low points, rather than a flat, undifferentiated, uniformity. If the overall risk being examined represents, for example, road accident fatalities in a state, then analysis will show that the risk is concentrated in some particular region or at certain hours of the day, or that there is a particular problem with teenagers driving their parents' cars late at night, or that seventeen major intersections account for a significant proportion of the fatalities. The dimensions in which the lumpiness is revealed are deliberately not stated in the figure, because no one knows what they are until the analytic operation (strategic intelligence analysis) finds them. What one wants from the analysis is the dimensions that reveal the *lumpiest* surface, so that the significant components (risk concentrations) can be picked as priority projects.

What does the figure show regarding the nature of the risk control account? How will a tax agency show that it suppressed noncompliance in a particular industry segment? How will a state police agency explain how it reduced accident fatalities from the level at time t_0 to the lower level at time t_1? The account they can give is that they picked important problems—represented by components A, B, C, and D—and fixed them. The agency's contribution to the suppression of the risk surface is that it identified and chose four major subcomponents of that risk. Bear in mind that projects A, B, C, and D need not all have been defined in the *same* dimensions. In fact, they could all have been defined in quite *different* dimensions, which is impossible to show in a simple diagram: one might address a geographic focus, one a particular class of victims, one a particular cause, one a particular transmission mechanism. (The four projects thus defined might also overlap. Never mind.)

Once the connecting risk control fabric is in place, the overall account of risks controlled falls into place. It has two major ingredients. First, there is the sum of the project accounts, each one showing the evidence of a problem's existence, the measures put in place to monitor progress, the action plan selected to address it, and the evidence that the underlying condition improved. Usually, these individual accounts do not prove, or claim to prove, causality. They merely show that a significant concentration existed before; that the agency organized attention, resources, and creativity around it; and that afterward it did not exist or had been substantially mitigated.

The second ingredient is the explanation of why the sum of these projects amounts to something substantial. That explanation uses the analytic story to reveal why particular subcomponents were chosen and then points to the managerial infrastructure as the mechanism that administered the portfolio of relevant projects. The agency thus *connects the performance account* by *describing the operational connections*. (That sounds simpleminded, yet it explains why most agencies have not produced such a performance account: they still lack the requisite operational connections.)

For major risk areas, the figure's middle layer may be oversimplified. A, B, C, and D might represent risk concentrations still significantly above the level of actionable projects, in which case these higher-level components would then be subdivided, and subdivided again, until they are sufficiently disaggregated for assignment as problem-solving projects. For major risks that spawn portfolios of portfolios (rather than the simple portfolio of projects, as illustrated), this middle layer may be more complex, multilayered, and textured. But however complex or textured this middle layer, the projects at the lowest level of aggregation draw upon the full range of regulatory tools available (represented by the lowest layer in the figure). Any one project may not use all the tools, but most projects would use several.

What happens to the performance account that each individual function can give? Without the intervening project account structure, the measurement puzzle for these functions consists of trying to draw direct connections between their activities (for example, F_1 in the diagram) and macrolevel changes in the outcome surface. Without the intervening project layer as part of the account, such connections cannot be drawn. Individual functions can only claim the localized and immediate consequences of their particular actions, and have no convincing way of claiming any part of broader, more significant, changes. The middle layer of the figure—the heart of the risk control operation—is absent, so they cannot use it as part of their performance account.

With the intervening analytic and operational infrastructure in place, individual functions can claim their risk control credits through the mechanism of the project account apparatus. In the figure, function F_1 contributed to projects A and B, each of which addressed and reduced specific risk concentrations. Those two projects, to which F_1 contributed, formed an important part of the agency's efforts in driving the overall risk level down between time t_0 and time t_1. Function F_1 was not alone in contributing to projects A and B and therefore has to share this credit with other functions, maybe with other agencies, and maybe with nongovernmental contributors. Over time, an important issue for managers of function F_1 will be to determine what proportion of their time and energy is spent in support of risk reduction projects. If the answer is not much, they should want to know why.

As James Q. Wilson suggests, at times the overall surface may move in the opposite direction, due to external factors outside the agency's control.[12] In that case, the agency will still be able to claim the sum of its problem-solving successes. Over time, however, if the agency continues to rack up its successes, and the risk surface continues to move in the opposite direction (or does not move in the right direction fast enough), then observers are entitled to question the agency's methods for selecting projects. If, in Wilson's account, police succeed in generating neighborhood-level security, neighborhood by neighborhood, but aggregate crime rates rise nevertheless, then there must be other types of crime that the neighborhood-oriented strategy fails to address. For an environmental agency, if drinking water quality continues to deteriorate even as the majority of drinking water projects succeed, then management should reexamine the bases for problem selection and definition.

The risk control performance account invites two special forms of scrutiny. When the performance account consisted of enforcement statistics, everyone knew that regulators were working hard and that they were productive, but it was not possible to tell from those statistics whether the agency was working *smart* or working on the *right things*. An account of risks controlled lays out for all to see whether the agency worked smart (that is, was able to solve the problems it identified) and whether it worked on the right things (that is, picked important problems that contributed substantially to major risk-reduction goals).

A Balanced Set of Performance Measures

The account of risks controlled or reduced will never be the whole of a regulatory or enforcement agency's performance story. Even though risk control represents a major piece of the regulatory mission, risk control successes have to be augmented by a broader range of performance measurement categories. Regulators should monitor customer or client satisfaction, although they should distinguish the myriad forms of regulatory encounter and avoid lumping together the opinions of enforcement targets and violators with the opinions of complainants or others. They should also monitor employee satisfaction, just as any other agency, to ensure that work is meaningful, challenging, and rewarding.

With respect to routine inspection processes (which will continue to absorb substantial resources), regulators must measure both types of error—the costs of holding up legitimate traffic and the costs of letting through illegitimate traffic—and make improvements on both fronts simultaneously. With respect to targeting systems, regulators should ensure that the majority of inspections and enforcement actions are targeted on high-risk areas and that the noncompliance problems addressed are plausibly connected to significant harms. But they must also preserve a random component and other proactive intelligence gathering techniques that help them reassess their priorities and redirect their attention over the long term. At a functional and process level, regulators should continue to measure productivity and efficiency, even as the emphasis shifts toward measuring the functional contributions to risk reduction.

Even if the story of risks controlled is not the whole story, it seems clear that risk control lies at the heart of the regulatory mission. The story of important problems solved, and important risks reduced, and the story of how particular parts of them were tackled, has been the missing piece in the story of regulatory effectiveness. Risk control accomplishments are the elusive *business results* for which regulators have been searching.

CHAPTER TWENTY-ONE

Conclusion

RISK CONTROL AND problem solving provide a model for regulatory and enforcement operations not contemplated by the vogue prescriptions for regulatory reform.

Occasions when agencies have identified specific risks or problems and devised effective interventions have been noted and even celebrated, but academics and practitioners alike have paid insufficient attention to the organizational challenge of making problem solving and risk reduction the core of normal operations. Politicians and legislatures have also failed to appreciate the enormous benefits to society that might accrue from development of the risk control art as a core professional skill for regulators.

The Agency Level

Some agencies—several of them described in these pages—have begun to implement a risk-centered or problem-solving strategy. Executives in these agencies, having discovered that they lacked much of the institutional apparatus necessary to support such operations and that they needed to reformulate many of their administrative systems, created (or formalized) systems for problem identification and selection, separate from their agency's core operational processes. They established criteria by which managers could determine which problems were important and which were less so. They trained managers to make, and defend, their choices. They reallocated resources from other work to problem-solving projects. They invented protocols for periodic managerial review of projects under way and mechanisms for closing projects.

These officials encountered problem-solving work as *different* and realized that their agencies could never demonstrate a problem-solving competence if staff just did their jobs as their jobs had traditionally been defined. They also experienced problem solving as methodologically rigorous and intellectually demanding. They found they needed to fight constantly against the temptation to define problems in ways that fit existing organizational structures or traditional program areas, rather than in dimensions inherent in the problems themselves. They realized their agencies' paucity of analytic skills and the importance of generating tailor-made and creative analyses. They learned the value of *analytic insights with a view to action*. They also understood the inadequacy of traditional enforcement bean counts for monitoring operations and developed more sophisticated and multitiered performance accounts. The *business results* section of these performance accounts took the form of demonstrated reductions in risks, hazards, or harms—coupled with plausible stories of how each reduction was accomplished.

They also discovered that their notions of enforcement discretion, and the ways in which that discretion had normally been constrained, failed to create the latitude necessary for effective risk control operations. They learned that, under a risk control framework, enforcement discretion was more often subsumed by the exercise of less familiar forms of discretion, each of which needed to be acknowledged publicly: the right to set the mission, the right to choose what to work on, and the right to choose how to work on it.

The Legislative Level

For their part, legislators seeking to support or promote these new kinds of regulatory behavior need to make some critical adaptations of their own. Although they should continue to demand results that count (demonstrations of effectiveness), they must leave regulators room to try different approaches, and avoiding locking them in to specific tools or tactics. They must engage agency executives, on a continuing basis, over the question of which problems are most important, and why. They must accept the need for experimentation and recognize that very few intervention plans work the first time. They must accept that closing projects and switching tactics are essential parts of the business and should not be construed as failure.

Legislators should also anticipate the artful structuring of discretion (which some may mistake for unauthorized rule making). They should accept the need for such structuring as an essential instrument of risk control operations, even while they carefully monitor its use. They should work to persuade their colleagues that risk-based use of discretion (producing rational inconsistencies) is preferable to an arbitrary or undeclared exercise of discretion. They should seek to convert as much agency funding as possible into more fungible forms, not bound to specific programmatic or functional areas. And they should learn to live with the reality that regulation and enforcement, done right, will never please everyone—and that targets of enforcement will line up at their doors, complaining they were not well served as customers.

A Thought on Timeliness

My 1994 volume, *Imposing Duties*, was published before the issues of reforming or reinventing regulatory practice were accepted as a subject worthy of interdisciplinary contemplation. My hope is that this book is not too late, that the prescriptions for organizational reform are not yet so rigid as to preclude consideration of a risk orientation as the foundation for the development and improvement of regulatory practice.

During the time it has taken to write this book, several events have occurred that suggest that the kind of performance demanded of regulators remains anything but clear. In April 1999 the Federal Appeals Court for the District of Columbia announced its decision regarding the Occupational Safety and Health Administration's cooperative compliance program, which established criteria that would alter the risk of an inspection. The court determined that the program was a rule and vacated the case for lack of adherence to rule-making procedures. The decision shows that the artful structuring of regulatory discretion is not by any means accepted as an instrument of regulatory operations.

In May 1999 a divided appeals court panel invalidated the Environmental Protection Agency's 1997 clean air rules (which toughened standards relating to ozone and particulate matter) on the grounds that the rules were based on "no intelligible principle" and represented an unconstitutional delegation of legislative authority to the executive branch.[1] The decision, if it stands, throws open to question the right (or duty) of regulators to make rules based on unavoidably imperfect risk assessments.

Also reported in May 1999, the Internal Revenue Service, with its latest reorganization plans driven predominantly by customer service principles, experienced its own substantial bean dip phenomenon. In the first six months of fiscal year 1999, the rate of taxpayer asset seizures by the collections staff plunged by 98 percent from the average rate for fiscal year 1997, steepening a decline begun in fiscal year 1998. The rate of levies placed on taxpayer bank accounts and paychecks fell by 75 percent, and the agency's use of claims against assets declined by 64 percent over the same period.[2] IRS executives explained that the declines resulted from declines in overall staffing, the reallocation of enforcement resources to taxpayer assistance, and the fact that staff were worried that upsetting taxpayers could put their jobs at risk. Immediately (as always) the bean dip phenomenon provoked concerns about the agency's commitment to enforcement and its regulatory effectiveness, displacing (at least for a moment) the countervailing worries about overly aggressive regulatory style.

As IRS executives work to demonstrate that the agency has not lost its teeth, once again one is reminded that concerns about customer satisfaction—important though they are—cannot provide a foundation upon which to build effective regulatory strategy. Client satisfaction always has to be integrated with, and in some instances weighed against, mission accomplishment.

The search by practitioners for satisfactory frameworks for regulatory reform is not over. Most prescriptions for reform do not accommodate the underlying nature of the regulatory mission. These issues will remain high on the public policy agenda for several years to come.

A Framework for Reform

In the context of that continuing debate, I offer the problem-solving or risk management framework for consideration. It casts a considerable amount of light on the more intractable problems of regulatory practice: how to manage discretion, how to report performance, how to structure and organize regulatory work, and how to balance customer service with mission accomplishment. As a few agencies have discovered and reported, a risk management framework provides a new foundation for their interactions with those they regulate.

The adoption of this framework—particularly making it work in practice—will not be easy. The two typical responses given by practitioners have been either, "There's nothing new about that; we've been doing that for years," or "We could never do that here." At this stage of the reform debate, I much prefer the second response to the first, because it indicates that practitioners have at least grasped the seriousness and complexity of the risk control challenge. My colleague David Kennedy (who directed the Boston gun project and has since been working with other cities on replication) observes that law enforcement practitioners with whom he works find the problem-solving business "unrelentingly difficult." The degree of difficulty explains, at least in part, the tendency of enforcement and regulatory agencies to back away from the challenge and to clutch at reductions and simplifications of it. David Kennedy says that if ordinary mortals are to be able to do this (operational problem solving), the research community "must somehow make it easier for them."

This book will not necessarily make it easier except perhaps by explaining what *it* is and by illuminating the more obvious obstacles. With a clearer view of the challenge, regulators and their overseers and all those affected by their conduct will be in a better position to decide whether it is worth the effort. But make no mistake: judging by the experience of those who have gone before, it will be a considerable effort. After reviewing a draft of this manuscript, Joe Dear, who headed OSHA during the introduction of problem solving to that agency, commented that I should put in a warning: "Trying these methods is more difficult than you can imagine. You must really be desperate to have an impact, or be totally dissatisfied with your program's status quo to make this undertaking worthwhile." From what I know of regulatory and enforcement practitioners, a great many of them are desperate to have an impact and are as dissatisfied with the status quo as they have been with other recent formulations of their business.

Reviewers of this text have said that the analysis extends beyond social regulation and law enforcement into the field of economic regulation—or even beyond the regulatory field altogether, into broader questions of organizational behavior and management. For two reasons, I do not press these claims, although I would be delighted if they turned out, upon deeper examination, to be true. First, those other areas lie outside my areas of knowledge. The agencies I have had experience with are enforcement agencies or instruments of social regulation. Second, there is so much work still to be done in the field of social regulation that I must leave it to others to determine where else, and how else, to apply any of this framework.

My hope is that a significant number of major regulatory agencies, both in the United States and abroad, will show within a few years what the fully developed, mature version of a risk control operation looks like and what kinds of legislative support and systems of accountability it takes to make it tick.

Notes

Preface

1. Malcolm K. Sparrow, *Imposing Duties: Government's Changing Approach to Compliance* (Praeger, 1994).

2. Jay A. Sigler, review of *Imposing Duties, American Review of Public Administration*, vol. 25 (June 1995), pp. 204–06.

3. Ibid., p. 205.

4. Ibid., p. 206.

5. Harvey Brooks, "The Dilemmas of Engineering Education," *IEEE Spectrum* (February 1967), p. 89.

Introduction

1. See Mark H. Moore, *Creating Public Value: Strategic Management in Government* (Harvard University Press, 1995), pp. 31–38.

2. Philip K. Howard, *The Death of Common Sense: How Law Is Suffocating America* (Random House, 1994), p. 186.

3. Eugene Bardach and Robert A. Kagan, eds. *Social Regulation: Strategies for Reform* (San Francisco: Institute for Contemporary Studies, 1982), pp. 17–18.

4. Marc K. Landy, Marc J. Roberts, and Stephen R. Thomas, *The Environmental Protection Agency: Asking the Wrong Questions* (Oxford University Press, 1990), p. 3.

5. Eugene Bardach and Robert A. Kagan, *Going by the Book: The Problem of Regulatory Unreasonableness* (Temple University Press, 1982), p. 7.

6. Ibid., p. 28.

7. Neal Shover, Donald A. Clelland, and John Lynxwiler, *Enforcement or Negotiation: Constructing a Regulatory Bureaucracy* (State University of New York Press, 1986), pp. 1–2.

8. Ibid., p. 9.

9. David J. Enriquez, "Government Perspective: The Policymaker's Perspective on Administrative and Regulatory Reform in Europe," *Columbia Journal of European Law* (Summer 1998), pp. 613–15.

10. Organization for Economic Cooperation and Development, "Recommendation of the Council of the OECD on Improving the Quality of Government Regulation" (Public Management Service, 1995), p. 10. For a study of the distance between law and its implementation, see Eugene Bardach, *The Implementation Game: What Happens after a Bill Becomes a Law* (MIT Press, 1977).

11. National Academy of Public Administration, *Setting Priorities, Getting Results: A New Direction for the Environmental Protection Agency*, Report to Congress (Washington, D.C.: NAPA, 1995), p. 6.

12. OECD, "Recommendation of the Council of the OECD on Improving the Quality of Government Regulation," p. 18.

13. Murray L. Weidenbaum and Andrew Haggard, "Modernizing Government Regulation: Mini-Forum: Regulatory Reform," *Public Manager,* vol. 27 (June 1998), p. 13.

14. Robert A. Kagan, *Regulatory Justice: Implementing a Wage-Price Freeze* (Russell Sage, 1978), pp. ix–x.

15. Derek Bok, personal letter to the author, June 14, 1999.

16. Dan. 2:1, King James Version (Cambridge University Press).

17. Ibid., p. 9.

18. Ibid., p. 5.

Chapter One

1. Eugene Bardach and Robert A. Kagan, eds., *Social Regulation: Strategies for Reform* (San Francisco: Institute for Contemporary Studies, 1982), p. 3.

2. P.L. 91-596, 84 Stat. 1590 (1970), codified at 29 U.S.C. 651-78 (1994).

3. Ian Ayres and John Braithwaite, *Responsive Regulation: Transcending the Deregulation Debate* (Oxford University Press, 1992), p. 11.

4. Bardach and Kagan, *Social Regulation,* p. 5.

5. Thomas Hopkins, *Regulatory Costs in Profile*, Policy Study 132 (St. Louis: Washington University, Center for the Study of American Business, 1996), p. 10.

6. Clyde Wayne Crews Jr., "Ten Thousand Commandments: Towards Accountability and Disclosure in the Regulatory State," Miniforum on Regulatory Reform, *Public Manager: The New Bureaucrat,* vol. 27 (June 1998), p. 5.

7. Organization for Economic Cooperation and Development, *OECD Report on Regulatory Reform: Synthesis* (Paris, 1997), p. 14.

8. Ibid., p. 40.

9. William Clifford and John Braithwaite, *Cost-Effective Business Regulation* (Canberra: Australian Institute of Criminology, 1981), p. 8.

10. Committee for Economic Development, *Modernizing Government Regulation: The Need for Action* (New York: Research and Policy Committee, 1998), p. 1.

11. Sidney A. Shapiro and Randy S. Rabinowitz, "Punishment versus Cooperation in Regulatory Enforcement: A Case Study of OSHA," *Administrative Law Review*, vol. 49, no. 4 (1997), p. 721.

12. Kalypso Nicolaïdis, "Mutual Recognition of Regulatory Regimes: Some Lessons and Prospects," *OECD Proceedings: Regulatory Reform and International Market Openness* (Paris: OECD, 1996).

13. Clifford and Braithwaite, *Cost-Effective Business Regulation*, p. 6.

14. Philip K. Howard, *The Death of Common Sense: How Law Is Suffocating America* (Random House, 1994), p. 11.

15. Clinton was referring to Executive Order 12866 (1993), which requires agencies to submit to the Office of Management and Budget an assessment of the potential benefits and costs of significant regulatory actions and requires more extensive analysis if the rules are considered "economically significant."

16. John D. Graham and Jennifer Kassalow Hartwell, "Risk Management: Green or Dirty?" in John D. Graham and Jennifer Kassalow Hartwell, eds., *The Greening of Industry: A Risk Management Approach* (Harvard University Press, 1997), p. 276.

17. Robert W. Hahn, "Achieving Real Regulatory Reform," *University of Chicago Legal Forum* (1997), pp. 143–51.

18. Robert W. Crandall and others, *An Agenda for Federal Regulatory Reform* (Washington, D.C.: American Enterprise Institute, 1997), p. 1.

19. Office of Policy Analysis *Unfinished Business: A Comparative Assessment of Environmental Problems* (Environmental Protection Agency, 1987).

20. Stephen G. Breyer, *Breaking the Vicious Circle: Toward Effective Risk Regulation* (Harvard University Press, 1993), pp. 24–27.

21. Estimates are based on a baseline mortality risk of less than one per million exposed and expressed in 1990 constant dollars.

22. Louise B. Russell, *Is Prevention Better Than Cure?* (Brookings, 1986), p. 67.

23. Robert W. Hahn and Robert E. Litan, *Improving Regulatory Accountability* (Washington, D.C.: American Enterprise Institute, 1997), p. 4.

24. Project XL sponsors can be single industrial facilities, multiple facilities, corporations, industry sectors, federal facilities, communities, or states.

25. National Academy of Public Administration, *Resolving the Paradox of Environmental Protection: An Agenda for Congress, EPA, and the States*, Report to Congress (Washington D.C., 1997), p. 13.

26. This motto is the fourth of four core principles of the National Performance Review's reinventing regulation initiative, printed on small plastic cards and distributed beginning February 21, 1995.

27. P. L. 103–62.

28. Ibid., sec. 3(a).

29. Howard, *The Death of Common Sense*, p. 28.

30. Ibid., pp. 180–81.

31. Committee for Economic Development, *Modernizing Government Regulation*, p. 3.

32. Ibid., p. 4.

Chapter Two

1. John Micklethwait and Adrian Wooldridge, *The Witch Doctors: Making Sense of the Management Gurus* (Random House, 1996), p. 291.

2. Ibid., p. 290.

3. Organization for Economic Cooperation and Development, *OECD Report on Regulatory Reform: Synthesis* (Paris, 1997), p. 13.

4. David Osborne and Ted Gaebler, *Reinventing Government: How the Entrepreneurial Spirit Is Transforming the Public Sector* (Addison-Wesley, 1992).

5. Ibid., p. xviii.

6. Omitted here are community-owned government, competitive government, and enterprising government.

7. Neal Shover, Donald A. Clelland, and John Lynxwiler, *Enforcement or Negotiation? Constructing a Regulatory Bureaucracy* (State University of New York Press, 1986), p. 117.

8. Ibid., pp. 11, 88.

9. Eugene Bardach and Robert A. Kagan, *Going by the Book: The Problem of Regulatory Unreasonableness* (Temple University Press, 1982), p. 300.

10. Shover, Clelland, and Lynxwiler, *Enforcement or Negotiation*, p. 5.

11. Ibid.

12. James Q. Wilson, *Varieties of Police Behavior: The Management of Law and Order in Eight Communities* (Harvard University Press, 1978), pp. 140–227. The reinventing government movement's emphasis on customer service brings regulatory conduct close to Wilson's service style.

13. Robert A. Kagan, *Regulatory Justice: Implementing a Wage-Price Freeze* (Russell Sage, 1978), p. 165.

14. Ian Ayres and John Braithwaite, *Responsive Regulation: Transcending the Deregulation Debate* (Oxford University Press, 1992), p. 20.

15. Shover, Clelland, and Lynxwiler, *Enforcement or Negotiation*, pp. 136–39.

16. Bardach and Kagan, *Going by the Book*, pp. 54–56.

17. Ayres and Braithwaite, *Responsive Regulation*, p. 5.

18. Ibid., p. 4.

19. John Braithwaite, *To Punish or Persuade: Enforcement of Coal Mine Safety* (State University of New York Press, 1985), p. x.

20. Ayres and Braithwaite, *Responsive Regulation*, p. 19.

21. Ibid., p. 6.

22. Braithwaite, *To Punish or Persuade*, p. 39.

23. Ayres and Braithwaite, *Responsive Regulation*, pp. 54–100. Peter Grabosky of the Australian Institute of Criminology proposes extending Braithwaite's enforcement pyramid to a third dimension to represent degrees of involvement of third parties. See Peter N. Grabosky "Inside the Pyramid: Towards a Conceptual Framework for the Analysis of Regulatory Systems," *International Journal of the Sociology of Law*, vol. 25 (1997), pp. 195–201.

24. Peter N. Grabosky, "Using Non-Governmental Resources to Foster Regulatory Compliance," *Governance: An International Journal of Policy and Administration*, vol. 8 (October 1995), pp. 527–50.

25. Ibid., p. 528.

26. Michael O'Hare, "Informational Strategies as Regulatory Surrogates," in Eugene Bardach and Robert A. Kagan, eds., *Social Regulation: Strategies for Reform* (San Francisco: Institute for Contemporary Studies, 1982), p. 221.

27. See Ayres and Braithwaite, *Responsive Regulation*, pp. 101–32.

28. An example of such a program is EPA Region 1's StarTrack program. See Environmental Protection Agency, "U.S.E.P.A.—New England StarTrack Program Guidance Documents," draft (Boston: EPA Region I, 1997–98).

29. Thomas Schelling, "Prices as Regulatory Instruments," in Thomas Schelling, ed., *Incentives for Environmental Protection* (MIT Press, 1983); Peter N. Grabosky "Regulation by Reward: On the Use of Incentives as Regulatory Instruments," *Law and Policy*, vol. 17 (July 1995), pp. 257–82.

30. Cary Coglianese, "Assessing Consensus: The Promise and Performance of Negotiated Rulemaking," *Duke Law Journal*, vol. 46 (April 1997), pp. 1255–349.

Chapter Three

1. See Alasdair Roberts, "REGO Around the World," *Government Executive* (January 1999), pp. 45–51.

2. Donald F. Kettl, *Reinventing Government? Appraising the National Performance Review* (Brookings, 1994), p. viii.

3. Ibid.

4. See Harvey Simon, "Regulatory Reform at OSHA" (John F. Kennedy School of Government case program, 1997), case C.

5. Ibid., p. 2.

6. Philip K. Howard, *The Death of Common Sense: How Law Is Suffocating America* (Random House, 1994).

7. Susannah Zak Figura, "The New OSHA," *Government Executive* (May 1997), pp. 35–38.

8. The Ballenger bill is formally titled the Safety and Health Improvement and Regulatory Reform Act of 1995.

9. The Senate proposal was introduced by Judd Gregg (Republican of New Hampshire) and Nancy Kassebaum (Republican of Kansas).

10. Figura, "The New OSHA," p. 36.

11. Simon, "Regulatory Reform at OSHA," case C, p. 3.

12. See George S. Hawkins, "The Eagle Agenda: An Agenda for the Future of Environmental Protection," unpublished paper (Boston: EPA Region I, 1996). Hawkins was senior adviser to Region I Office of Assistance and Pollution Prevention.

13. Elizabeth Glass Geltman and Andrew E. Skroback, "Reinventing the EPA to Conform with the New American Environmentality," *Columbia Journal of Environmental Law,* vol. 23, no. 1 (1998), pp. 1–56.

14. Ibid., p. 3.

15. Ayres and Braithwaite, *Responsive Regulation,* pp. 8–9.

16. Ibid., p. 11.

17. "President's Memorandum on Regulatory Reform: Regulatory Reinvention Initiative," March 4, 1995, *Public Papers of the Presidents of the United States* (1995).

18. William Clinton and Al Gore, *Blair House Papers* (National Performance Review, 1997), p. 15.

19. Ibid., pp. 15–16.

20. Senior regulatory official, correspondence with author, March 1999.

Chapter Four

1. Customs Service, "People, Processes, Partnerships: A Report on the Customs Service for the 21st Century" (Department of the Treasury, 1994), pp. 8, 9. Emphasis in original.

2. Customs Service, "U.S. Customs Service Expands Air Passenger Program," news release (August 1, 1994).

3. Fred T. Goldberg Jr., "Tax Systems Modernization," Statement before the Subcommittee on Commerce, Consumer and Monetary Affairs, House Committee on Government Operations, July 9, 1991, pp. 12, 13.

4. Internal Revenue Service, "Compliance 2000: Orientation Guide," IRS Publication 9102, catalog no. 15644C (Department of the Treasury, 1993), p. 7.

5. Ibid., p. 9.

6. National Commission on Restructuring the Internal Revenue Service, *A Vision for a New IRS* (Department of the Treasury, 1997), p. v.

7. Ibid., p. 15.

8. Ibid., p. 67.

9. Ibid., p. 68. Keating was quoting language used in an editorial in the May 19, 1997, issue of *Accounting Today*.

10. Customer Service Task Force, "Reinventing Service at the IRS," IRS Publication 2197, catalog no. 25006E (Department of the Treasury, 1998).

11. William H. Webster, "Review of the Internal Revenue Service's Criminal Investigation Division," IRS Publication 3388 (Department of the Treasury, 1999), pp. 2, 3.

12. Institutional Participation and Oversight Service, "IPOS: The Gatekeeper" (Department of Education, 1998), p. 1.

13. Henry Mintzberg, "Governing Management," *Harvard Business Review* (May–June 1996), pp. 75–83.

14. Mark H. Moore, *Creating Public Value: Strategic Management in Government* (Harvard University Press, 1995), p. 37.

15. Neal Shover, Donald A. Clelland, and John Lynxwiler, *Enforcement or Negotiation? Constructing a Regulatory Bureaucracy* (State University of New York Press, 1986), p. 11.

16. John Braithwaite and Peter Grabosky, *Occupational Health and Safety Enforcement in Australia* (Canberra: Australian Institute of Criminology, 1995), pp. 79–80.

17. John Braithwaite, *Corporate Crime in the Pharmaceutical Industry* (London: Routledge and Kegan Paul, 1984), pp. 2, 4.

Chapter Five

1. Richard Bolstein and John Hill, "Estimating the Number of Occurrences of a Rare Event: U.S. Customs Violations at Border Crossings," *Proceedings of Section on Quality and Productivity, American Statistical Association* (1996), pp. 23–27.

2. Michael Hammer and James Champy, *Reengineering the Corporation: A Manifesto for Business Revolution* (HarperCollins, 1993).

3. Ibid., p. 28.

4. Ibid., p. 32.

5. Ibid., p. 66.

6. Michael H. Lane, *Customs Modernization and the International Trade Superhighway* (Westport, Conn.: Quorum Books, 1998), p. 47.

7. Hammer and Champy, *Reengineering the Corporation*, p. 102.

8. Lane, *Customs Modernization and the International Trade Superhighway*, p. 49.

9. Hammer and Champy, *Reengineering the Corporation*, p. 35.

10. *Merriam Webster's Collegiate Dictionary*, 10th ed.

11. Herman Goldstein, *Problem-Oriented Policing* (McGraw-Hill, 1990), p. 15.

12. See Malcolm K. Sparrow, Mark H. Moore, and David M. Kennedy, *Beyond 911: A New Era for Policing* (Basic Books, 1990).

13. Goldstein, *Problem-Oriented Policing*, p. 15.

14. When Goldstein flew from Wisconsin to visit Customs Service headquarters in Washington, D.C., the Office of Enforcement greeted him with classic law enforcement humor. After planting a packet of drugs in the distinguished professor's luggage, they intercepted him in the public concourse of Dulles airport with a drug-sniffing dog, to his surprise and subsequent delight.

15. Inar Morics and other senior managers, interviews with author, 1993. For details, see Malcolm K. Sparrow, *Imposing Duties: Government's Changing Approach to Compliance* (Praeger, 1994), p. 38.

16. "OSHA's Enemies Find Themselves in High Places," *Washington Post*, July 24, 1995.

Chapter Six

1. Details of the program available at ⟨http://www.ksg.harvard.edu/innovations⟩.

2. Innovations detailed in this chapter are drawn from the Innovations in American Government competition applications, John F. Kennedy School of Government, supplemented by site evaluation reports (not available publicly). The Kennedy School case program has prepared detailed teaching cases based upon several of the winners. Where available, these are cited separately.

3. Malcolm K. Sparrow, *Imposing Duties: Government's Changing Approach to Compliance* (Praeger, 1994), back cover.

4. Some studies have been unable to relate this reduction directly to the Maine 200 program, particularly as the criteria for recordable incidents changed during this period. See, for example, John Mendeloff, "A Preliminary Evaluation of the Top-200 Program in Maine," Report to the Office of Statistics (Occupational Safety and Health Administration, 1996).

5. See Harvey Simon, "Regulatory Reform at OSHA" (John F. Kennedy School of Government case program, 1997), cases A and B.

6. See Esther Scott, "Protecting Pension Benefits: The Pension Benefit Guaranty Corporation Meets General Motors" (John F. Kennedy School of Government case program, 1997), cases A and B.

7. See David M. Kennedy, "Fighting Fear in Baltimore County" (John F. Kennedy School of Government case program, 1990).

8. Florida Department of Environmental Protection, *Secretary's Quarterly Performance Report*, vol. 1 (Tallahassee, September 1998), p. 1.

Chapter Seven

1. Herman Goldstein, *Problem-Oriented Policing* (McGraw-Hill, 1990).

2. "President's Memorandum on Regulatory Reform: Regulatory Reinvention Initiative," March 4, 1995, *Public Papers of the Presidents of the United States* (1995), p. 3.

Chapter Eight

1. "President's Memorandum on Regulatory Reform: Regulatory Reinvention Initiative," March 4, 1995, *Public Papers of the Presidents of the United States* (1995).

2. Remarks by President Clinton on reinventing worker safety regulation, Stromberg Sheet Metal Works, Inc., Washington, D.C., May 16, 1995. Text of speech available through White House Virtual Library.

3. Scott Allen, "Inspections, Fines by EPA Drop in N.E.," *Boston Globe*, April 26, 1996.

4. George S. Hawkins, "The Eagle Agenda: An Agenda for the Future of Environmental Protection," unpublished paper (Boston: EPA Region I, 1996).

5. Ron Seely, "Observers Say Customer-Based Approach Hurts Enforcement," *Wisconsin State Journal*, February 15, 1997.

6. Stephen Barr, "Aiming to Enforce Change at Customs: Shake-Up Underway; Scrutiny Looms," *Washington Post*, February 17, 1999.

7. Malcolm K. Sparrow, "The EPA's Evolving Use of Information" (John F. Kennedy School of Government, Program on Strategic Computing and Telecommunications in the Public Sector Program, 1991), p. 31.

8. Allen, "Inspections, Fines by EPA Drop in N.E."

9. James E. Donelson, "Collection Actions," statement (Washington, D.C.: National Commission on Restructuring the IRS, February 26, 1997), p. 7.

10. *Practices and Procedures of the Internal Revenue Service*, Hearings before the Subcommittee on Taxation and IRS Oversight of the Senate Committee on Finance, 105 Cong. 1 sess., December 3, 1997, Serial 98-5361-8 (Government Printing Office, 1998), pp. 3, 105–06, 123–28, 153, 155–56, 162–63, 206–09, 212–13, 303–04, 310, 317–18, 320–22, 325–26, 330, 333, 351–56.

11. "Review of the Use of Statistics and the Protection of Taxpayer Rights in the Arkansas-Oklahoma District Collection Field Function," Internal Audit Reference no. 380402 (Internal Revenue Service, December 5, 1997). Two further internal IRS reports assess the broader uses of such performance measures throughout the agency: "Use of Enforcement Statistics in the Collection Field Function," Internal Audit Reference no. 081904 (January 12, 1998); "Examination Division's Use of Performance Measures and Statistics," Internal Audit Reference no. 084303 (July 7, 1998).

12. Customer Service Task Force, "Reinventing Service at the IRS," IRS Publication 2197, catalog no. 25006E (Department of the Treasury, 1999), p. 75.

13. For proposed regulations to establish a balanced system for measuring organizational and individual performance at the IRS, see 26 CFR, pt. 801. (REG 119192-98) RIN 1545-AW80.

14. Confirmation hearing for Donald C. Alexander before the Senate Committee on Finance, 93 Cong. 1 sess., May 15, 1973, Serial 73-5361-15 (Government Printing Office, 1973), pp. 4–5. For a fuller account of the history of this issue at the IRS, see Charles Rossotti, "Modernizing America's Tax Agency," publication 3349 (1-1999), catalog no. 27171U (Internal Revenue Service, 1999), app. 2.

15. These observations and analyses stem from my work with the EPA Office of Enforcement and Compliance Assurance, the IRS Criminal Investigation Branch, the Customs Service, the Florida Department of Environmental Protection, and Revenue Canada.

16. For example, the Florida Department of Environmental Protection used the following hierarchy in their November 1994 *Strategic Assessment of Florida's Environment:* actions by federal or state regulatory agency, responses of the regulated community or society, changes in discharge or emission standards, changes in ambient conditions or in quantities of natural resources, changes in uptake or assimilation, and changes in health, ecology, or other benefits.

Chapter Nine

1. The Tax Reform Act of 1986 required social security numbers for dependents older than five years. Subsequent changes in law gradually lowered the threshold to one year of age (for 1991 returns).

2. See James E. Donelson, "Quality of Audit," statement (National Commission on Restructuring the IRS, February 26, 1997), p. 7.

3. See Customs Service, "Strategic Problem Solving Guide," revised (February 1997).

4. John Micklethwait and Adrian Wooldridge, *The Witch Doctors: Making Sense of the Management Gurus* (Random House, 1996), p. 322.

5. See Malcolm K. Sparrow, *Imposing Duties: Government's Changing Approach to Compliance* (Praeger, 1994), pp. 115–18.

Chapter Ten

1. Herman Goldstein, *Problem-Oriented Policing* (McGraw-Hill, 1990), chap. 4.

2. John E. Eck and William Spelman, *Problem-Solving: Problem-Oriented Policing in Newport News* (Washington, D.C.: Police Executive Research Forum, 1987).

3. Adrian Leigh, Tim Read, and Nick Tilley, "Problem-Oriented Policing," Crime Detection and Prevention Series 75 (London: Police Research Group, 1996), p. 17.

4. Eck and Spelman, *Problem-Solving,* p. 7.

5. Herman Goldstein, "Problem-Oriented Policing: The Rationale, the Concept, and Reflections on Its Implementation" (London: Police Research Group, 1996), p. 1.

6. Herb Appenzeller, ed., *Risk Management in Sport: Issues and Strategies* (Durham, N.C.: Carolina Academic Press, 1998), p. 9. The framework Appenzeller adopted was developed in G. L. Head and S. Horn, *Essentials of Risk Management* (Malvern, Pa.: Insurance Institute of America, 1991).

7. J. B. R. Matthews, *Risk Management in Dentistry* (Oxford: Wright Books, 1995), p. 11.

8. Ibid., p. 10.

9. Ibid., p. 12.

10. Malcolm K. Sparrow, *Imposing Duties: Government's Changing Approach to Compliance* (Praeger, 1994), p. 45.

11. Florida Department of Environmental Protection, "Environmental Problem-Solving Booklet" (Tallahassee, February 1998), sec. 5. Also available at (http://www.dep.state.fl.us/ospp/eps/epslist.htm).

12. Other sources explore these difficulties. See Goldstein, *Problem-Oriented Policing;* Sparrow, *Imposing Duties,* chap. 2.

13. Goldstein, *Problem-Oriented Policing,* p. 66.

14. FDEP's problem-solving forms can be found in Florida Department of Environmental Protection, "Environmental Problem Solving Booklet," section 7.

15. Charles Pollard, "Problems Solved," *Police Review.* June 28th, 1996, pp. 19–20.

16. Sandford Borins, *Innovating with Integrity: How Local Heroes Are Transforming American Government* (Georgetown University Press, 1998), p. 20.

17. Eugene Bardach, *Getting Agencies to Work Together: The Practice and Theory of Managerial Craftsmanship* (Brookings, 1998), p. 14.

18. Peter M. Senge, *The Fifth Discipline: The Art and Practice of the Learning Organization* (Doubleday, 1990), p. 58.

19. Ibid., p. 61.

Chapter Eleven

1. National Academy of Public Administration, *Setting Priorities, Getting Results: A New Direction for the Environmental Protection Agency,* Report to Congress (Washington, D.C., 1995), p. 145.

2. I am grateful to my colleague Mark. H. Moore, who elucidated this distinction.

3. John D. Graham, "Legislative Approaches to Achieving More Protection against Risk at Less Cost," *University of Chicago Legal Forum* 13 (1997), p. 18.

4. NAPA, *Setting Priorities, Getting Results,* pp. 23, 142.

5. Ibid., p. 142.

6. This paragraph is based on John D. Graham and Jennifer Kassalow Hartwell, *The Greening of Industry: A Risk Management Approach* (Harvard University Press, 1997), pp. vii, 9, 281.

7. More detailed guidance for managers conducting project reviews can be found in Florida Department of Environmental Protection, "Environmental Problem Solving Booklet" (Tallahassee, February 1998), sec. 7. Also available at (http://www.dep.state.fl.us/ospp/eps/epslist.htm).

8. Herman Goldstein, "Problem-Oriented Policing: The Rationale, the Concept, and Reflections on Its Implementation" (London: Police Research Group, 1996), pp. 4–5.

9. Robert D. Behn, "Creating an Innovative Organization: Ten Hints for Involving Frontline Workers," *State and Local Government Review,* vol. 27 (Fall 1995), pp. 221–34, table 1.

Chapter Twelve

1. David M. Kennedy, "Juvenile Gun Violence and Gun Markets in Boston," *NIJ Research Preview* (National Institute of Justice) (March 1997), p. 1.

2. The summary project account that follows draws heavily on descriptive articles prepared by David M. Kennedy, the project director, and upon classroom discussions of the project, with Kennedy present, in the John F. Kennedy School of Government's Executive Program on Regulatory Reform. For a detailed but early account of the project, see David M. Kennedy, "Pulling Levers: Chronic Offenders, High Crime Settings, and a Theory of Prevention," *Valparaiso University Law Review,* vol. 31 (1997), pp. 1–53. For a more recent briefing on the project, see Kennedy, "Juvenile Gun Violence and Gun Markets in Boston."

3. Kennedy, "Juvenile Gun Violence and Gun Markets in Boston," p. 4; Kennedy, "Pulling Levers," pp. 5, 6.

4. Ibid., p. 15.

5. Ibid., p. 31.

6. Ibid., p. 27.

7. Ibid., p. 41.

Chapter Thirteen

1. Malcolm K. Sparrow, *Imposing Duties: Government's Changing Approach to Compliance* (Praeger, 1994), p. ix.

2. Ibid., p. 33.

3. David Osborne and Ted Gaebler, *Reinventing Government: How the Entrepreneurial Spirit Is Transforming the Public Sector* (Addison-Wesley, 1992), pp. 219–49.

4. Customer Service Task Force, "Reinventing Service at the IRS," IRS Publication 2197, catalog no. 25006E (Department of the Treasury, 1998), p. 69.

5. Mark H. Moore and Darrel W. Stephens, *Beyond Command and Control: The Strategic Management of Police Departments* (Washington, D.C.: Police Executive Research Forum, 1991), p. 31.

6. Richard J. Bonnie, Carolyn E. Fulco, and Catharyn T. Liverman, eds., *Reducing the Burden of Injury: Advancing Prevention and Treatment* (National Academy Press, 1999), p. 2.

7. Ibid., p. 29.

8. Ibid., p. 42.

9. Ibid., p. 22.

10. Sue Mallonnee and others, "Surveillance and Prevention of Residential Fire Injuries," *New England Journal of Medicine*, vol. 335, no. 1 (1996), pp. 27–31.

11. Robert I. Mehr and Bob A. Hedges, *Risk Management: Concepts and Applications* (Homewood, Ill.: Richard D. Irwin, 1974), p. 7.

12. Bonnie, Fulco, and Liverman, *Reducing the Burden of Injury*, pp. 29–30.

13. Ibid., p. 90.

14. Russell, *Is Prevention Better Than Cure?* (Brookings, 1996), pp. 19-20.

15. Ibid., p. 20.

16. Malcolm K. Sparrow, *License to Steal: Why Fraud Plagues America's Health Care System* (Boulder, Colo.: Westview Press, 1996), esp. chap. 8.

17. Marie-Christine Ryckaert, "How Can Information Technology Contribute to Controlling New Emerging Diseases?" Unpublished paper submitted for the course Information Systems: The Public Manager's Perspective, John F. Kennedy School of Government, Harvard University, Spring 1998, p. 1.

18. Ibid. pp. 3–7.

19. Ibid. p. 9.

20. Russell, *Is Prevention Better Than Cure?* p. 41.

21. Ibid., pp. 2–5.

22. John D. Graham, "Making Sense of Risk: An Agenda for Congress," in Robert W. Hahn, ed., *Risks, Costs, and Lives Saved: Getting Better Results from Regulation* (Oxford University Press, 1996), p. 186.

23. Russell, *Is Prevention Better Than Cure?* p. 111.

Chapter Fourteen

1. Sidney A. Shapiro and Randy S. Rabinowitz, "Punishment versus Cooperation in Regulatory Enforcement: A Case Study of OSHA," *Administrative Law Review*, vol. 49, no. 4 (1997), pp. 716, 756.

2. Jon G. Sutinen, "Fisheries Compliance and Management: Assessing Perfor-mance," Report to the Australian Fisheries Management Authority (Kingston: University of Rhode Island, Department of Environmental and Natural Resource Economics, August 1996), p. 12.

3. Wayne Thomas, "Statement on Geographic Allocation of IRS Resources," testimony before the National Commission on Restructuring the IRS, January 9, 1997, p. 6.

4. Alan H. Plumley, *The Determinants of Individual Income Tax Compli-ance: Estimating the Impacts of Tax Policy, Enforcement, and IRS Responsive-ness,* IRS Publication 1916, catalog no. 22555A (Department of the Treasury, August 1996).

5. Ibid., p. 41.

6. Sutinen, "Fisheries Compliance and Management," p. 19.

7. Peter N. Grabosky and Russell G. Smith, "Telecommunications and Crime: Regulatory Dilemmas," *Law & Policy*, vol. 19 (July 1997), p. 329.

Chapter Fifteen

1. Adrian Leigh, Tim Read, and Nick Tilley, "Problem-Oriented Policing," Crime Detection and Prevention Series 75 (London: Police Research Group, 1996), p. 39.

2. Ibid., p. v.

3. Ibid., p. 13.

4. Herman Goldstein, "Problem-Oriented Policing: The Rationale, the Con-cept, and Reflections on Its Implementation" (London: Police Research Group, 1996), p. 3.

5. Remarks by President Clinton on reinventing worker safety regulation, Stromberg Sheet Metal Works, Inc., Washington, D.C., May 16, 1995. Text of speech available though White House Virtual Library.

6. For a copy of the memorandum, and for a more detailed account of the struggles that ensued within OSHA, see Harvey Simon, "Regulatory Reform at OSHA" (John F. Kennedy School of Government case program, 1997), case C.

7. I use here the language of strategic public management and strategic inno-vation as developed by Mark H. Moore and other colleagues of mine at the John F. Kennedy School and elsewhere. For anyone not familiar with that lan-guage, I recommend Mark H. Moore, *Creating Public Value: Strategic Manage-ment in Government* (Harvard University Press, 1995).

8. Donald L. MacDonald, *Risk Control in the Overseas Operation of Ameri-can Corporations* (University of Michigan, Graduate School of Business Admin-istration, 1979), p. x.

9. J. B. R. Matthews, *Risk Management in Dentistry* (Oxford: Wright Books, 1995).

10. Richard B. Felder, "Building Experience with Risk Management," *Pipeline and Gas Journal,* September 1, 1998, pp. 44–49.

11. Ibid., p. 46.

12. Rick Kowalewski, "Using Outcome Information to Redirect Programs: A Case Study of the Coast Guard's Pilot Project under the Government Performance and Results Act" (U.S. Coast Guard, Office of Marine Safety, Security, and Environmental Protection, April 1996), p. 8.

13. Ibid., p. 1.

14. Ibid., p. 12.

15. Michael D. Maltz, *Measuring the Effectiveness of Organized Crime Control Efforts,* Monograph 9 (University of Illinois at Chicago, Office of International Criminal Justice, 1990), p. 19.

16. Ronald V. Clarke, quoted in Gordon Hughes, *Understanding Crime Prevention* (Philadephia: Open University Press, 1998), p. 60.

17. Ronald V. Clarke, "Situational Crime Prevention," in Michael Tonry and David Farrington, eds., *Building a Safer Society: Strategic Approaches to Crime Prevention* (University of Chicago Press, 1995), p. 97.

18. Goldstein, "Problem-Oriented Policing: The Rationale, the Concept," p. 7.

19. Peter Senge, *The Fifth Discipline: The Art and Practice of the Learning Organization* (Doubleday, 1990), pp. 63–64.

20. Trevor Boucher, "Risk Management on a Market Segmented Basis," in Peter Grabosky and John Braithwaite, eds., *Business Regulation and Australia's Future* (Canberra: Australian Institute of Criminology, 1993), pp. 231–44.

21. Ibid., p. 244.

Chapter Sixteen

1. David M. Kennedy, "Fighting Fear in Baltimore County," (John F. Kennedy School of Government, case program, 1990).

2. On the problem of fear, see Mark H. Moore and Darrel W. Stephens, *Beyond Command and Control: The Strategic Management of Police Departments* (Washington, D.C.: Police Executive Research Forum, 1991), p. 8.

3. Mike Lane, "Funding of Strategic Problem Solving Initiatives," memorandum (Customs Service, June 11, 1996).

4. Eugene Bardach and Robert A. Kagan, *Going by the Book: The Problem of Regulatory Unreasonableness* (Temple University Press, 1982), p. 153. Bardach and Kagan drew upon the field research work of Steven Kelman, "Regulating Job Safety and Health: A Comparison of the U.S. Occupational Safety and Health Administration and the Swedish Worker Protection Board," Ph.D. diss., Harvard University, 1978), p. 335.

5. See James Q. Wilson, *Varieties of Police Behavior: The Management of Law and Order in Eight Communities* (Harvard University Press, 1978), p. 80;

Malcolm K. Sparrow, "Integrating Distinct Managerial Styles: The Challenge for Police Leadership," *American Journal of Police*, vol. 12, no. 2 (1992), pp. 1–16.

6. Malcolm K. Sparrow, *Imposing Duties: Government's Changing Approach to Compliance* (Praeger, 1994), pp. 115–18.

Chapter Seventeen

1. Donald F. Kettl, *Reinventing Government? Appraising the National Performance Review* (Brookings, 1994), p. 24.

2. Alan A. Altshuler, foreword to Michael Barzelay, *Breaking through Bureaucracy: A New Vision for Managing in Government* (University of California Press, 1992), p. viii.

3. Eugene Bardach and Robert Kagan, *Going by the Book: The Problem of Regulatory Unreasonableness* (Temple University Press), p. 37.

4. Ibid., p. 75.

5. James Q. Wilson, *Varieties of Police Behavior: The Management of Law and Order in Eight Communities* (Harvard University Press, 1978), p. 72.

6. National Academy of Public Administration, *Resolving the Paradox of Environmental Protection: An Agenda for Congress, EPA, and the States*, Report to Congress (Washington, D.C., 1997), pp. 11–17

7. The Internet site promised potential investors they would triple their money in fifteen months if they invested in "millennium bug insurance," which was to be offered to blue chip companies as insurance against losses from the Y2K computer bug.

8. Kettl, *Reinventing Government?* p. 24.

9. Barzelay, *Breaking through Bureaucracy*, p. 6.

10. Mark H. Moore, *Creating Public Value: Strategic Management in Government* (Harvard University Press, 1995), p. 299.

11. Ibid., p. 301.

12. For example, Landy and others urge EPA to recognize its obligation to propose and set its own direction. "Statutes do not and cannot fully guide their behavior. Thus they possess substantial power that needs to be understood, managed, and used to advance democratic purposes." Marc K. Landy, Marc J. Roberts, and Stephen R. Thomas, *The Environmental Protection Agency: Asking the Wrong Questions* (Oxford University Press, 1990), p. 6.

13. National Academy of Public Administration, *Setting Priorities, Getting Results: A New Direction for the Environmental Protection Agency*, Report to Congress (Washington, D.C., 1995), p. 1.

14. Ibid., p. 125.

15. Ibid., p. 160.

16. See Harvey Simon, "Regulatory Reform at OSHA" (John F. Kennedy School of Government, case program, 1997), case C.

17. Herman Goldstein, "Problem-Oriented Policing: The Rationale, the Concept, and Reflections on Its Implementation" (London: Police Research Group, 1996), pp. 10, 11.

18. See Malcolm K. Sparrow, *Imposing Duties: Government's Changing Approach to Compliance* (Praeger, 1994), pp. 23–24.

19. For a summary description of the cooperative compliance program and the arguments made for and against it, see the report of U.S. Chamber of Commerce v. Labor Department (98-1036a) in the Occupational Safety and Health Reporter (Bureau of National Affairs), May 26, 1999, p. 1549. The U.S. Court of Appeals ruling is available at ⟨http://www.ll.georgetown.edu/fed-ct/circuit/dc/opinions/98-1036a.html⟩.

20. Cynthia Omberg and Ellen Byerrum, "Future of OSHA Compliance Program Unclear in Wake of Appeals Court Stay," Daily Labor Report (Bureau of National Affairs), March 2, 1998, pp. 1–4.

21. Brian Friel, "OSHA Gives Up on Regulatory Reform Program," Daily Briefing, A Service of Government Executive Magazine, April 21, 1999 ⟨http://www.govexec.com/dailyfed/⟩.

Chapter Eighteen

1. Sun Tzu, *The Art of War*, trans. Samuel B. Griffith (Oxford University Press, 1963), p. 88. Epigraph quote is from p. 39.

2. John Bacon, "The French Connection Revisited," *International Journal of Intelligence and Counter-Intelligence*, vol. 4, no. 4 (1990), pp. 507–23; Malcolm K. Sparrow, "Network Vulnerabilities and Strategic Intelligence in Law Enforcement," *International Journal of Intelligence and Counter-Intelligence*, vol. 5, no. 3 (1991), pp. 255–74.

3. David M. Kennedy, "Closing the Market: Controlling the Drug Trade in Tampa, Florida" (John F. Kennedy School of Government, 1991); Malcolm K. Sparrow, *Imposing Duties: Government's Changing Approach to Compliance* (Praeger Books, 1994), pp. 49–52.

4. Rick Kowalewski, "Using Outcome Information to Redirect Programs: A Case Study of the Coast Guard's Pilot Project under the Government Performance and Results Act" (Coast Guard, Office of Marine Safety, Security and Environmental Protection, April 1996), p. 8.

5. David Herbster, project leader for Team SOS, communication with author.

6. Marilyn B. Peterson, *Applications in Criminal Analysis: A Sourcebook* (Greenwood Press, 1994), pp. 273, 275.

7. Frederick T. Martens, "The Intelligence Function," in Paul P. Andrews Jr. and Marilyn B. Peterson, eds., *Criminal Intelligence Analysis* (Loomis, Calif.: Palmer Enterprises, 1990), pp. 5–6.

8. Kowalewski, "Using Outcome Information to Redirect Programs," p. 4.

9. Ibid., p. 1.

10. Mark H. Moore, *Buy or Bust* (D. C. Heath, 1977), pp. 168-69.

11. Peterson, *Applications in Criminal Analysis*, pp. 4-5.

12. Angus Smith, ed., *Intelligence-Led Policing: International Perspectives on Policing in the 21st Century* (Lawrenceville, N.J.: International Association of Law Enforcement Intelligence Analysts, 1997), p. 1.

13. Ibid., p. 3.

14. Russ Porter, "Getting Started in Intelligence-Led Policing," in Smith, *Intelligence-Led Policing*, p. 27.

15. Richard Anderson, "Intelligence-Led Policing: a British Perspective," in Smith, *Intelligence-Led Policing*, pp. 5-8.

16. John E. Eck, *Using Research: A Primer for Law Enforcement Managers* (Washington, D.C.: Police Executive Research Forum, 1984), pp. 5-6.

17. See D. Roe, W. Pease, K. Florini, and E. Silbergeld, "Toxic Ignorance" (Environmental Defense Fund, 1997); W. Pease, "The Chemical Scorecard" (Environmental Defense Fund, 1998).

18. Bruce N. Ames and Lois Swirsky Gold, "The Causes and Prevention of Cancer: Gaining Perspectives on the Management of Risk," in Robert W. Hahn, *Risks, Costs, and Lives Saved: Getting Better Results from Regulation* (Oxford University Press, 1996), p. 28.

19. Herman Goldstein, *Problem-Oriented Policing* (McGraw-Hill, 1990), p. 84.

20. National Electronic Injury Surveillance System data for 1997, *Consumer Product Safety Review*, vol. 3 (Fall 1998), p. 6.

21. Bill Bryson, *Notes from a Big Country* (Doubleday, 1998), p. 19.

22. Richard A. Weintraub, "The Problem of Sudden Death in Competitive Athletes," in Herb Appenzeller, ed., *Risk Management in Sport: Issues and Strategies* (Durham, N.C: Carolina Academic Press, 1998), pp. 187-208.

23. National Institute for Occupational Safety and Health, Education and Information Division, "Trac-Safe: A Community-Based Program for Reducing Injuries and Deaths from Tractor Overturns," Publication 96-108 (Centers for Disease Control and Prevention, 1996), pp. 11-12.

24. Richard J. Bonnie, Carolyn E. Fulco, and Catharyn T. Liverman, eds., *Reducing the Burden of Injury: Advancing Prevention and Treatment* (National Academy Press, 1999), p. 22.

25. Sparrow, *Imposing Duties*, pp. 118-22.

26. Goldstein, *Problem-Oriented Policing*, pp. 84-88.

27. Peter N. Grabosky and Russell G. Smith, "Telecommunications and Crime: Regulatory Dilemmas," *Law and Policy*, vol. 19 (July 1997), p. 326.

28. Consumer Product Safety Commission, "Saving Lives through Smart Government: Success Stories" (March 1996), p. 23.

29. For an account of the IRS's attempts to control the problem of fraudulent tax returns claiming the earned income tax credit, see Malcolm K. Sparrow, *License to Steal: Why Fraud Plagues America's Health Care System* (Boulder, Colo.: Westview Press, 1996), chap. 3.

30. For a defense of the IRS's taxpayer compliance monitoring program see Malcolm K. Sparrow, Testimony, *Hearing before the Subcommittee on Oversight of the House Committee on Ways and Means*, 104 Cong. 1 sess., July 18, 1995, Serial 104-30 (Government Printing Office, 1996), pp. 75–80.

31. Ronald V. Clarke and David Weisbrud, "Diffusion of Crime Control Benefits: Observations on the Reverse of Displacement," in Ronald V. Clarke, ed., *Crime Prevention Studies*, vol. 2 (Monsey, N.Y.: Criminal Justice Press, 1994).

Chapter Nineteen

1. "Environmental News: Environmental Enforcement Records Set for 1996," press release, Environmental Protection Agency Communications, Education, and Public Affairs, February 25, 1997.

2. Ibid. p. 8.

3. "EPA Set Record in '96 of 262 Criminal Cases on Pollution Charges," *Wall Street Journal*, February 26, 1997.

4. OECA's search for more compelling measures resulted in its measures strategy project, initiated in January 1997 and directed by Deputy Assistant Administrator Michael Stahl. See Office of Enforcement and Compliance Assurance, "Measuring the Performance of EPA's Enforcement and Compliance Assurance Program," Final Report (National Performance Measures Strategy, 1997).

Chapter Twenty

1. Michael D. Maltz, *Measuring the Effectiveness of Organized Crime Control Efforts*, Monograph 9 (University of Illinois, Office of International Criminal Justice, 1990), p. 39.

2. James Q. Wilson, "The Problem of Defining Agency Success," in Bureau of Justice Statistics, *Performance Measures for the Criminal Justice System* (Department of Justice, Office of Justice Programs, 1993), p. 160.

3. Ibid., p. 163.

4. Rick Kowalewski, "Using Outcome Information to Redirect Programs: A Case Study of the Coast Guard's Pilot Project under the Government Performance and Results Act" (U.S. Coast Guard, Office of Marine Safety, Security and Environmental Protection, April 1996), p. 5.

5. Ibid., p. 7.

6. Ibid., p. 3.

7. OSHA strategic plan, fiscal years 1997–2002, revised, September 18, 1999 (http://www.osha.gov/oshinfo/strategic/).

8. Florida Department of Environmental Protection, *Secretary's Quarterly Performance Report*, vol. 1 (Tallahassee, September 1998), p. 1.

9. Kirby Green, "Good, Watch, and Focus Designation for the Sixth Secretary's Quarterly Performance Report" (Tallahassee, March 26, 1999), p. 1.

10. Dave Herbster, letter to author, May 4, 1999, p. 1.

11. See General Accounting Office, "Managing for Results: Analytic Challenges in Measuring Performance," GAO/HEHS/GGD-97-138 (May 1997), pp. 2–4; "The Government Performance and Results Act: 1997 Government-wide Implementation Will Be Uneven," GAO/GGD-97-109 (June 1997), p. 6; "Managing for Results: Regulatory Agencies Identified Significant Barriers to Focusing on Results," GAO/GGD-97-83 (June 1997), pp. 4–5.

12. Wilson, "The Problem of Defining Agency Success."

Chapter Twenty-One

1. "A Reach on Regulation," *Washington Post*, May 19, 1999.

2. Albert B. Crenshaw and Stephen Barr, "New Commitment to 'Service' May be Taxing IRS," *Washington Post*, May 19, 1999.

Index